Constructing a Theology of Prayer

Monographs in Baptist History

VOLUME 17

Ours is a day in which not only the gaze of Western culture but also increasingly that of Evangelicals is riveted to the present. The past seems to be nowhere in view. Hence, it is dismissed as being of little value for our rapidly changing world. Such historical amnesia is fatal for any culture, but particularly so for Christian communities whose identity is profoundly bound up with their history. The goal of this new series of monographs, Studies in Baptist History, seeks to provide one of these Christian communities, that of evangelical Baptists, with reasons and resources for remembering the past. The editors are deeply convinced that Baptist history contains rich resources of theological reflection, *praxis*, and spirituality that can help Baptists, as well as other Christians, live more Christianly in the present. The monographs in this series will therefore aim at illuminating various aspects of the Baptist tradition and in the process provide Baptists with a usable past.

Constructing a Theology of Prayer

Andrew Fuller's (1754–1815)
Belief and Practice of Prayer

Matthew C. Bryant

PICKWICK *Publications* · Eugene, Oregon

CONSTRUCTING A THEOLOGY OF PRAYER
Andrew Fuller's (1754–1815) Belief and Practice of Prayer

Monographs in Baptist History 17

Pickwick Publications
An Imprint of Wipf and Stock Publishers
199 W. 8th Ave., Suite 3
Eugene, OR 97401

www.wipfandstock.com

PAPERBACK ISBN: 978-1-7252-7638-3
HARDCOVER ISBN: 978-1-7252-7639-0
EBOOK ISBN: 978-1-7252-7640-6

Cataloging-in-Publication data:

Names: Bryant, Matthew C., author.

Title: Constructing a Theology of Prayer: Andrew Fuller's (1754–1815) Belief and Practice of Prayer / by Matthew C. Bryant.

Description: Eugene, OR: Pickwick Publications, 2021 | Series: Monographs in Baptist History 17 | Includes bibliographical references.

Identifiers: ISBN 978-1-7252-7638-3 (paperback) | ISBN 978-1-7252-7639-0 (hardcover) | ISBN 978-1-7252-7640-6 (ebook)

Subjects: LCSH: Prayer—Christianity. | Fuller, Andrew, 1754–1815. | Baptists—History.

Classification: BX6495.F75 B79 2021 (print) | BX6495.F75 (ebook)

JANUARY 12, 2021

To my parents, Mike and Lisa, my first teachers in theology and prayer. Your faith and example in prayer first taught me to call on the name of Jesus.

To Mercy Talitha, remember your name. You are God's little girl. God has used your life to stoke my heart to pray more earnestly.

To Josiah Matthew, remember your name. Call out to God. He will support.

To Lily Marie, remember your name. Just as God provides for the lilies of the field, he will provide for you.

To my bride, Lindsay. Your sacrifice in this project have far surpassed any efforts on my part. Thank you for your love and friendship. Your companionship through life's journey has been, and remains, my greatest earthly treasure.

To Christ, the author and perfecter of our faith, may the fruits of this labor continue by your grace in the power of your Spirit to form me as an instrument fit for your use in this world until I am removed to the next. In all things, may I never be ashamed to call on your name.

Contents

Acknowledgments

As this book was originally completed as my doctoral dissertation, I would like to express my deepest appreciation for my guidance committee. Dr. Adam Harwood, my chair, sharpened me as a scholar and a Christ-follower. Dr. Jeffrey Riley provided sage counsel and continued support from my initial visit to New Orleans in October 2014 to the completion of the original work. Finally, Dr. Michael Haykin deserves special thanks for agreeing to be an external reader as a member of my guidance committee. His correspondence early in the research proposal phase encouraged me to commit to the present study of Andrew Fuller and his theology of prayer.

I would also like to thank my faith families at King Street Church in Chambersburg, Pennsylvania; Edgewater Baptist Church in New Orleans, Louisiana; and The Village Baptist Church in Fayetteville, North Carolina. King Street, your kind support made the beginning of this journey a reality. Edgewater, your support nurtured my faith on the way and helped make the completion of thestudy a reality. The Village, your encouragement has made it possible to see the study adapted for publication.

Abbreviations

THEB   Crosby, Thomas. *The History of English Baptists*. 4 vols. Bellingham, WA: Logos Bible Software, 2011.

HEB   Ivimey, Joseph. *A History of the English Baptists*. 4 vols. London, 1811–1830.

Works   Fuller, Andrew. *The Complete Works of the Rev. Andrew Fuller*. Edited by Joseph Belcher. 3 vols. Harrisonburg, VA: Sprinkle, 1988.

Introduction

THE FOLLOWING STUDY IS the first full treatment of Andrew Fuller's (1754–1815) theology of prayer. Fuller is a central figure in a rich Baptist heritage. Joseph Ivimey, author of one of the earliest Baptist histories, praises the effect of Fuller's writings, his example as a preacher, and his prominence in the formation and sustainment of the Baptist Missionary Society.[1] He stated "that the denomination . . . never had so distinguished an ornament."[2] Ivimey also predicted that Fuller "will ever be remembered with esteem and veneration by all who feel an interest for the salvation of the heathen and prosperity of the denomination."[3] His bold prediction continues to come to fruition with the recovered interest in Fuller Studies since the mid-twentieth century, an interest that continues to grow.[4]

Hypothesis

While Fuller never explicitly wrote a theology of prayer, a construction of Fuller's theology of prayer is possible by analyzing four points of data:

1. Fuller's understanding of the nature and moods of Christian prayer as represented in his sermons on prayer and expositions of the prayers in Scripture;[5]

1. The Baptist Missionary Society was founded originally under the title: The Particular Baptist Society for Propagating the Gospel amongst the Heathen, but soon after became known as the Baptist Missionary Society. Hereafter, abbreviated as BMS.

2. Ivimey, *HEB*, 4:532.

3. Ivimey, *HEB*, 4:532–34.

4. Finn, "Renaissance in Andrew Fuller Studies," 44–61. I refer to Fuller Studies as a proper noun and thus it will be capitalized throughout.

5. In Fuller's *Thoughts on Preaching*, he distinguishes between an *exposition* and a *sermon*. He encourages the young preacher to utilize both. First, an *exposition* was the "expounding of the Scriptures," in order to *"enter into their true meaning."* Fuller states

1

2. Fuller's understanding of major Christian doctrines, considering their implications for prayer;

3. Fuller's writings that explicitly address the topic of prayer, considering implications for corollary doctrines; and

4. Fuller's practice of prayer, considering the implications for corollary Christian doctrines.

A construction of Fuller's theology of prayer through an analysis of corollary doctrines will shed light on a multifaceted aspect of Fuller's spirituality. Fuller states, "Prayer is a kind of religious exercise which is necessary to accompany all others."[6] Whether in leading corporate prayer, fellowshipping with fellow ministers, preparing sermons, or reflecting on systematic divinity, Fuller prioritized prayer as essential to communing with God and thinking correctly about God.

Definition of Terms

"By 'theology of prayer' the writer," to borrow James Leo Garrett's words, "does not mean an explanation of praying that divests it of its profundity and mystery but rather an exposition of the major Christian doctrines in their bearing upon prayer."[7] An analysis of select major doctrines and their bearing on Fuller's belief and practice concerning prayer will produce a multifaceted construction of Fuller's theology of prayer. Additionally, the analysis will allow readers to consider how Fuller's understanding of "the basic Christian doctrines affect and are affected by Christian prayer."[8] In

---

that he made it a habit to deliver an exposition "of a chapter, or part of a chapter" each Lord's day. Fuller stated that the "scope of the sacred writers is of greater importance in understanding the Scriptures than the most critical examination of terms." A *sermon*, on the other hand, Fuller considered as the "discoursing on the Divine subjects." Fuller stated that a sermon's "*subjects*" could be doctrinal or practical. Fuller prized simplicity in his preaching. He states, "*One thing at once* is a maxim in common life, by which the greatest men have made the greatest proficiency. Shun, therefore, a multitude of divisions and subdivisions. He who aims to say every thing [*sic*] in a single discourse, in effect says nothing." Perhaps Fuller's most piercing recommendation for the young minister was to remember that "there is a great difference between reading the Scriptures *as a student*, in order to find something to say to the people, and reading them *as a Christian*." Indeed, Fuller's advice is sound for a preacher in any era. See Fuller, *Works*, 1:712–19. For more on Fuller's preaching, especially as it related to his pastoral theology and evangelical influences, see Grant, *Andrew Fuller*, 77–104.

6. Fuller, *Works*, 3:655.
7. Garrett, "Theology of Prayer," 3.
8. Garrett, "Theology of Prayer," 4.

other words, a *theology of prayer* considers how prayer informs and is informed by the major doctrines of the Christian faith.

The term "corollary" is being used assuming the reciprocal relationship between prayer and doctrines of the Christian faith. One's doctrine of God, the Son, the Holy Spirit, humanity, the church, and eschatology will inform by systematic reflection one's belief and practice concerning prayer. Likewise, one's belief and practice concerning prayer will inform systematic reflection on these doctrines of the Christian faith.

Delimitations

Since nearly all doctrines have prayer as their corollary, the construction will be limited to six major doctrines of the faith: the doctrine of God the Father, the Son, the Spirit, humanity, the church, and last things. Garrett's study utilized these same six points to construct his own theology of prayer. Garrett divided them as follows, "The God and Father of All Prayer," "Jesus Christ and Prayer," "The Holy Spirit and Prayer," "The Person Who Prays," "The Church at Prayer," and "Prayer and the Eschaton."[9] The construction will not treat comprehensively each of the six doctrines. Instead, the construction will survey the major contours of the doctrines, highlighting the areas where Fuller's theology of prayer demonstrates reciprocity with said doctrines.

Status of Research

A construction of Fuller's theology of prayer is on the edge of two fields of theological inquiry, systematic theology and spiritual theology. The theological construction is systematic. The subject matter, prayer, is the most basic expression of one's faith. To use Fuller's words, "Prayer is pouring out of the soul before God."[10] Elsewhere, Fuller states, "Prayer is the ascending of the heart to God. It is one of the ordinary means of our communion with God. A great part of the religious life consists in the exercise of it, either in public or in private, either vocal or mental."[11] Prayer is multifaceted. The practice of prayer is indispensable regarding one's communion with God, and the manner and matter of prayer affects one's systematic reflection on

---

9. Garrett, "Theology of Prayer," 3–17.

10. Fuller, *Works*, 1:579.

11. Fuller, *Works*, 3:620.

God. As Patrick Miller expresses well in the introduction of *They Cried to the Lord*:

> Prayer is not, however, only a matter of spirituality and the prac-
> tice of piety. It also has to do with faith, that is, with whom we
> trust and what we believe . . . So prayer and theology exist in re-
> lation to each other in a correcting circle, the one learning from
> the other and correcting the other. Religious faith seeks not to
> think one way and to pray another but to come before God in
> a manner that is consistent with what we believe and profess
> about God and God's way and to think about God in a way that
> is shaped by the experience of actual encounter in prayer.[12]

An experience and encounter with God was of great importance to Fuller. The doctrinal and experimental were not contradictory in his thinking.[13] Thus, an analysis of Fuller's theology of prayer must respect the reciprocal relationship between his doctrine and prayer.

Spiritual Theology

A study on Fuller's theology of prayer falls within the realm of spiritual the-
ology. Simon Chan's and Glen Scorgie's definitions and distinctions between spirituality and spiritual theology are helpful in clearly situating the study in the latter domain of spiritual theology. "Spirituality," according to Chan, is "the kind of life that is formed by a particular type of spiritual theology. Spirituality is the lived reality, whereas spiritual theology is the systematic reflection and formalization of that reality."[14] Consider also Scorgie's definitions: "Spirituality, precisely because it is a historical and experiential phenomenon, lends itself to descriptive, non-evaluative study. By contrast, spiritual theology is prescriptive, constructive, and prophetic. The former describes what has been and what is, while the latter proposes what ought to be."[15] While the study will encompass descriptive accounts of Fuller's prayer

---

12. Miller, *They Cried to the Lord*, 1.

13. For example, Fuller states in his sermon, *The Nature and Importance of an In-
timate Knowledge of Divine Truth*, "From these instances, out of many others, you will easily perceive that doctrinal and experimental preaching are not so remote from each other as some persons have imagined; and that to extol the latter, at the expense of the former, is to act like him who wishes the fountain to be destroyed, because he prefers the stream." See Fuller, *Works*, 1:170.

14. Chan, *Spiritual Theology*, 16.

15. Scorgie, "Overview of Christian Spirituality," 27–29.

life—a key aspect of one's spirituality—the chief aim is to construct Fuller's theology of prayer through systematic reflection.

The study falls within the field of spiritual theology in another sense. Chan explains that spiritual theology, in a narrow sense, refers to the "systematic reflection and formalization" of one's spirituality, as aforementioned.[16] However, in a broad sense, spiritual theology "refers to a certain way in which all theological reflection ought to be undertaken," that is, without a rugged divide between the disciplines of theological inquiry, systematic, moral, biblical, philosophical, and so forth.[17] Fuller and his contemporaries were first- or second-generation recipients of such formal divisions in theological reflection, granted the divisions of Fuller's day was more commonly a bifurcation between the systematic and the practical.[18] Fuller recognized the value of systematic theology, what he referred to as systematic divinity; yet practical concerns were never far from view.[19] For example, in January of 1780, Fuller famously prayed and committed himself "to take up no principle at secondhand; but to search for everything at the pure fountain of *thy word*." Fuller continued in his prayer, "O Lord, never let me, under the specious pretence of preaching *holiness*, neglect to promulge the truths of thy word; for this day I see, and have all along found, that holy practice has a necessary dependence on sacred *principle*."[20] Fuller understood that both belief and practice were bound in a dependent relationship, that is, "holy practice has a necessary dependence on sacred principle." Fuller further explicated what he meant in one of his *Dialogues and Letters between Crispus and Gaius*.[21] In a dialogue titled, "The Connexion between Doctrinal, Experimental, and Practical Religion," Crispus asks of Gaius, "Will you give me your thoughts on the influence of truth on holy practice?" Gaius responds:

16. Chan, *Spiritual Theology*, 16.

17. Chan, *Spiritual Theology*, 16.

18. Pelikan states, "The two branches of theology," that is, dogma and ethics, "were not permanently separated until the work of the seventeenth-century Protestant theologian, Georg Claixtus, but the distinction between doctrine and life had been in force long before that division of labor was effected." Pelikan, *Christian Tradition,* 3.

19. For example, see Fuller's sermon *On the Importance of an Intimate Acquaintance with Divine Truth*, and his *Letters on Systematic Divinity* in Fuller, *Works*, 1:160–74, 684–711. *Systematic divinity* and *systematic theology* may be used interchangeably throughout this study considering Fuller's definition of systematic divinity—"the studying of truth in a systematic form." Fuller, *Works*, 1:164.

20. Fuller, *Works*, 1:20.

21. The collection of these dialogues and letters may be found in Fuller, *Works*, 2:647–80.

> Perhaps there is no proposition but what has some *consequence* hanging upon it, and such consequence must be expected to correspond with the nature of the proposition. A truth in natural philosophy will be productive of a natural effect. Divine truth, when cordially imbibed, proves the seed of a godly life. For example: If there be a God that judgeth in the earth, he is to be loved, feared, and adored. If man be a sinner before God, it becomes him to lie low in self-abasement. If salvation be of grace, boasting is excluded. If we be bought with a price, we are not our own, and must not live unto ourselves, but to him who died for us, and rose again. Religious sentiments are called *principles*, because, when received in the love of them, they become the springs of holy action.[22]

Clearly, doctrinal and practical concerns were never far apart in Fuller's thinking. The holy practice of prayer has a necessary dependence on sacred principle, sound theology. Fuller held orthopraxis in tow with orthodoxy.

Systematic Theology

In Protestant systematic theologies, prayer commonly is treated under the heading of providence.[23] The location is appropriate because what one believes about God and the way he works in the world naturally impacts one's belief and practice regarding prayer. Dennis Okholm's comparative study of Karl Barth and Norman Pittenger's theologies of providence and petitionary prayer is representative of this type of systematic reflection.[24] Terrance Tiessen's *Providence and Prayer* is, perhaps, the most comprehensive representation of this type of study.[25] Tiessen explores eleven "models of providence

---

22. Fuller, *Works*, 2:653.

23. A notable exception here are the few who treat prayer as an individual chapter. For example, Calvin's *Institutes*, III.20, "Prayer, Which Is the Chief Exercise of Faith, and by Which We Daily Receive God's Benefits." Grudem's *Systematic Theology* also treats prayer under its own heading. See, chapter 18, "Prayer: Why Does God Want Us to Pray? How Can We Pray Effectively?" Even still, Grudem's chapter on prayer (ch. 18) follows his chapter on providence (ch. 16) and miracles (ch. 17). See Calvin, *Institutes*, 559–605; and Grudem, *Systematic Theology*, 315–96.

24. Okholm, "Petitionary Prayer and Providence in Two Contemporary Theological Perspectives."

25. Tiessen, *Providence & Prayer*. Even Catholic theologians, according to Garrett, who historically define prayer more in terms of contemplation, must interact with questions related to providence and prayer. For a recent example, see Selman, *Providence and Prayer*. Garrett broadly juxtaposes the tendency of the Catholic tradition toward contemplation and Protestant tradition toward petition when defining prayer.

and prayer," including his own, and provides parameters and examples of petitionary prayers based on the model of providence represented.[26] Such an analysis provides an excellent test of consistency and internal coherence for one's belief and practice regarding providence and petitionary prayer. Considering how prayer relates to other corollary doctrines, especially providence, is a systematic approach to constructing a theology of prayer.

Exploring the reciprocity between providence and prayer thoroughly explicates one manner—form and function—of prayer, namely, petitionary prayer. Although such studies are fruitful, inadvertently one could misconstrue a theology of prayer as a theology of asking. Prayer, certainly, is more than just asking.[27] Studies that treat prayer as the corollary of providence may inadvertently fail to recognize the various manners of prayer beyond petition.

Stanley Grenz, in *Theology for the Community of God*, presents a broad systematic treatment of prayer. Grenz treats prayer, first, as a corollary to the doctrine of the Trinity. Grenz stated that "our affirmation of the doctrine of the Trinity forms the foundation for the way we pray" because "cognizance of the doctrine of the Trinity will facilitate a consciousness of whom we address in prayer."[28] Grenz affirms that while prayer may be addressed to all three persons of the Trinity, according to Scripture, "we normally ought to address the Father in prayer."[29] Grenz's most systematic analysis of prayer comes under the heading of Christology and Jesus's ongoing work: "Our theological concern is that we always pray in accordance with our Lord's functions within the divine program."[30] Jesus's ongoing ministry of intercession is a continuation of his earthly ministry. Jesus prayed for the Twelve "but also for 'those who will believe . . . ' Our exalted Lord continues that ministry as he now pleads for us in heaven."[31] Regarding the modes of prayer, one may always address Jesus in prayers of adoration because "such prayers are not dependent on the work of Christ, for they focus on his eternal reality as the divine Son."[32] Likewise, prayers of thanksgiving are permissible if thanks is rendered for Jesus's completed and ongoing work. Prayers of confession—while "we may at times be drawn to confess sin to him [Jesus]"—are

Garrett, "Theology of Prayer," 3–4.
26. Tiessen, *Providence & Prayer*, 20.
27. Garrett, "Theology of Prayer," 3–4.
28. Grenz, *Theology for the Community of God*, 74–75.
29. Grenz, *Theology for the Community of God*, 75.
30. Grenz, *Theology for the Community of God*, 355.
31. Grenz, *Theology for the Community of God*, 354.
32. Grenz, *Theology for the Community of God*, 355.

"generally preferable" to address the Father because "sin is always against God our Father . . . and he is the one who forgives sin."[33] According to Grenz, "Our primary theological difficulty lies with petition."[34] With parameters similar to that of thanksgiving, Grenz proposes that petitions be addressed to Christ solely with respect to his ongoing work.[35] Grenz's lengthiest treatment of prayer comes under the heading of ecclesiology; specifically, the mandate of the church in "worship, edification, and outreach through evangelism and service."[36] Prayer is an "aspect" of worship, "foundational to the edifying mandate," "crucial" in the task of evangelism, and "indispensable to our service as the people of God in the world."[37] Grenz's treatment of prayer is multifaceted and systematic, highlighting the reciprocal relationship between prayer and the doctrine of the Trinity. However, Grenz does not explicitly treat prayer under the headings of pneumatology or eschatology—both of these headings were of great import for Fuller and the eighteenth-century Particular Baptist theological milieu regarding prayer.[38]

Garrett's approach—constructing a theology of prayer through an analysis of the major doctrines of the faith—appears to be the most appropriate method of systematic analysis for accommodating the multifaceted nature of prayer. Garrett poses the question, "Is it possible to translate the second person reality of prayer into third person reality of theology without some contradiction or a certain distortion of prayer?"[39] Garrett's answer to the question is an implicit yes by exploring a number of prayers throughout the Old and New Testament. Garrett's thesis is that "after such foundational considerations as the nature and moods of Christian prayer,

33. Grenz, *Theology for the Community of God*, 356.

34. Grenz, *Theology for the Community of God*, 356. Grenz wrote a monograph on prayer, *Prayer: The Cry for the Kingdom*. The first edition, according to Grenz, was aimed primarily at addressing "the petitionary aspect of prayer," despite the fact that "the discipline of contemplative prayer . . . was becoming increasingly popular." Grenz's interest in petitionary prayer spawned in 1981 with the prospect of teaching a "course for seminarians on the theology and practice of prayer." Grenz, *Prayer*, xi. Grenz's first edition of *Theology for the Community of God* was completed in 1994. Grenz's deep reflection on the theology and practice of prayer in his systematic theology is perhaps the result of his focus on prayer early in his career in theological education and writing.

35. Grenz, *Theology for the Community of God*, 356.

36. Grenz, *Theology for the Community of God*, 509. For each prayer's relation to worship, edification, evangelism, and service see, 494–95, 497–98, 504–5, and 509–10, respectively.

37. Grenz, *Theology for the Community of God*, 494, 497, 504–5, and 509.

38. For example, consider two recent works focusing on these doctrinal points as they relate to Andrew Fuller. See Bruce, "The Grand Encouragement"; and Chun, *The Legacy of Edwards in the Theology of Fuller*.

39. Garrett, "Theology of Prayer," 3.

it becomes possible to ask how some of the basic Christian doctrines affect and are affected by Christian prayer."[40] Garrett explores prayer's relatedness to six major headings: "The God and Father of All Prayer," "Jesus Christ and Prayer," "The Holy Spirit and Prayer," "The Person Who Prays," "The Church at Prayer," and "Prayer and the Eschaton."

Peter Beck's dissertation on Jonathan Edwards's theology of prayer takes a similar approach to Garrett's theology of prayer.[41] Beck explores Edwards's theology of prayer by analyzing the corollary doctrines of the Father, the Son, the Spirit, and humanity. Beck's thesis is that Edwards's theology of prayer is complex, "one part of the whole." Beck states, "Theology proper, Christology, pneumatology, and anthropology all play a vital role in his theology of prayer and fall within the scope, even if in sketch form only."[42] Beck observes that Edwards's understanding of God's character and nature is the key factor in his theology of prayer. Nonetheless, his theology of prayer relies on other aspects of the doctrine of God and humanity.[43] Together, Garrett's and Beck's studies provide exemplary systematic approaches to follow in constructing Fuller's theology of prayer. Methodologically, Garrett's and Beck's constructions are replicable with a new subject and data.[44]

Recent Developments in Fuller Studies

Fuller Studies have flourished over the last fifty years. In his bibliographic essay, "The Renaissance in Andrew Fuller Studies," Nathan Finn thoroughly documents an increase in Fuller Studies since the 1980s.[45] Finn states that there remain a number of profitable areas left to be explored. The present study seeks to fill one of those voids, Fuller's theology of prayer.[46] Finn's

40. Garrett, "Theology of Prayer."

41. Beck, "Voice of Faith." The similarities between the two studies are seemingly coincidental since Beck's dissertation does not include Garrett's article in the bibliography. I reviewed Garrett's article before discovering Beck's dissertation. Much of my initial reflection was shaped by Garrett; however, Beck's dissertation provides a more comprehensive study to replicate and further supports the validity of such multifaceted approach to understanding one's theology of prayer. See also Beck, *The Voice of Faith*.

42. Beck, "Voice of Faith," 41.

43. Beck, "Voice of Faith," 285–94.

44. One such alteration will be considering Fuller's eschatology, where Beck's research did not devote a chapter to the eschatological dimensions of Edwards's theology of prayer. Beck cites Robert Bakke's work, *The Power of Extraordinary Prayer*, as having drawn out this emphasis in Edwards's theology of prayer. Beck, "Voice of Faith," 12–13. See Bakke, *Power of Extraordinary Prayer*.

45. Finn, "Renaissance in Andrew Fuller Studies."

46. Finn, "Renaissance in Andrew Fuller Studies," 54.

study is commended to the reader for a thorough survey of Fuller Studies from 1980 to 2014. What follows will expound on a number of the works surveyed by Finn. Additionally, an explanation of noteworthy developments in Fuller Studies will be summarized with particular reference to Fuller's theology of prayer.

One of the most significant developments in Fuller Studies is the publication of a critical edition of *The Complete Works of Andrew Fuller*, published by De Gruyter. Michael Haykin is spearheading this ongoing project as the general editor. Once complete, this "modern critical edition of the entire corpus of Andrew Fuller's published and unpublished works" will expand modern readership of Fuller's works.[47] Three of the sixteen volumes are published and available for study.[48] Two other works are set to be published within the next year.[49]

Peter Morden has written two biographical treatments of Fuller's life and thought. The first, *Offering Christ to the World: Andrew Fuller (1754– 1815) and the Revival of Eighteenth Century Particular Baptist Life*, represented the first book-length biographical introduction to Fuller's life and ministry since Gilbert Laws's *Andrew Fuller: Pastor, Theologian, Ropeholder*, and Arthur H. Kirkby's *Andrew Fuller*.[50] Morden's thematic treatment of Fuller's life and thought connects his influence "in theology, pastoral practice, spirituality and work as a missionary statesman" to the revival of eighteenth-century Particular Baptist life.[51] Morden's work distinguishes itself from prior surveys in its utilization of primary sources, his interaction with modern secondary works on Fuller's thought, and his highlighting of Fuller's ministry as an embodiment of evangelical priorities.[52]

---

47. Fuller, *Complete Works: Samuel Pearce*, xi.

48. "The Complete Works of Andrew Fuller," last modified January 1, 2012, accessed February 27, 2018, https://www.degruyter.com/view/serial/455677; Fuller, *Complete Works: Diary*; Fuller, *Complete Works: Apologetic Works 5*; and Fuller, *Complete Works: Samuel Pearce*.

49. See Fuller, *Complete Works: Apologetic Works 3*; Fuller, *Complete Works: Apologetic Works 1*.

50. Laws, *Andrew Fuller, Pastor, Theologian, Ropeholder*; Kirkby, *Andrew Fuller*. Both works are out of print. See also Finn's assessment, Finn, "Renaissance in Andrew Fuller Studies," 45, 49.

51. Morden, *Offering Christ to the World*, 4–6.

52. Morden, *Offering Christ to the World*, 181–84. Morden utilizes Bebbington's quadrilateral as the defining marks of evangelicalism. Bebbington states, "There are the four qualities that have been the special marks of Evangelical religion: conversionism, the belief that lives need to be changed; activism, the expression of the gospel in effort; biblicism, a particular regard for the Bible; and what may be called crucicentrism, a stress on the sacrifice of Christ on the cross. Together they form a quadrilateral of priorities that is the basis of Evangelicalism." See Bebbington, *Evangelicalism in Modern*

Morden's latest biography, *The Life and Thought of Andrew Fuller (1754–1815)*, traces key moments and influences on Fuller's formation as a pastor, theologian, author, and leader of the BMS. His book is the most definitive biographical treatment of Fuller to date. Nonetheless, Morden admitted that any detailed study will have "gaps."[53] For example, he delimited himself from careful consideration of Fuller's *The Gospel its Own Witness*, a key apologetic response to Deism and the likes of Thomas Paine's *The Age of Reason*.[54]

In both biographical accounts, Morden attests to the prominence of prayer within Fuller's thought and ministry.[55] Morden describes Fuller's influential role within the Prayer Call of 1784, and labeled prayer as a priority in Fuller's spiritual life.[56] In line with a number of scholars noting the influence of Jonathan Edwards on Fuller's thought, Morden connects Fuller's enthusiasm for prayer with an "Edwardsean postmillennial eschatology."[57] Edwards's influence on Fuller's eschatology and theology of prayer may be an area of fruitful study. The Prayer Call of 1784[58] was a catalytic event for the founding of the BMS.[59] Through John Ryland Jr., the Northamptonshire Baptist Association was introduced to Edwards's book calling for corporate prayer for the purpose of revival and the expansion of the Kingdom of Christ.[60] Morden's connection between Edwards, the prayer call, and Fuller's subsequent missional activism provides a number of helpful starting points to explore influences on Fuller's theology of prayer. Nonetheless, a comprehensive treatment of Fuller's theology of prayer is far beyond the scope of either of Morden's thorough biographical works.

A number of tribute works have increased the availability of secondary scholarly sources. In 2015, the 200th anniversary of Fuller's death, *Founders Journal* featured Andrew Fuller in its summer issue. The journal includes an

---

Britain, 2–3.

53. Morden, *The Life and Thought of Andrew Fuller*, 8.

54. Morden, *The Life and Thought of Andrew Fuller*, 8.

55. See Morden, *Offering Christ to the World*, 120–27, 172–75; Morden, *Life and Thought of Andrew Fuller*, 73–74, 97.

56. Morden, *Life and Thought of Andrew Fuller*, 111–15; Morden, *Offering Christ to the World*, 120–26.

57. Morden, *Offering Christ to the World*, 113. See Chun, *The Legacy of Edwards in the Theology of Fuller*; Nettles, "The Influence of Edwards on Fuller," 97–116.

58. For an excellent introduction to the major figures and events surrounding the Prayer Call of 1784, see Haykin, *One Heart and One Soul*, 153–71; and Payne, "The Prayer Call of 1784," 19–30.

59. Morden, *Offering Christ to the World*, 120–26.

60. Morden, *Life and Thought of Andrew Fuller*, 111–12.

introduction by Tom Nettles, an article by Michael Haykin, five small sketches from various authors engaging with primary sources from a variety of Fuller's letters, sermons, and apologetic defenses; and an article by Paul Brewster, "Andrew Fuller's Doctrine of God."[61] The following year, *The Journal of Baptist Studies* featured Fuller as the subject of its annual publication. The publication contains five articles by Michael Haykin, Peter Beck, Chris Chun, Brian Daniels, and G. Stephen Weaver.[62] Both journals are a testament to the growing interest and corpus of secondary literature on Fuller in recent years.

Prayer and Fuller Studies

Michael A.G. Haykin, rightly identified in Finn's essay as "the key scholar engaging a wider range of Fuller's theology and legacy," has authored and edited a number of works with particular reference to Fuller's theology of prayer.[63] First, Haykin's article, "A Socinian and Calvinist Compared: Joseph Priestley and Andrew Fuller on the Propriety of Prayer to Christ," and his chapter from *One God in Three Persons*, "To Devote Ourselves to the Blessed Trinity," represent the importance of prayer within Fuller's theological enterprise.[64] Haykin demonstrates Fuller's aptitude as an apologist, taking on "the leading form of heterodoxy within English Dissent in the last quarter of the eighteenth century," Socinianism.[65] Prayer is a vital part of Fuller's argument for the divinity of Christ. He argued for the propriety of praying to, and thus worshipping, Jesus as fully God.[66] Both of Haykin's works represent the reciprocity of Fuller's theology of prayer with the doctrine of the Trinity, particularly the divinity of Christ. His works leave the researcher wondering if, and in what ways, Fuller may demonstrate such reciprocity between prayer and other major Christian doctrines.

61. Nettles, "Introduction," 4–6; Haykin, "Reading Andrew Fuller," 7–8; Ballitch, "Analysis of Fuller's The Gospel Its Own Witness," 9–10; Weaver, "An Unsung, but Influential Sermon," 11–13; Smith, "Analysis of Fuller's Letters to Mr. Vidler," 14–5; Bruce, "Analysis of Fuller's Strictures," 16–19; Owens, "Fuller's Reply to Philanthropos," 20–21; Brewster, "Andrew Fuller's Doctrine of God," 22–47.

62. Haykin, "An Historical and Biblical Root of the Globalization of Christianity," 3–15; Beck, "Trans-Atlantic Friendships," 16–50; Chun, "Andrew Fuller on the Atonement," 51–71; Daniels, "The Doctrine of the Bible's Truthfulness," 72–98; Weaver, "C. H. Spurgeon: A Fullerite?," 99–117.

63. Finn, "Renaissance in Andrew Fuller Studies," 46.

64. Haykin, "A Socinian and Calvinist Compared,"178–98; Haykin, "To Devote Ourselves to the Blessed Trinity."

65. Haykin, "Devote Ourselves to the Blessed Trinity," 180.

66. For more on Andrew Fuller as an apologist of the faith, see Haykin, *At the Pure Fountain of Thy Word*.

Haykin has also edited a collection of Fuller's letters, *Armies of the Lamb: The Spirituality of Andrew Fuller.* Haykin introduces the work with a sketch of Fuller's life and spirituality.[67] Fuller's theological reflection and eventual publication of *The Gospel Worthy of All Acceptation* represents more than just an exposition of soteriological musings disconnected from his pastoral ministry. Indeed, Haykin argues, "*The Gospel Worthy . . .* was . . . a key factor in determining the shape of Fuller's ministry."[68] Fuller's work on *The Gospel Worthy* in these early years left an indelible mark on his "mission-centered spirituality."[69] Haykin argues that the centrality of the cross, cultivation of spiritual friendships, and the pursuit of an experimental knowledge of God were key marks of Fuller's spirituality.[70] One could argue that prayer informed or was informed by all four of these aspects of Fuller's spirituality—mission-focused, cross-centered, a cultivation of spiritual friendship,[71] and deep knowledge and experience of God. The letters themselves give insight into Fuller's spirituality through the lens of personal correspondence, of which prayer is the subject.[72]

Haykin's *One Heart and One Soul: John Sutcliff of Olney, His Friends and His Times* provides an essential basis for understanding some of the major figures who influenced Fuller within the Northamptonshire Baptist Association, that is, John Sutcliff, John Ryland Jr., William Carey, and Samuel Pearce.[73] Haykin devoted a chapter to exploring the Prayer Call of 1784, a pivotal event regarding the future creation of the BMS.[74] Fourth, Haykin's "The Concert of Prayer in the 18th Century: A Model for Praying Together" highlights the influence of Jonathan Edwards and his treatise, "An Humble Attempt," on the Prayer Call of 1784, a prayer movement with consequence well beyond British or Baptist boundaries, and well beyond the lives of its principal originators.[75]

---

67. Haykin, *Armies of the Lamb*, 23–54.

68. Haykin, *Armies of the Lamb*, 35.

69. Haykin, *Armies of the Lamb*, 35–36.

70. Haykin, *Armies of the Lamb*, 36–53; esp. 36–37, 42–43, and 47.

71. The enduring effect of Fuller's Christian friendships are seen clearly in the numerous memoirs that he wrote upon their deaths, in particular his *Memoirs of the Late Rev. Samuel Pearce.* See Haykin, "Editor's Introduction."

72. Haykin, *Armies of the Lamb*, esp. 91–109.

73. Haykin, *One Heart and One Soul.*

74. Haykin, *One Heart and One Soul*, 153–71. See also Edwards, *Humble Attempt*, 278–312. For more on the influence of Edwards on Fuller, see Nettles, "Influence of Jonathan Edwards on Andrew Fuller," 97–116; Chun, *Legacy of Edwards in the Theology of Fuller.*

75. Haykin, "Concert of Prayer," 123–45.

Prior to Haykin's work regarding the Prayer Call of 1784, E. A. Payne's brief account of the catalytic movement was the best introduction to principal events and persons surrounding the call.[76] Payne highlighted three outcomes of the prayer call. First, the prayer call was vital to the formation of the BMS. Second, the call reached beyond Northampton and Baptist connections. And, third, the movement exceeded the lives of the original progenitors of the movement, that is, "for several generations . . . in Baptist churches, the monthly missionary prayer-meeting remained one of the most vital and rewarding gatherings of all those held."[77] Haykin's and Payne's conclusions seem to be in harmony. Regarding Fuller's influence, Payne highlights Fuller's lesser-known work, *Persuasives to General Union in Extraordinary Prayer for the Revival and Extent of Real Religion*, as "mak[ing] abundantly clear what was in the mind of the little company."[78] Additionally, Payne regards the effect of Edwards's *An Humble Attempt* as most easily observable "in the case of Andrew Fuller."[79] "This Call to Prayer," according to Payne, "had a story behind it, and was issued by men themselves deeply conscious of the solemnity of the step they took and how costly and searching a thing Christian prayer must be to those who rightly embark upon it."[80]

Two PhD dissertations and one ThM thesis have focused on Fuller's pastoral theology,[81] all of which draw attention to the importance of prayer within Fuller's life and ministry. The following paragraphs will survey the primary thesis of each work, highlight the author's conclusions regarding Fuller's theology of prayer, and make a concluding assessment.

Paul Brewster's PhD dissertation, "Andrew Fuller (1754–1815): Model Baptist Pastor-Theologian," is a valuable work of retrieval. Brewster's thesis is "that British Baptist pastor Andrew Fuller is a model pastor-theologian, as demonstrated in his theological method, his leadership during a critical soteriological controversy, and his manner of relating doctrine and practice."[82] One of Fuller's primary means of relating doctrine and practice was through his preaching. Brewster provides a critical interaction with

---

76. See Payne, "Prayer Call of 1784."

77. Payne, "Prayer Call of 1784," 30.

78. Payne, "Prayer Call of 1784," 20.

79. Payne, "Prayer Call of 1784," 23.

80. Payne, "Prayer Call of 1784," 21.

81. James Lapsley's definition of pastoral theology—"theological inquiry into the care of persons in an ecclesial context, or by ecclesial representatives outside that full context"—may serve as good working definition, particularly regarding the studies surveyed below. See Lapsley, "Defining Pastoral Theology," 116–24.

82. Brewster, "Model Baptist Pastor-Theologian," 2–3. Brewster's dissertation was republished as a monograph in 2010. See Brewster, *Andrew Fuller.*

Fuller's dual function as a pastor and a capable theologian, both as a defender of orthodoxy and evangelical Calvinism. Fuller's work on *The Gospel Worthy* was influential in the "matter" and "manner" of his preaching, that is, the sermon matter "must contain the content of the gospel," and the manner must be "with the objective of bringing his hearers to the point of decision."[83] Brewster proposes that Baptist pastors will be better equipped theologically and practically by looking to good pastor-theologians who rightly see that "theology and church health are inextricably linked," and "that the theological soundness of Baptist congregations is directly dependent on the theological influences of the pastor."[84]

Brewster identifies the significance of prayer in a sub-section on Fuller's theological method. One must have "a proper spiritual frame of mind to understand the Scriptures rightly." One cannot have this right frame of mind, in Fuller's understanding, without prayer and the Word. Prayer and the Word are inseparable in Fuller's thinking. Brewster concludes, "As Fuller saw it, constant engagement in prayer and immersion in the Word of God was a *sine qua non* for the pastor-theologian."[85] Positively, the two pages that Brewster devoted to place of prayer and the Word in theological reflections highlighted the prominence of prayer in Fuller's piety and spirituality. Brewster posed two lengthy quotes, one from a letter to a young minister and another from his diary, as evidence for such piety. Additionally, Brewster recognized the importance of corporate prayer and spiritual friendships in Fuller's prayer life.[86] Addressing Fuller's practice of prayer under the major heading of "Andrew Fuller's Theological Method," Brewster treated prayer as a central component of Fuller's experience in theological reflection.[87] Brewster neglected to draw out clear points of systematic reflection on prayer.

Also in 2007, Keith Grant completed his master's thesis on Fuller's evangelical renewal of pastoral theology. In 2013, the thesis was published under the title, *Andrew Fuller and the Evangelical Renewal of Pastoral Theology*.[88] Grant's primary thesis is that "evangelical renewal did not only take place *alongside* the local church, but especially in congregational ecclesiology, there was a transformation *within* the existing pastoral office."[89]

83. Brewster, "Model Baptist Pastor-Theologian," 126–28.

84. Brewster, "Model Baptist Pastor-Theologian," 2.

85. Brewster, "Model Baptist Pastor-Theologian," 64.

86. Brewster, "Model Baptist Pastor-Theologian," 64.

87. Such clear points have already been highlighted in Haykin's work on Fuller's response to Socinianism and Joseph Priestley. See Haykin, "A Socinian and Calvinist Compared."

88. Grant, *Andrew Fuller*.

89. Grant, *Andrew Fuller*, 3. Emphasis original.

Grant stated that the "Northamptonshire pastor of the later eighteenth century exemplified the renewal of such an evangelical pastoral theology in the transformed dissenting churches, a renewal that was particularly evident in his preaching."[90] Grant stated, "Fuller's pastoral theology applied to preaching . . . was *plain* in composition and delivery, *evangelical* in content and concern, and *affectionate* in feeling and application."[91] Grant saw Fuller as helping to bring about a renewal in the pastoral theology of Particular Baptists, particularly with reference to their preaching; that is, Fuller now "used the language of 'obligation' and 'duty': urgent, affectionate, conversionist, and evangelical."[92]

Grant's work makes an excellent contribution to the field by exploring the development in Fuller's pastoral theology from the perspective of his preaching. Even still, his study did have a few minor weaknesses. For example, Grant's reasoning for Particular Baptists' seemingly delayed response to the revival lacked substance. This author agrees with Haykin, Grant's explanation was "all too simplistic." Grant stated that Gill and Brine's negative answer to the "Modern Question," along with "other elements of high Calvinist piety, meant that Particular Baptists were largely, though not entirely, unaffected by the revival until the late-eighteenth century."[93] One may consider that the revival's principal originators, Wesley and Whitefield, were members of the Established Church. This alone endowed a number of dissenting churches, not just Baptists, with a skeptical outlook on the revival at large. Nonetheless, Grant's study begs the question: If elements of high Calvinist piety are to blame for Particular Baptists missing the early years of the revival, then did his theology of prayer go through a similar evangelical transformation as Grant traces in his preaching ministry?

In 2009, Nigel Wheeler wrote a dissertation on Fuller's pastoral theology as expressed in his ordination sermons.[94] The study was the first of its kind, considering whether Fuller's pastoral theology was in continuity or discontinuity with his denominational predecessors. Wheeler draws upon an under-utilized source material, ordination sermons, in exploring the pastoral theology of British Particular Baptists. By exploring the ordination sermons of prior Particular Baptist ministers, Wheeler places Fuller's

90. Grant, *Andrew Fuller*, 77.

91. Grant, *Andrew Fuller*, 103. Emphasis original.

92. Grant, *Andrew Fuller*, 49–50.

93. Grant, *Andrew Fuller*, 27. In a review article, Haykin found this explanation of the delay in the revival amongst Particular Baptists as "all too simplistic." See Haykin, "Very Affecting and Evangelical," 42–45. For an introduction to the "Modern Question," see Nuttall, "Northamptonshire," 101–23.

94. Wheeler, "Eminent Spirituality and Eminent Usefulness."

pastoral theology in his most immediate ecclesial context, tracing areas of continuity and discontinuity between Fuller and his Particular Baptist heritage. In light of Grant's study, the importance of Wheeler's contextual study is quite apparent. Wheeler's study concludes that Fuller was more in continuity than in discontinuity with the pastoral theology of his denominational forbearers in the "seventeenth century and even those with high Calvinists leanings in the early part of the eighteenth century."[95] Wheeler's study provides a helpful analysis of the corpus of Fuller's ordination sermons and the ordination sermons of some of Fuller's immediate ecclesial influences within his own denomination, men like Nehemiah Coxe, Joseph Stennett, John Gill, and John Brine.[96] Wheeler describes prayer as a part of the structure of Particular Baptists' ordination sermons.[97] Another section treats public prayer as one of the pastoral duties prescribed in ordination sermons.[98] Wheeler's section on "Piety and Effectiveness" also provides a helpful starting point to explore some of Fuller's early influences regarding his private prayer life. Additional insights are left to be explored regarding Fuller's theology of prayer within his pastoral theology as a whole.[99]

---

95. Wheeler, "Eminent Spirituality and Eminent Usefulness," 239–40.

96. Wheeler's conclusions regarding Fuller's continuity within his Particular Baptist tradition presents an apparent contradiction with some of Grant's conclusions in *Andrew Fuller and the Evangelical Renewal of Pastoral Theology*. Wheeler states, "Fuller's demolition of High Calvinist dogma was in fact more of a renewal of earlier Baptist evangelical priorities and in this sense was more of a revitalization of pastoral theology within their tradition." See Wheeler, "Eminent Spirituality and Eminent Usefulness," 240. Resolving this contradiction and others is beyond the scope of the present study. Nonetheless, a section of the study considering Fuller's ecclesial tradition may provide circumstantial evidence to support either Wheeler or Grant's claims. Wheeler's conclusions may also challenge Bebbington's thesis that the Evangelical Revival has a clear beginning in the 1730s with a shift in the doctrine of assurance. He challenges Bebbington's thesis by providing support for those who trace the emergence of evangelicalism to persons, events, and so forth, which predate the likes of Wesley, Whitefield, and Edwards. Bebbington's thesis is that "the timing of their [Edwards and Wesley] remoulding of the doctrine of assurance according to empiricist canons has to be understood as a result of the spread of a new cultural mood." See Bebbington, *Evangelicalism in Modern Britain*, 52–54. The change in mood was the product of the Enlightenment, according to Bebbington. A number of works have challenged Bebbington's thesis. For the most comprehensive response to Bebbington's work by multiple contributors, see Haykin and Stewart, *Advent of Evangelicalism*.

97. Wheeler, "Eminent Spirituality and Eminent Usefulness," 108–9.

98. Wheeler, "Eminent Spirituality and Eminent Usefulness," 151.

99. Wheeler, "Eminent Spirituality and Eminent Usefulness," 189ff.

Importance of the Study

A study of Andrew Fuller's theology of prayer will contribute to the growing corpus of research on this significant figure in Baptist and Evangelical
thought. In addition to filling a void in the burgeoning field of Fuller Studies, a number of benefits arise from such an exploration. With no major
study on Fuller's theology of prayer, the research will provide new perspectives concerning the continuity and discontinuity of Fuller's belief and practice. A construction of his theology of prayer through analysis of corollary
doctrines will provide a unique test of consistency and coherence to Fuller's
theology as a whole.

Replicating Garrett and Beck's method of analysis provides a secondary benefit. The dissertation will draw conclusions regarding the usefulness
of their methodology in constructing one's theology of prayer.

As Payne convincingly details in "The Prayer Call of 1874," there is a
story behind the formation of a prayer movement, which eventually led to
the formation of the BMS. Likewise, there is a theology that develops and
matures along the same lines. The story behind the BMS deserves retelling
from this systematic angle, understanding the sacred principles that undergirded the holy practice.[100]

Finally, a study of Fuller's theology of prayer may help the church
today as it considers prayer as an essential aspect of the pastor and congregation's vitality and effectiveness in ministry. In agreement with Brewster,
Fuller may serve as an excellent mentor for today, particularly in developing
an evangelical theology of prayer. Perhaps a decline in evangelical activism
can be traced to a decline in a critical stimulus for evangelical activism,
prayer. Garrett's words summarize the hope for any study of one's theology
of prayer: "The purpose of a theology of Christian prayer is that Christians
may pray more effectively. So may it be."[101] To be sure, Garrett's adverbial
modification is a succinct summary of my hope, that Christians may pray
more and pray more *effectively*.

Methodology

The researcher will replicate Garrett's and Beck's systematic, multifaceted
approach to understanding one's theology of prayer with a new subject and
data; namely, Fuller and his works. The dissertation will differ from Beck's

---

100. As Fuller saw it, "holy practice has a necessary dependence on sacred principle." Fuller, *Works*, 1:20.

101. Fuller, *Works*, 1:17.

by mirroring the doctrines identified by Garrett as the major corollary Christian doctrines of prayer; namely, the Trinity, humanity, the church, and eschatology.

What Is the Data?

The main body of data comes from the three-volume collection of Andrew Fuller's works edited by Joseph Belcher, *The Complete Works of Andrew Fuller*.[102] This collection, along with the available publications from *The Complete Works of Andrew Fuller*, edited by Haykin, serves as the primary source for exploration. Memoirs and biographical works by John Ryland Jr., J. W. Morris, and Fuller's son, Andrew Gunton Fuller, serve as invaluable records of Fuller's life and ministry.

Secondary data comes from a number of recent books, articles, and dissertations on Fuller's life and thought. Several of these works have been aforementioned in the "State of Research."

Criteria for Admissibility of the Data

Brewster and Wheeler both demonstrate the significance of using Fuller's sermons as essential for understanding his theology. Special attention will be given to Fuller's sermons related to prayer and the selected major doctrines of the faith. Fuller's exposition on the Lord's Prayer and numerous sermons on Paul's Epistles related to prayer deserve a close reading for Fuller's explicit teaching regarding prayer. Likewise, Fuller's diary and biographical works by Ryland, Morris, and A.G. Fuller will provide critical data regarding Fuller's prayers and practice of prayer.

Acquiring the Data

Fuller's *Works* are available and searchable within *Logos Bible Software* through tagged words, Boolean Operators, and Proximity Operators. In addition to giving select works a careful read, the researcher will make full use of the search functions to explore each instance of words synonymous with prayer.[103] A.G. Fuller's memoirs of his father are part of the *Works* on *Logos*.

---

102. Fuller, *Works*, vols. 1–3.

103. Words selected to search include, "pray(s)," "prayer(s)," "praying," "petition(s)," "intercede(s)," "implore(s)," "calling on," "crying to," "entreat(s)," "supplicate(s)," "watch," and "importune(s)."

Ryland and Morris's memoirs of Fuller are available and searchable on *Hathi Trust Digital Library*.[104] The researcher has transcribed every prayer or mention of prayer to include prayer meetings and days of prayer from the newly published *Diary of Andrew Fuller, 1780–1801*, edited by Michael D. McMullen and Timothy D. Whelan.[105] For ease of reference, the transcription of each prayer is included in the appendix.

Interpreting the Data

The study is a replication of Beck's multifaceted approach to constructing a theology of prayer with a new subject and data. Differing from Beck, the researcher will include a chapter on ecclesiology and eschatology. Additionally, the researcher utilized Garrett's doctrinal categories.

Methodologically, Garrett constructs a theology of prayer with three components: (1) a preliminary examination of "the nature and moods of Christian prayer"; (2) a framework of major Christian doctrines, considering the implications for prayer with each doctrine; and (3) explanations of the prayers and teachings on prayer in Scripture, considering the implications for corollary Christian doctrines. The researcher will adapt Garrett's methodology to suit the needs of the present study. The researcher will first prioritize setting Fuller within his ecclesial context and evaluating the dominant attitudes and thoughts regarding prayer in the eighteenth century, particularly in the Baptist tradition. Fuller's theology of prayer will be constructed through (1) exploring Fuller's understanding of the nature and moods of Christian prayer as represented in his expositions on the prayers of Scripture; (2) analyzing Fuller's understanding of major Christian doctrines, considering their implications for prayer; (3) analyzing Fuller's writings on prayer, considering implications for corollary doctrines; and (4) analyzing Fuller's practice of prayer, considering the implications for corollary Christian doctrines. The researcher will follow this pattern in the collection of the data and presentation of the findings. Each chapter will survey the select doctrinal point from Fuller's perspective; consider implications for prayer; analyze Fuller's relevant expositions of prayers and teachings on prayer; and analyze Fuller's practice regarding prayer for implications with select doctrine.

---

104. See Ryland, *Work of Faith*; Morris, *Memoirs*.
105. Fuller, *Complete Works: Diary*.

1

Foundational Considerations
for Fuller's Theology of Prayer

THE FOLLOWING CHAPTER SETS out to accomplish two things: (1) situate
Fuller within his ecclesial context, especially as it relates to prayer; and
(2) introduce Fuller's practice of prayer. Situating Fuller within his ecclesial context means briefly surveying beliefs and practices regarding prayer
from late-seventeenth and early-eighteenth-century Britain in general and
specifically those within the Particular Baptist tradition and the Northamptonshire Baptist Association. Finally, introducing Fuller's practice of prayer
means surveying the pertinent literature regarding his thoughts and actions
regarding prayer with respect to his private duty as a Christian and public
duty as a pastor. The reader will be introduced to Fuller's major works concerning prayer and his practice of prayer through a brief spiritual biography.
Fuller's ecclesial context and personal practice of prayer are foundational for
considering his theology of prayer.

Fuller's Ecclesial Context

The following section explores Fuller's ecclesial context concerning basic
beliefs and practices regarding prayer. Surveying the beliefs and practices
regarding prayer in Britain's broader ecclesial landscape in the late-
seventeenth century sets the stage for understanding Baptist beliefs and
practices regarding prayer from the late-seventeenth to early-eighteenth
century.

The brief survey will progress chronologically from the Act of Uniformity 1662 to the mid-eighteenth century. Additionally, the survey will move from more general beliefs and practices regarding prayer to the specific beliefs and practices of the Particular Baptist tradition. The survey concludes by considering Fuller's immediate context: the early years and figures of the Northamptonshire Baptist Association.

Prayer in Britain

In the late-seventeenth century, Britain was divided broadly into two ecclesial groups, Anglicans and Nonconformists. The Anglicans were those belonging to the Establishment, that is, the Church of England. The Nonconformists, or Dissenters, as they were lumped together, included Baptists, Congregationalists, and Presbyterians.[1] The divide between eighteenth-century Anglicans and Nonconformists may be traced to the seventeenth-century divide between Anglicans and Puritans. Horton Davies traces the divide between Puritans and Anglicans to the liturgical divide between the Magisterial Reformers, Luther and Calvin. He states,

> The results of the Lutheran and Calvinist liturgical reforms are admittedly different . . . The real difference between Lutheran and Calvinist reforms in worship may be summed up as follows: Luther will have what is not specifically condemned by the Scriptures; whilst Calvin will have only what is ordained by God in the Scriptures. That is their fundamental disagreement. It is of vital importance in the history of Puritan worship, since the Puritans accepted the Calvinist criterion, whilst their opponents, the Anglicans, accepted the Lutheran criterion.[2]

In the seventeenth century, the divide between Anglicans and Nonconformists continued along these same lines and was accentuated by differing opinions regarding prayer. Davies states, "If the main theological difference between Puritan and Anglican worship consists in the attempt of the Puritans to model their worship more closely on the Biblical criterion, this resolved itself practically in the Puritan emphasis on free prayer over against the 'stented forms' of the Establishment."[3] Although some Puritans advocated for their own prayer books or various revisions of the *BCP*, their

1. Davies, *English Free Churches*, 1.

2. See Davies, *Worship of the English Puritans*, 16. For more on how the Puritans' theology of worship was inherited from Calvin's theology of worship see Davies, *Worship of the English Puritans*, 13–24.

3. Davies, *Worship of the English Puritans*, 98.

use and appropriateness was a source of controversy in the British Isles for nearly a century prior to the Act of Uniformity.[4] John Bunyan's dialogue with the several Justices during his imprisonment reflects the divide in belief regarding set and extemporaneous forms of prayer. The clerk read the charge against Bunyan. Among other items, Bunyan was accused of not attending services of the Church of England and holding "several unlawful meetings and conventicles, to the great disturbance and distraction of the good subjects of this kingdom contrary to the laws of our sovereign lord the King."[5] Bunyan recorded the discussion that ensued:

> *The Clerk.* When this was read, the clerk of the sessions said unto me, What say you to this?
>
> *Bun.* I said, that as to the first part of it, I was a common frequenter of the church of God. And was also, by grace, a member with the people over whom Christ is the Head.
>
> *Keelin.* But, saith Justice Keelin, who was the judge in that court? Do you come to church, you know what I mean; to the parish church, to hear Divine service?
>
> *Bun.* I answered, No, I did not.
>
> *Keel.* He asked me why?
>
> *Bun.* I said, because I did not find it commanded in the Word of God.
>
> *Keel.* He said, We were commanded to pray.
>
> *Bun.* I said, But not by the Common Prayer Book.
>
> *Keel.* He said, How then?
>
> *Bun.* I said, With the Spirit. As the apostle saith, "I will pray with the Spirit, and with the understanding" (1 Cor 14:15).
>
> *Keel.* He said, We might pray with the Spirit, and with the understanding, and with the Common Prayer Book also.

4. For more on the use of prayer books within nonconformity, especially among Puritans of the sixteenth century, see Peaston, *Prayer Book Tradition in the Free Churches*, esp. 16–34. *The Book of Common Prayer* is hereafter abbreviated as *BCP*. The Church of England authorized numerous versions of the *BCP*. For clarity, *BCP* will be used to refer to the book generically rather than specific editions.

Chapter 6 will interact with the controversy surrounding the use of set or free forms of prayer as the dispute relates to one's theology of prayer and doctrine of the Spirit. Puritans and Separatists of the late-sixteenth and early-seventeenth century saw the rise and use of the *BCP* as an ecclesial intrusion that quenched the work of the Spirit. See Davies, *Worship and Theology*, 19; and Davies, *Worship of the English Puritans*, 55–56, 67–69.

5. Bunyan, *Relation of His Imprisonment*, 54.

> *Bun.* I said that the prayers in the Common Prayer Book were
> such as were made by other men, and not by the motions of the
> Holy Ghost, within our hearts; and as I said, the apostle saith, he
> will pray with the Spirit, and with the understanding; not with
> the Spirit and the Common Prayer Book.[6]

The authority of Scripture in worship has implications for the use, adaptation, or rejection of a state-authorized prayer book. These implications were
borne out in the Anglican, Puritan, and Separatist's beliefs and practices
regarding prayer.[7]

The Book of Common Prayer[8] was at the center of British beliefs and
practices regarding prayer in the late-seventeenth century. According to
Judith Maltby, the BCP was the decisive influencer of religious thought in
England. She states,

> To its detractors, the Prayer Book provided too much continuity
> with England's medieval and "popish" past. However, it was the
> experience of suppression which successfully turned Common
> Prayer into an undisputed identifier of an emerging Anglican
> self-consciousness. A liturgy which was composed to serve at
> "all times and in all places" would become after 1660 a way of
> distinguishing oneself from dissenting neighbours.[9]

Even though banned from use in 1645, the BCP remained woven into the
religious life of England throughout the era of the Commonwealth. Shortly
after the Restoration in 1660, Charles II commissioned a convocation of

---

6. Bunyan, *Relation of His Imprisonment*, 54.

7. Anglicans, following the Act of Uniformity 1662, adopted wholesale the *BCP*,
while the majority of Puritans rejected the use of a state-authorized prayer book because such a device found no justification in Scripture. One of the main differences
between Separatists and Puritans, aside from the Separatists' willingness to separate for
the sake of Reformation, was the "radical opposition to set or 'stinted' forms of prayer."
See Davies, *English Free Churches*, 38–39. Separatists are, as Garrett states, "those English Puritans who, not being willing to continue to await thoroughgoing reforms in the
Church of England, separated therefrom by constituting congregations or conventicles
on the basis of a church covenant and congregational polity." Garrett, *Baptist Theology*,
16. *A True Confession*, a Separatist confession that "expressed Calvinistic doctrine and
congregational polity" was distinctively helpful in the crafting of a Particular Baptist
confession in 1644. Garrett, *Baptist Theology*, 19. For more on Separatists and their
influence on early Baptists, see Garrett, *Baptist Theology*, 16–22; and McBeth, *Baptist
Heritage*, 25–31. Garrett's survey focuses on the theological influence of Separatism
on Baptists. McBeth's survey focuses on the principle characters of the Separatist
movement.

8. For a comprehensive look at the *BCP*'s use and development, see Hefling and
Shattuck, *Oxford Guide to The Book of Common Prayer*; Jacobs, *Book of Common Prayer*.

9. Maltby, "The Prayer Book."

Anglican and Presbyterian divines to discuss modifications to a proposed Book of Common Prayer, what would become a shibboleth of sorts between Anglicans and Nonconformists. The heart of the theological disagreement dividing these two groups was the authority of Scripture regarding matters of worship and the nature of the church. The two traditions' differing views regarding the authority of Scripture in matters of worship and the nature of the church were manifest clearly in Britain's divergent beliefs and practices regarding prayer.

The Act of Uniformity—the full name being "An Act for the Uniformity of Public Prayers and Administrations of Sacraments and other Rites and Ceremonies: and for establishing the form of making, ordaining, and consecrating Bishops, Priests, and Deacons, in the Church of England"—required the following:

> Every parson, vicar, or other minister whatsoever, who now hath and enjoyeth any ecclesiastical benefice or promotion within this realm of England, or places aforesaid, shall in the church, chapel, or place of public worship belonging to his said benefice or promotion, upon some Lord's day before the feast of St. Bartholomew, which shall be in the year of our Lord God, one thousand six hundred and sixty two, openly, publicly, and solemnly read the morning and evening prayer appointed to be read by and according to the said Book of Common Prayer, at the times thereby appointed; and after such reading thereof, shall openly and publicly, before the congregation there assembled, declare his unfeigned assent and consent to the use of all things in the said book contained and prescribed in these words and no other.[10]

Those who failed to assent and consent publicly to the BCP were "deprived of all his spiritual promotions. And that from thenceforth . . . to present or collate to the same, as though the person or persons so offending or neglecting were dead."[11] Each new minister within the Church of England likewise was to assent and consent publicly to the BCP "within two months next after that he shall be in the actual possession of the said ecclesiastical benefice or promotion."[12] Effectively furthering the divide, the Act of Uniformity forced Puritan ministers either to conform or be removed from the Anglican order. Ministers were ejected from their parishes or political posts upon refusal "to

10. Act of Uniformity, III. All quotations of the Act of Uniformity 1662 are taken from Bayne, *Documents Relating to the Settlement*, 386–403.

11. Bayne, *Documents Relating to the Settlement*, 389.

12. Bayne, *Documents Relating to the Settlement*, 390.

be re-ordained, . . . and to declare 'unfeigned assent and consent' to the Book of Common Prayer, as in all things agreeable to the Word of God."[13] The ejection occurred on August 24, 1662, St. Bartholomew's Day, a day known as the Great Ejection. The Act of Uniformity—just one of "the five-stringed whip" (as Clarendon Code was known)—impacted Presbyterian ministers more so than Congregationalists or Baptists whose understanding of the "gathered church" and its relation to the state was more akin to the Separatists.[14] Nonetheless, the irony of the Act of Uniformity, as Davies stated, is that "it aimed at compelling religious uniformity; it succeeded in consolidating religious Nonconformity as a force in the national life of England."[15]

Prayer in the Particular Baptist Tradition

English Particular Baptists, broadly speaking, belong to the Nonconformist tradition of worship, a tradition inherited from English Puritans and Separatists.[16] The affinity of English Particular Baptists with Puritans is seen clearly by the framers of the Second London Confession of Faith choosing to model their confession after the Westminster Confession of Faith with a few adoptions from the Savoy Declaration.[17] The SLC is one of the most far-reaching Particular Baptist doctrinal confessions.[18] The SLC's statements on worship both represented and shaped the basic beliefs and practices regarding prayer for Particular Baptists of the late-seventeenth century into the eighteenth century. The following section will consider several articles from the SLC's chapter 22, "Of Religious Worship and the Sabbath," to present a baseline of Particular Baptist beliefs and practices regarding prayer; that is, they viewed prayer as an aspect of worship, Trinitarian, made in accordance with God's will, accompanied frequently with humiliation and fasting, and practiced everywhere—in private, with family, and in public worship gatherings.

13. Davies, *English Free Churches*, 93.

14. Davies, *English Free Churches*, 90–93; Davies, *Worship and Theology*, 24–29.

15. Davies, *English Free Churches*, 93.

16. See White, *Protestant Worship*, 117–20; Davies, *Worship and Theology in England*, 19–24.

17. Hereafter, the *Second London Confession of Faith* will be abbreviated as SLC. Likewise, the *Westminster Confession of Faith* will be abbreviated as WCF. For an introduction to the SLC with comparison of similarities and differences to the WCF and *Savoy Declaration*, see Garrett, *Baptist Theology*, 71–80.

18. David Dockery says, "This statement has served as one of the most influential shaping documents for Baptist Theology." Dockery, "Looking Back, Looking Ahead," 339.

An Aspect of Worship

Particular Baptists viewed prayer as an aspect of worship. The SLC treats prayer under the chapter addressing worship and the Sabbath. The belief that prayer is an aspect of worship is not unique to Baptists; nonetheless, the SLC, like the WCF and Savoy Declaration, clearly articulates prayer as belonging to the larger heading of worship. Locating prayer under this heading is significant with regard to the fracture in the ecclesial landscape, which developed along the line of the authority of Scripture and with particular reference to worship. For Particular Baptists, like other Nonconformists, Scripture is the authority for practice and belief regarding worship. Therefore, the Scripture is the authority for Particular Baptist practice and belief regarding prayer.[19]

Trinitarian

Particular Baptists ascribed worship to the Trinity—"In this divine and infinite Being there are three subsistences, the Father, the Word (or Son) and Holy Spirit, of one substance, power, and Eternity, each having the whole Divine Essence."[20] Chapter 22, Article 2 states: "*Religious Worship* is to be given to *God* the *Father*, *Son* and *Holy Spirit*, and to him alone; not to *Angels*, *Saints*, or any other *Creatures*; and since the fall, not without a *Mediator*, nor in the *Mediation* of any other but Christ alone."[21] Prayer, therefore, is Trinitarian by merit of being an aspect of worship.

Prayer, also, is naturally Trinitarian by virtue of God's design. The SLC's article on God and the Trinity ends with the statement, "The Trinity is the foundation of all our Communion with God, and comfortable dependence

---

19. In this respect, it is worth noting the close affinity in worship that Particular Baptists shared with other Dissenters, especially Independents. Davies observes that aside from the mode of baptism, distinguishing between Particular Baptist and Independent practices of worship is difficult. See Christopher J. Ellis, citing a specific example of the similarities between Baptists and Independents, states that Isaac Watts, an Independent, exercised "a wide influence among eighteenth-century dissenting circles, both through his hymns and his *Guide to Prayer*." See Ellis, *Gathering*, 53. Also worth noting here, Watts had an observable influence upon Fuller. Aside from quoting Watts in his diary, Fuller recommended to a young minister in lacking the proper words for preaching to "read, good and easy authors; Dr. Watts especially." See Fuller, *Works*, 3:443. Additionally, Fuller's library record on August 28, 1798 lists six works or collections of works by Watts. It appears as though Watts's *A Guide to Prayer* was not among these collections. Fuller, *Complete Works: Diary*, 1:216–17.

20. SLC 2.3. All SLC quotations are from McGlothlin, *Baptist Confessions*, 215–89.

21. SLC 22.2. Italics original.

on him."[22] One is hard-pressed to think of an action more fitting than prayer to further one's communion with God or represent a comfortable dependence on him. Prayer is a regular means of communion with God and a beautiful expression of dependence on him. Chapter 22, Article 3 expresses the Trinitarian-nature of prayer well: "Prayer . . . is to be made in the Name of the Son, by the help of the Spirit, according to his Will."[23] Benjamin Keach preached a sermon regarding the glory given to God the Father, Son, and Holy Spirit when prayer is given in the pattern prescribed by the SLC. According to Keach, persons approaching the Father by merit of their relationship to Christ glorify the Father by approaching as a child approaches a father. They exalt Christ through calling on his name. And they glorify the Spirit by dependence on him to "call on Jesus Christ aright."[24]

In Accordance with God's Will

Chapter 22, Article 3 states that a prayer is only accepted if made "according to his Will; with understanding, reverence, humility, fervency, faith, love, and perseverance; and when with others, in a known tongue."[25] The article expresses that not only is the content of one's petition to be in accordance with God's will, but also the disposition of the heart. This seems to be the heart of Bunyan's protest against the BCP:

> I said that the prayers in the Common Prayer Book were such as were made by other men, and not by the motions of the Holy Ghost, within our hearts; and as I said, the apostle saith, he will pray with the Spirit, and with the understanding; not with the Spirit and the Common Prayer Book.[26]

To expand Bunyan's argument, the BCP may supply a form of prayer, but the Spirit supplies the understanding, reverence, humility, fervency, faith, love, and perseverance necessary for prayer according to God's will.

The next article moves from the heart of the one praying to articulate specific things revealed in Scripture appropriate for prayer. Chapter 22, Article 4 states, "Prayer is to be made for things lawful, and for all sorts of men living, or that shall live hereafter; but not for the dead, nor for those

22. SLC 2.3.
23. SLC 23.3.
24. Keach, *Parables*, 440–41.
25. SLC 22.3.
26. Bunyan, *Relation of His Imprisonment*, 54.

of whom it may be known that they have sinned the sin unto death."[27] The main belief and practice expressed with regard to prayer here is fidelity to Scripture. One may pray for all things lawful, all people, and the unborn because Scripture either commands or exemplifies such prayer as according to God's will. Conversely, one may not pray for the dead nor one who has "sinned the sin unto death" because Scripture prohibits such prayer as contrary to God's will.

Frequently with Humiliation and Fasting

The fifth article states that "solemn humiliation, with fastings; and thanksgiving upon special occasions, ought to be used in an holy and religious manner" as part of one's "religious worship of God."[28] The SLC adapted the WCF's final clause with few changes. The WCF states that "besides religious oaths, vows, solemn fastings, and thanksgivings upon several occasions; which are, in their several times and seasons, to be used in an holy and religious manner."[29] Aside from the exclusion of "religious oaths, vows," the SLC changed "several" to "special occasions" of thanksgiving and omitted "which are, in their several times and seasons." The special occasions of prayer and fasting in which Particular Baptists regularly participated include ordination of ministers and extraordinary circumstances.

Regarding the ordination of ministers, both General and Particular Baptists historically practiced fasting and prayer as a normative part of the setting apart and ordination of her ministers. Thomas Helwys's confession from Amsterdam in 1611 states, "That these *officers* are to be chosen when there are persons qualified according to the rules in Christ's testament, by election and approbation of that *church* or congregation whereof

---

27. SLC 22.4.

28. SLC 22.

29. WCF 21.5. WCF quoted from Schaff, *Creeds*, 3:647–48. The exclusion of religious oaths and taking of vows under this article may be a reflection of careful editing—since chapter 23 addresses lawful oaths and vows—or possibly be a response to the abuses and misuses of religious oaths that had to be taken on the Sabbath day in the Act of Uniformity. Additionally, Particular Baptists were concerned with hedging out occasional conformity among their ranks. Particular Baptists rejected the practice of occasional conformity before the Occasional Conformity Act (1711) made occasional conformity politically untenable. In SLC's chapter 23, article 3, the caution is given: "Whosoever takes an oath warranted by the word of God, ought duly to consider the weightiness of so solemn an act, and therein to avouch nothing but what he knows to be truth; *for that by rash, false, and vain oaths, the Lord is provoked, and for them this land mourns.*"

they are members, with fasting, prayer, and laying on of hands."[30] Likewise, a 1656 confession from a company of Particular Baptist churches in and around Somerset County included fasting and prayer along with the laying on of hands as the duty of the church for setting apart her ministers for ordination.[31]

Regarding extraordinary circumstances, Benjamin Keach wrote in a published sermon that there are seven such "special times for extraordinary prayer":

1. When we are afflicted.

2. When we are tempted.

3. When we look for, and suddenly expect to be called to great sufferings.

4. When the enemies threaten us, and seek to invade us, or come in lake a flood upon us.

5. When heavy judgments are upon us, or upon the land.

6. In times when great and wonderful things are expected, or strange revolutions for the church's deliverance may be near.

7. When we are about some great work for God, or desire that he would put forth his miraculous working power, as in healing the sick, or casting out unclean spirits.[32]

Keach opens the sermon with these words, "My brethren, I enter upon this parable at a season when the subject may appear to all very seasonable: what is at this time more necessary than extraordinary prayer, or crying unto God."[33] While uncertain as to the exact circumstances precipitating Keach's sermon, he dates the introduction of his collection of sermons on August 20, 1701.[34] Keach continues, "We seem to be in an evil and amazing hour; what God is about to do with England, with other nations, and with his own people, we know not; we are in a cloud; things look black abroad, and bad at home."[35]

Two of the Western Association's circular letters, June of 1714 and July of 1715, illustrate well another example of extraordinary circumstance.

---

30. Crosby, *History of the English Baptists*, 2:395.

31. Crosby, *History of the English Baptists*, 1:436.

32. Keach, *Parables*, 436–37.

33. Keach, *Parables*, 434.

34. Keach, *Parables*, x.

35. Keach, *Parables*, 434. Keach may be referencing the start of the War of Spanish Succession (1701–1714).

Joseph Ivimey preserved the context of the letters in the *History of English Baptists*. The first letter, June 1714, was written in what would be the last year of Queen Anne's reign. The letter asks for a united effort and set-apart day for humiliation, fasting, and prayer. The churches were to pray first and foremost "that God would pour down of his Holy Spirit upon his people abundantly."[36] Through the pouring out of the Holy Spirit, the churches were to ask for renewal and healing from a "lukewarm, carnal, and worldly spirit."[37] Additionally, they were to pray that God thwart "the malicious designs of our enemies," for the blessing of Queen Anne, for the preservation of "the nation from popery and tyranny," and for delay of God's judgment against the nation.[38] Almost a year after the Queen's death, the Western Association circulated another letter. The second letter from July 1715, as Ivimey states well, reflects "the predictions of their faithful watchmen, just before the close of the former reign . . . But he [God], who passeth by the transgressions of the remnant of his heritage, because he delighteth in mercy, was pleased again to stay his rough wind in the day of his east wind, and in the midst of his deserved wrath to manifest undeserved mercy."[39] The letter states:

> You may remember what surprising apprehensions we had of the designs of our and the nation's enemies, against our civil and religious privileges about twelve months since, and you cannot forget how the Lord did appear for us in time of distress and fear; and by a marvellous providence had disappointed our enemies, outdone our faith, and prevented our fears! And we must acknowledge that we are a people served by the arm of the Lord alone.[40]

In response to physical and spiritual warfare, the languishing spiritual condition of their people, the uncertainty as to the state of the Protestant monarchy, and continual threats to their religious liberty the Western Association rallied for a concerted effort to seek the Lord in prayer for his mercy. Their prayer was an affirmation of dependence on the Lord for sustainment through extraordinary trials. After twelve months, the Association felt as though they could clearly see the "arm of the Lord alone" bringing them to a point of thanksgiving and praise. They chose in 1715 to call again for a concerted effort in prayer and thanksgiving:

36. Ivimey, *HEB*, 3:107.
37. Ivimey, *HEB*, 3:107.
38. Ivimey, *HEB*, 3:107.
39. Ivimey, *HEB*, 3:106.
40. Ivimey, *HEB*, 3:108.

> To bless our most gracious God for hearing and so seasonably answering the prayers of his people; and earnestly to pray for the King, viz. that God may direct his council, bless parliament, disappoint the designs of the nation's enemies abroad and at home, revive the work of reformation in these nations, and the power of godliness amongst his people, send forth more labourers into his harvest, and bless the gospel with great success.[41]

The special occasions of extraordinary prayer for the Western Association included times of perceived hardship and blessing. Indeed, when one considers the origins of Baptists in England through the nineteenth century, it is hard to imagine a time or place that did not warrant extraordinary prayer, whether from great hardship or blessing.

At All Times and All Places

Chapter 22, Article 6 states:

> Neither *Prayer*, nor any other part of Religious worship, is now under the Gospel tied unto, or made more acceptable by, any place in which it is performed or towards which it is directed; but God is to be worshipped every where [*sic*] in *Spirit*, and in truth; as in private families daily, and in secret each one by himself, so more solemnly in the public Assemblies, which are not carelessly, nor willfully, to be neglected, or forsaken, when God by his word, or providence calleth thereunto.[42]

The statement clearly articulates a concern for liberty in prayer. Religious liberty is an uncontested priority in the Baptist tradition, and for many early Baptists the practice of prayer was where the contest of religious liberty was worked out.

Particular Baptists believed that prayer, like all worship, is to be free. Prayer ought to be free from the constraints of set times and places. Of even more significance to the seventeenth-century Particular Baptist, prayer ought to be free from set forms. Whether the prayer is public or private, the essential belief regarding prayer expressed by the SLC is that prayer ought to be offered up "in *Spirit*, and in truth." Consider Keach's words from his sermon, again from "The Parable of the Importunate Widow." He states: "My brethren, I understand not that reading out of a book, is any more praying, than the reading a sermon out of a book is preaching. When I pray, I will

---

41. Ivimey, *HEB*, 3:108–9.
42. SLC 22.6.

pray with the Spirit: that is, my spirit shall pray by the aid and assistance of the Spirit of God."[43] Keach's argument seems to echo Bunyan's sentiments from the dialogue above; that is, one cannot pray in Spirit with a prayer book. Bunyan, in *I Will Pray with the Spirit*, goes as far as recommending that persons avoid reciting the Lord's Prayer for fear of not praying in the Spirit.[44] The primary concern for Particular Baptists of the late-seventeenth century, like Keach, and the Baptists that came before them, like Bunyan, was to be obedient to God and his institution of prayer. For Bunyan and Keach, and the majority of Particular Baptist, this meant the complete rejection of set forms of prayer.

At the start of the eighteenth century, a mediated position between set and extempore prayer became more tenable among some Dissenting circles. For example, consider Isaac Watts's *A Guide to Prayer*. Although the Independent minister's work provided examples and recommended prayers, his guide served as a manual rather than a prescribed set of prayers. His preface to the reader exemplifies just how contentious the debate between set and free forms of prayer became:

> But if the leaders of one party had spent as much in learning to pray, as they have done in reading liturgies, and vindicating their imposition; and if the warm writers of the other side, together with their just cautions against quenching the spirit, had more cultivated this divine skill themselves, and taught Christians regularly, how to pray; I believe the practice of free prayer had been more universally approved, and the fire of this controversy had never raged to the destruction of so much charity.[45]

To resolve the deficiencies left by the prior party divisions, Watts aimed "to write a prayer-book without forms . . . To maintain a middle way between the distant mistakes of contending Christians."[46] Regardless of Watts's influence on Particular Baptists in the eighteenth century, on the main, eighteenth- and nineteenth-century Baptists continued to follow the example of their seventeenth-century predecessors.

The majority position among Baptists of the seventeenth century was for free, if not extempore, prayer.[47] Baptists opposed the use of a state-im-

---

43. Keach, *Parables*, 436.

44. Bunyan, *I Will Pray with the Spirit*, 635.

45. Watts, *Guide to Prayer*, A2–A3.

46. Watts, *Guide to Prayer*, A3.

47. Isaac Watts distinguished between free and extempore prayers in his *A Guide to Prayer*. "*Conceived* or *free prayer*," as defined by Watts, "is when we have not the words of our prayer formed beforehand, to direct our thoughts, but we conceive the matter or

posed prayer book, which dictated the set forms, times, and places of prayer. Indeed, as Ellis indicated, a median position between set and extempore prayer among Baptists did not surface until the twentieth century.[48] Andrew Fuller's most immediate ecclesial context, the Northamptonshire Baptist Association, was certainly no exception.

Prayer in the Northamptonshire Baptist Association (1765–1775)

The following section, while brief, sets out to establish the Northampton-shire Baptist Association as a wellspring of prayer: a heritage of prayer laid in its origin, filled with ministers devoted to prayer, and her churches united in prayer.

A Heritage of Prayer

If one considers the subject of prayer within the Northamptonshire Baptist Association, the Prayer Call of 1784 warrants distinction as perhaps the most catalytic occasion of prayer in the association's history.[49] Elwyn, in fact, considered the prayer call as "one of the most decisive events in the life of Dissent in that period, and probably for all of Christendom."[50] Elwyn stated that the creation of the Baptist Missionary Society, London Mission-ary Society, and Baptist Union precipitate "from this awakened interest and activity in prayer."[51] And while 1784 is a watershed moment, the associa-tion from her origin was one of great interest and activity in prayer. Indeed,

---

substance of our address to God, first in our minds, and then put those conceptions into such words and expressions as we think most proper"; "*Extemporary prayer*," accord-ing to Watts, "is, when we, without any reflection or meditation before-hand, address ourselves to God, and speak the thoughts of our hearts, as fast as we conceive them." See Watts, *Guide to Prayer*, 34. Emphasis original. Since a number of Watts's works were circulated and recommended among Particular Baptist circles, his distinction would be known although not necessarily embraced by eighteenth-century Baptists. Ellis, *Gathering*, 273n18. To borrow Ellis's language, all spontaneous prayer is free prayer. However, not all free prayer is spontaneous prayer. Ellis, *Gathering*, 107.

48. Ellis states, "Virtually all prayer in Baptist churches before the twentieth century was free prayer." Ellis, *Gathering*, 107.

49. For introductions to the principle figures and circumstances preceding and pro-ceeding from the prayer call, see Payne, "The Prayer Call of 1784"; Haykin, *One Heart and One Soul*, 153–71.

50. Elwyn, *Northamptonshire Association*, 17–18.

51. Elwyn, *Northamptonshire Association*, 17–18.

the association inherited by Fuller, John Ryland Jr., John Sutcliff, and their contemporaries was an association steeped in a heritage of prayer, a heritage that would continue for a many number of years beyond Fuller, Ryland, and Sutcliff.[52]

Elwyn concludes from his study of the association's Circular Letters, "It is quite clear that prayer was very important to the association by the number of references to it, but specifically in two letters, those of 1787 and 1820, and of course in the issuing of the Prayer Call of 1784."[53] The following section will look at three other circular letters to support Elwyn's claim. These three letters predate 1775, supporting the claim that Fuller entered into an association with a heritage of deep interest and activity in prayer.[54] The first letter is from 1765, the first Circular Letter of the association, written by John Evans. Evans, not to be confused with John Evans who wrote *The History of all Denominations*, was a minister at Foxton in Leicestershire.[55] The second letter is from 1770, written by John Martin (1741–1820). Martin wrote the letter while a minister at Sheepshead in Leicestershire.[56] The third is from 1774, written by the same aforementioned John Evans. What is clear from these circular letters is that the ministers made prayer as a primary activity and concern at their meetings. They saw prayer as key to the renewal of the church and nation. Prayer was also a means of uniting the efforts of a broadly scattered association of churches.

Prayer as a Primary Interest and Activity

Initial plans for an association of Particular Baptists in Northamptonshire date back to October 17, 1764.[57] "Six ministers," according to Elwyn, "pastors of the Churches at Sutton in the Elms, Ansby, Foxton, Walgrave and Kettering; and whose names were Woodman, Hall, Evans, Deacon, Walker and Brown, met at Kettering, and formed a plan of the association."[58] The following year they met for the first time. The first circular letter and minutes of the association clearly present prayer as a centerpiece for the association's

52. Elwyn, "Particular Baptists of Northamptonshire," 376–80.

53. Elwyn, "Particular Baptists of Northamptonshire," 376.

54. Fuller, by connection with Soham Baptist Church, joined the association in 1775.

55. Elwyn, *Northamptonshire Association*, 12; Ivimey, *HEB*, 4:17.

56. Ivimey, *HEB*, 4:343. Ivimey's *History* provides a brief survey of Martin's life and ministry. See Ivimey, *HEB*, 4:342–50.

57. Elwyn, *Northamptonshire Association*, 11.

58. Elwyn, *Northamptonshire Association*, 11.

gatherings. Indeed, prayer not only seems to have been a primary activity of the first meeting, but the primary subject of both sermons. Moses Deacon's sermon came from Acts 2:42. Also on prayer, William Walker's text was 2 Thess 3:1.[59] Their interest in prayer came from fidelity to Scripture as a guide to their duties as ministers to be in prayer for their churches. Conversely, they expressed the need for churches to pray for their ministers. The Circular Letter 1765 stated:

> And as you should attend church meetings and all prayer in pub-
> lic, family, and secret, for yourselves, so also for your ministers
> as we heard fervently recommended by our esteemed brother
> Mr. Walker, on 2 Thes. iii. 1; and, doing thus, you seek your own
> good; and we trust we have been agreeing on earth so to pray
> for you according to Matt xvii. 19 as redound to your profit.[60]

Prayer was for the good of the ministers and the good of the church members, for by prayer they believed one received the blessing of "the Spirit of truth and his grace that is good to establish the heart."[61]

Prayer was a primary activity of the association's gatherings. The minutes from 1765, the first meeting state that those in attendance "had four meetings for prayer and conference, besides the more public solemnity, wherein several spent time in prayer, with praise, and 2 Sermons before mentioned."[62] Consider the centrality of prayer evidenced by the appended minutes from the Circular Letter in 1770:

> In the evening, May 22, we met about six o'clock for prayer, and
> reading the letters from the churches. The next morning we
> met, at six o'clock, for prayer and other business. The same day
> the public meeting began about ten o' clock: Brother Hopper
> preached from Revelation iii. 11 . . . And Brother Medly preached
> from Psalm lxxxv. 6 . . . At six o'clock Brother Craner preached
> from Revelation ii. 7 . . . May the 24th, we met at six o' clock in
> the morning, for prayer, and communicating, as Ministers; our
> experiences to each other in the past year, which we still find to
> be of considerable use and service to our souls—Note, In these
> opportunities eleven Brethren were engaged in prayer.[63]

59. The Circular Letter from 1765 is printed in Elwyn's history of the Association, see Elwyn, *Northamptonshire Association*, 13–14.

60. Evans, "Circular Letter 1765."

61. Evans, "Circular Letter 1765."

62. Elwyn, *Northamptonshire Association*, 14.

63. Martin, "Circular Letter 1770."

For three days, the meetings commenced with a time of prayer. The recorder of the minutes took special note not only to include the times of prayer but the number of men engaged in prayer throughout the meeting. The minutes from the 1774 meeting described a similar pattern of time set aside for prayer in the mornings, prayer interwoven through the public worship meeting, and the conclusion of the whole.[64]

Prayer as the Key to Renewal

The three letters also reveal the association's belief that prayer is key for renewal of the church and state. The Circular Letter 1765 stated, "We desire all church members will most contentiously attend all prayer meetings and the Lord's Table, for your revival."[65] The letter later stated, "We also think it would be very seasonable to appoint days of humiliation and prayer on account of the church and state."[66] The Circular Letter 1770 issued "a call for fervent prayer to God," and to set aside a day, "Wednesday the 3d of October, as a day of fasting and prayer."[67] "The circumstances of some of our churches, and the affairs of our nation," the letter stated, "made it our duty."[68] Again in 1774, the association "agreed to recommend days of fasting; the nature of which might, to good effect, be explained in a discourse the preceding Lord's day, as we desire they may be well attended, and all church meetings, whilst our liberties are continued."[69] It seems as though their fasting and prayer for renewal was never limited in scope just to their association. Payne's analysis of the Prayer Call of 1784 highlights the call for revival beyond the Baptist interest. The three association letters may indicate that the association's vision for revival, while not as far reaching as Fuller's or Carey's pleas following the Prayer Call of 1784, likewise reached beyond the borders of their own associational interest.

An Association United in Prayer

Prayer was also a means for uniting the efforts of geographically scattered churches. Prayer united the association and her ministers in their labors

---

64. Evans, "Circular Letter."
65. Evans, "Circular Letter 1765."
66. Evans, "Circular Letter 1765."
67. Martin, "Circular Letter 1770."
68. Martin, "Circular Letter 1770."
69. Evans, "Circular Letter 1774."

while together and apart. The Circular Letter 1765 tells of the advantage to the founding members at the first meeting: "Dear brethren, through the goodness of our God we came together according to our former appointment; and we think we have had much of the Lord's presence to assist and refresh us in our prayer-meetings and conferences, as well as in the more public opportunity."[70] The Circular Letter 1770 ended the report section from the association's meeting with the following encouragement, "We now close the meeting by drawing up and sending among you our annual letter, which is, and will be accompanied with our united prayers, that what is seasonable in it, the Lord would also make successful."[71] The early founders of the association ensured prayer was of primary interest and activity at their meetings. They encouraged prayer as the key for renewal among the churches and the nation. Prayer, also, was key for the unity of the association's ministers and their churches.

Fuller's Practice of Prayer

The following section will introduce the reader to the prominence of prayer in Fuller's spirituality through looking at his practice of prayer in both private and public arenas. In the Baptist tradition, the study of worship in general, and prayer specifically, is limited by the lack of written prayers since most Baptists are proponents of free or extempore prayer.[72] Fuller was no exception to this practice. However, the content of his diary not only discloses some of what Fuller said *about* prayer, but also provides the content or abbreviated substance of some his prayers.[73] Fuller's sermons and writings had much to say on the subject of prayer. Fuller's works, then, serve as a rich mine for not only understanding his belief and practice regarding prayer, but also representing an aspect of Baptist spirituality that is typically difficult to observe.

70. Evans, "Circular Letter 1765."

71. Martin, "Circular Letter 1770." A number of Circular Letters included some teaching of doctrine in addition to a report from the meeting and minutes. For a list of the Association's Circular Letters from 1765–1891, see Elwyn, *Northamptonshire Association*, 99–106. Elwyn's list supplies readers with the date of the meeting, the moderator of the meeting, the general subject of the Circular Letter, and the author of the letter.

72. Ellis, *Gathering*, 104. For a thorough chapter surveying prayer in the Baptist tradition, see Ellis, "From the Heart," 103–24.

73. Morden, *Life and Thought of Andrew Fuller*, 73.

Fuller's Works Addressing Prayer

Fuller's Diary

Fuller's diary and the memoirs published in the years following his death have preserved critical data concerning Fuller's practice of prayer. The manuscript of Fuller's diary was in three volumes. Of the three volumes, only the third volume remains extant. The first was lost. The second was destroyed by Fuller. The third was preserved but never published in its entirety until 2016, in Michael McMullen and Timothy Whelan's edited volume of Fuller's diary.[74] McMullen and Whelan's editorial work is a significant contribution to the ongoing work in Fuller Studies. The first entry in Fuller's diary is dated January 10, 1780, a little over ten years after the probable date of his conversion in November 1769.[75] The last entry is from June 26, 1801, roughly fourteen years prior to his death in May 1815.[76] Prayer was a primary subject addressed in Fuller's diary. From January 1780 to June 1801, Fuller's diary contains at least 188 entries related to prayer, either public or private. Some of these entries are descriptive accounts of happenings of prayer. For example, Fuller repeatedly recorded on Mondays that he attended the prayer meeting at Soham. Usually, he mentioned his attitude only regarding the effect of the meeting with little to no account of prayers given in the meeting itself. Other accounts of his diary are deeply personal and reveal a great deal about the attitude and content of Fuller's prayers, most of them private. For example, on June 22, 1780, Fuller prayed:

> O that I might feel more the power of religion, and know more of the love of Christ, which passeth knowledge! I think I see divine excellence in such a life. O that thou wouldest bless me indeed, enlarge my coast! I am going, God willing, to visit a friend today. O that a spirit of watchfulness, savour, and fellowship with Christ, may attend me![77]

Perhaps the only subject to be addressed more than prayer is the preaching of sermons and expositions.

---

74. McMullen and Whelan, "Introduction." For details on the preservation of Fuller's diary, see McMullen and Whelan, "Introduction," xiii.

75. Fuller, *Works*, 1:4.

76. Fuller, *Works*, 1:102.

77. Fuller, *Complete Works: Diary*, 1:4.

Fuller's Sermons

Another critical source for understanding Fuller's belief and practice regarding prayer are his sermons on prayer and expositions of the prayers of Scripture.[78] Both his sermons and expositions concerning prayer articulate Fuller's understanding of the nature and moods of Christian prayer and present practical application for his congregation regarding the practice of prayer.[79]

Fuller's exposition of the Lord's Prayer is his most comprehensive examination of a prayer in Scripture.[80] *The Nature and Importance of Walking by Faith* is perhaps Fuller's most significant sermon concerning his theology of prayer.[81] Fuller preached the sermon at the Northamptonshire

---

78. See note above on p. 25 for Fuller's distinction between a sermon and exposition.

79. Tangential to the use of Fuller's sermons and expositions is the general neglect of the British sermon in academia. Keith Francis and William Gibson, editors of *The Oxford Handbook of the British Sermon 1689–1901*, attest to the neglect within "scholarly circles" of the British sermon, that is, "until the last decade." Francis and Gibson, *Oxford Handbook of the British Sermon*, 5, 611. James Bradley and Richard Muller echo Francis and Gibson's analysis: "In late-eighteenth-century Britain, however, neither published nor unpublished sermons have been examined in sufficient detail." Bradley and Muller, *Church History*, 66. Wheeler's dissertation on Fuller's pastoral theology, as represented in his ordination sermons, not only begins to address the lacuna with regard to Fuller and Particular Baptist ordination sermons. Wheeler's work also demonstrates the great value of sermons for theological analysis. Wheeler, "Eminent Spirituality and Eminent Usefulness," 1.

80. Fuller, *Works*, 1:577–83. Early in the research for this monograph, Haykin shared via email a paper on Fuller's exposition of the Lord's Prayer that Dustin Benge and he worked on together. Benge and Haykin, "A Most Blessed Exercise."

81. According to the editor, Joseph Belcher, Fuller was inspired to preach on the text, 2 Cor 5:7, from an experience on his way to the association meeting in Nottingham where the road led through a flooded stream. A local man, knowing the true height of the flood and seeing Fuller's hesitancy, encouraged Fuller to continue riding through the water. The water reached horse's saddle but, trusting the man, Fuller continued. He made it safely to the other side. Belcher stated, "Taking the man at his word, the traveller proceeded, and the text was suggested 'We walk by faith, not by sight.'" See note from Fuller, *Works*, 117. The seven-volume edition published in New-Haven, 1824, and the two-volume edition published in Boston, 1833, do not include a note describing the origins of Fuller's sermon text or subject. See Fuller, *Complete Works*, 7:9–38; Fuller, *Complete Works*, 2:171–83. Belcher's two-volume edition published in Philadelphia, 1845 seems to be the first inclusion of such an account. Belcher does not supply a source. The story may have been shared by one of Fuller's friends or family, as Belcher was furnished with numerous original manuscripts in the organization and publication of Fuller's collected works. See "Advertisement to the First Collected English Edition," in Fuller, *Complete Works*, 1:xx. Fuller's diary, as a related point to consider, reflects that he preached a sermon on the topic, "walking by faith," about one month before his encounter with the stranger on the road. Fuller wrote in his diary on April 25, 1784, "A very good forenoon both in prayer & preaching on *walking by faith*"

Association meeting at Nottingham, June 2, 1784. The Prayer Call of 1784 originated from this meeting.[82] Appended to Fuller's sermon was perhaps his most germane writing on the subject of prayer.

Fuller's Writings

In the wake of the Prayer Call being issued from the association meeting in 1784, Fuller appended *A Few Persuasives to a General Union in Prayer for the Revival of Real Religion*.[83] The published sermon and added plea for united prayer for the revival of real religion was Fuller's first major publication.[84] Note that prayer was the subject of Fuller's first major publication.

Prayer was a central concern in a number of other writings, from circular letters to short treatises to major apologetic works. For example, both the private and public practice of prayer was of central concern in his circular letter in 1785, "Causes of Declension in Religion and Means of Revival."[85] Likewise, Fuller's treatise, *The Backslider: Or an Inquiry into the Nature, Symptoms, and Effects of Religious Declension, with the Means of Recovery*, treated prayer extensively.[86] Fuller also used prayer in his apologetic arguments against Socinianism in *The Calvinistic and Socinian Systems Examined and Compared, as to Their Moral Tendency*.[87] Of significance in the disagreement between Trinitarian orthodoxy and Socinian heterodoxy is the worship of Christ. Fuller argued that "according to the New Testament . . . the primitive Christians are characterized by their 'calling upon the name of the Lord Jesus.'"[88] More examples could be given, but the three above establish that prayer was not a passing concern for Fuller's theological reflection and writing.

(emphasis original). See Fuller, *Complete Works: Diary*, 1:42. Having preached from 2 Cor 5:7 a month prior, Fuller's change of sermon would have been much easier.

82. Ryland, *Circular Letter 1784*.

83. Fuller, *Works*, 1:117–34. The added persuasives are separated from the sermon in Belcher's edited *Works*. Additionally, the copy in *Works* contains a few abridged paragraphs and some paragraphs deleted entirely. Compare with Fuller, *Works*, 3:666–70.

84. Morden, *Life and Thought of Andrew Fuller*, 77.

85. Fuller, *Works*, 3:318–25.

86. Fuller, *Works*, 3:635–59.

87. Fuller, *Works*, 2:108–242. Haykin's article is a valuable introduction to Joseph Priestley as a principal proponent of the Socinian heterodoxy in Fuller's day. See Haykin, "A Socinian and Calvinist Compared."

88. Fuller, *Works*, 2:180–81. The principal arguments from this work will be explored in chapter 3, "The Son and Prayer."

Conclusion

Prayer held a place of prominence in Fuller's life and ministry. His diary reflects a private life devoted to prayer. Fuller's sermons and expositions touching on the subject of prayer reflect the central role prayer played in his public ministry. Likewise, the place of prayer in his various writings reflect that prayer was never far from view.

A Spiritual Biography: "In All Thy Ways Acknowledge Him"

Numerous authors have set out to establish a brief account of the principal events in Fuller's life and ministry. Distinct from those accounts, the following is an attempt to highlight the significance of prayer in Fuller's spiritual journey, a journey of imperfectly, yet persistently, acknowledging the Lord in all his ways, especially through prayer.

Early Years (1754–1769)

John W. Morris, one of Fuller's first biographers, wrote, "Like many other great and original characters, Mr. Andrew Fuller arose out of obscurity, without any flattering prospect of future eminence."[89] Fuller was born February 6, 1754, the son of a tenant farmer, his parents Robert and Philippa Fuller of Wicken in Cambridgeshire.[90] Fuller's childhood education was negligible. Ryland stated that despite the fact that he did not have "the advantages of early education, he rose to high distinction among the religious writers of his day, and . . . left monuments of his piety and genius which will survive to distant posterity."[91] While "eminent as Mr. Andrew Fuller afterwards became for his piety and usefulness," Morris states, "His youthful days were spent in sin and vanity."[92] Fuller recorded that it was not until he was fourteen years old that he "began to have much serious thought about futurity."[93]

---

89. Morris, *Memoirs*, 1.
90. Ryland, *Work of Faith*, 8.
91. Ryland, *Work of Faith*, xii.
92. Morris, *Memoirs*, 2–3.
93. Fuller, *Works*, 1:2.

Fuller often described these early years as prayerless. In a letter to Charles Stuart, Fuller described a moment of intense and fleeting conviction from c.1767.[94] He wrote:

> But, strange as it may appear, though my face that morning was, I believe, swollen with weeping, yet before night all was gone and forgotten, and I returned to my former vices with as eager a gust as ever. Nor do I remember that for more than half a year afterwards I had any serious thoughts about the salvation of my soul. *I lived entirely without prayer*, and was wedded to my sins just the same as before, or rather was increasingly attached to them.[95]

Fuller, later in the same letter, described an account from the following year, c.1768:

> This, like the former, overcame my mind with joy. I wept much at the thoughts of having backslidden so long, but yet considered myself now as restored and happy. But this also was mere transient affection. I have great reason to think that the great deep of my heart's depravity had not yet been broken up, and that all my religion was without any abiding principle. *Amidst it all, I still continued in the neglect of prayer*, and was never, that I recollect, induced to deny myself of any sin when temptations were presented.[96]

Indeed, prayerlessness was wedded with Fuller's own recollection of his depravity. In turn, after his conversion, Fuller would come to see the prayer-filled life as a shibboleth of the life of faith.

Conversion, Baptism, Early Formation (1769–1774)

Conversion. Prayer was a recurring subject of significance in Fuller's conversion, baptism, and the early years of his spiritual formation. Upon moving to Soham, Fuller attended the Baptist church there with his parents. The church was newly formed and "under the pastoral care of Mr. John

---

94. Fuller also wrote a second letter to C. Stuart, the second of which completed the telling of his early days leading up to his conversion. The substance of both letters can be found in Andrew Gunton Fuller's *Memoirs* in Fuller, *Works*, 1:2–6. Ryland's memoir more clearly divides the two letters from other correspondence in A.G. Fuller's account, see Ryland, *Work of Faith*, 11–20. Michael Haykin also included both letters in an edited collection of Fuller's letters. See Haykin, *Armies of the Lamb*, 59–74.

95. Fuller, *Works*, 1:3. Emphasis added.

96. Fuller, *Works*, 1:4.

Eve."[97] Fuller seemed to connect the delay in his conversion to the manner of preaching he heard at Soham. Fuller stated that "Mr. Eve, . . . who being what is here termed *high* in his sentiments, or tinged with false Calvinism, had little or nothing to say to the unconverted. I therefore never considered myself as any way concerned in what I heard from the pulpit."[98] Without a clear direction from the pulpit, Fuller was left to wrestle with his eternal state in the confines of his heart. Describing the internal turmoil leading to his conversion in 1769, Fuller stated, "I was not then aware that *any* poor sinner had a warrant to believe in Christ for the salvation of his soul"[99]—a topic that will be of highest importance in the early years of his ministry.[100] In November 1769, Fuller finally resolved to go before the Lord to plea for mercy. He stated, "It seems to resemble that of Esther, who went into the king's presence *contrary to the law*, and at the hazard of her life . . . I must—I will—yes, I will trust my soul—my sinful soul in his hands. If I perish, I perish."[101] Upon doing so, Fuller was overwhelmed with a deep sense of true repentance and sorrow regarding his sin. Likewise, he was overcome with joy, joy at having realized, "I had *thought* I had found the joys of salvation heretofore; but now I *knew* I had found them, and was conscious that I had passed from death unto life."[102]

Baptism. In the year following his conversion, March 1770, Fuller witnessed his first baptism.[103] He stated, "I was fully persuaded that this was the primitive way of baptizing, and that every Christian was bound to attend to this institution of our blessed Lord. About a month after this I was baptized myself, and joined the church at Soham, being then turned of sixteen years of age."[104] Within the next few days, Fuller experienced his first taste of persecution for his Dissenting, and specifically Baptist, convictions. As he rode along the road, some men along the way mocked him for having

97. Ryland, *Work of Faith*, 9.

98. Fuller, *Works*, 1:2. In his *History of the English Baptists*, Joseph Ivimey, a late contemporary of Fuller's, traced this manner of preaching to John Skepp. Ivimey described Skepp's manner of preaching as "[a] *non-invitation, non-application* scheme," stating that "it was by him introduced among the Baptists." See Ivimey, *HEB*, 3:262–67. Grant's discussion regarding the correlation between the high Calvinist preaching scheme and the delay in the Evangelical Revival impacting Particular Baptists is worthy of consideration; however, his thesis is not without contestation. See Grant, *Andrew Fuller*, 26–28; Wheeler, "Eminent Spirituality and Eminent Usefulness," 236–40.

99. Morris, *Memoirs*, 13.

100. Morris, *Memoirs*, 13.

101. Fuller, *Works*, 1:5–6.

102. Fuller, *Works*, 1:6.

103. Fuller, *Works*, 1:7.

104. Fuller, *Works*, 1:7.

been "dipped."[105] Infuriated as he was, Fuller's response was stayed when a Scripture passage came to mind, which in turn brought on conviction, tears, and prayer for forgiveness.[106] As Fuller continued to ride, more thoughts came to his mind regarding future temptations that he would undoubtedly face. Fuller stated:

> While poring over these things, and fearful of falling into the snares of youth, I was led to think of that passage, "*In all thy ways acknowledge him, and he shall direct thy paths.*" This made me weep for joy; and for forty-five years I have scarcely entered on any serious engagement without thinking of these words, and entreating divine direction. I have been twice married, and twice settled as the pastor of a church; which were some of the leading ways in which I had to acknowledge the Lord; and in each, when over, I could say, as Psal. 119:26, "*My ways have I declared, and thou heardest me.*"[107]

Indeed, Prov 3:6 would be a guide for Fuller on his journey—not just as a principle, but also as a foundation for holy practice—a prayer for divine direction on the way.[108]

Early formation. Soon after his baptism, a controversy at Soham thrust Fuller to the heart of theological reflection and prayer. Fuller was forced to think and pray more earnestly. He was forced to reflect on the corollary nature of theological principles and the practice of prayer. The controversy began when Fuller, now a member at Soham, observed a fellow church member "drinking to excess."[109] Fuller, "one of the first who knew of it," confronted the man regarding "the evil of his conduct."[110] The drunkard excused his own actions by stating that he was not his "own keeper" and unable to prevent himself from drinking. Fuller took the case to Eve, who sided with Fuller, commending him as having handled the situation properly. The church, however, sided with the drunkard.

---

105. Fuller, *Works*, 1:7.

106. Fuller, *Works*, 1:7–8.

107. Fuller, *Works*, 1:8.

108. Fuller, *Complete Works: Diary*, 1:28, 186. See entries dated May 1, 1781 and July 18, 1794. Haykin made note of Fuller's informing Sutcliff of his prayer for him regarding difficulties in Olney pertaining to High Calvinists. Among other things prayed, part of Fuller's prayer written was a line from Prov 3:6. See Haykin, *One Heart and One Soul*, 150.

109. Fuller, *Works*, 1:8. Morden, *Life and Thought of Andrew Fuller*, 34. Morden's inquiry into the Church Book at Soham revealed this member to be James Levit.

110. Fuller, *Works*, 1:8.

The church, according to Fuller, "readily excused me, as being a babe in religion; but thought the pastor ought to have known better, and to have been able to answer the offender without betraying the truth."[111] The truth, as the church saw it, was "that the greatest and best of characters, as recorded in Scripture, never arrogated to themselves the power to keeping themselves from evil, but constantly prayed for keeping grace."[112] Numerous prayers in Scripture, the church reasoned, reflect on the principle of humanity's internal and external inability to obey God's commands. Eve, "on the other hand, . . . distinguished between internal and external power. He allowed that men had no power of themselves to perform any thing [*sic*] spiritually good; but contended that they could yield external obedience, and keep themselves from open acts of sin."[113] The church was divided over the issue, and Fuller was deeply disturbed by the events.

For Fuller, the controversy was not merely a passing misunderstanding. Fuller's unsettled position drove him to pray and reflect earnestly on the matter. Fuller stated, "I prayed much, and labored hard to solve this difficulty."[114] In hindsight, he recognized that "though, during these unpleasant disputes, there were many hard thoughts and hard words on almost all hands, yet they were ultimately the means of leading my mind into those views of divine truth which have since appeared in the principal part of my writings."[115] Additionally, Fuller recognized that the disputes "excited me to read, and think, and pray, with more earnestness than I should have done without them."[116] Fuller was thrust into a season of solemn prayer and reflection as he sought to resolve a difficult theological controversy within the congregation and within his own mind.

Fuller was not alone in seeking to resolve the controversy. Joseph Diver, a future deacon in the church and an elder confidant who was baptized the same day as Fuller, sought to help him. He encouraged Fuller to reflect on the theological principles dividing the church with specific application to prayer. The church, against their pastor, resolved that humans had neither internal nor external power to keep from sinning. "To support these ideas," Fuller stated, "They alleged the prayers of the faithful to be kept from evil, even presumptuous sins."[117] He wrote:

111. Fuller, *Works*, 1:9.
112. Fuller, *Works*, 1:9.
113. Fuller, *Works*, 1:10.
114. Fuller, *Works*, 1:9.
115. Fuller, *Works*, 1:10.
116. Fuller, *Works*, 1:10
117. Fuller, *Works*, 1:10.

[Diver] would reason with me, "We ought to hate evil, and love the Lord; but it is the grace of God alone that can make us what we ought to be." . . . "*Thus it is*," said he, "*that we should turn every precept into a prayer*, instead of inferring from it a sufficiency in ourselves to conform to it. All our conformity to the divine precepts is of grace; it will never do to argue from our obligations against our dependence, nor from our dependence on grace against our obligations to duty. If it were not for the restraining goodness and preserving grace of God, we should be a kind of devils, and earth would resemble hell."[118]

Fuller's diary is a testament to the lasting influence of Diver's counsel "that we should turn every precept into prayer."[119] Nearly thirteen years later, August 26, 1783, Fuller wrote a paper at the request of John Ryland Jr. concerning the harmony of Scripture's "commands, petitions, and promises."[120]

Pastorate at Soham (1774–1782)

Soon after this controversy, Eve resigned from the pastorate at Soham. The Baptist church of Soham was without a pastor from 1771 until 1775. Fuller's formal ministry began in 1774 with the request to preach the funeral for an elderly woman in the congregation. "As the members were nearly of one mind respecting me," Fuller stated, "they agreed to set apart the twenty-sixth of that month, which was previous to the funeral, for fasting and prayer and then they called me to the ministry."[121] Fuller was ordained as the pastor of Soham in 1775 following a one-year trial period in 1774.[122] In that year, "being now devoted to the ministry," Fuller stated, "I earnestly besought the Lord to be my guide; and those words in Prov 3:6, were very sweet to me, . . . In most of the important turns of my life, I have thought of that passage with renewed tenderness."[123]

During his pastorate at Soham, the prayers recorded in Fuller's diary reveal several pastoral priorities and personal struggles. Considering the sum total of his prayers from 1780 until 1782, the most constant themes were related to knowing the Lord's will regarding his remaining in Soham or

118. Fuller, *Works*, 1:9–10. Emphasis added.

119. Fuller's most significant precept turned into prayer, Prov 3:6, was noted immediately following his baptism. Fuller's paper will be treated more fully in chapter 5.

120. Ryland, *Work of Faith*, 218–21.

121. Fuller, *Works*, 1:12.

122. Ryland, *Work of Faith*, 20–24.

123. Fuller, *Works*, 1:12.

departing for Kettering, confessing sin, and seeking mercy. Ryland described Fuller's time at Soham as such that "every serious Christian must admire the conscientious manner in which he acted, the self-denying scrupulosity which kept him so long in suspense, the modest manner in which he asked counsel of his senior brethren, and the importunity with which he implored divine direction."[124]

Fuller's private life at Soham fluctuated from spiritual mountain tops to dark valleys. For example, consider the disparity between these two prayers, both within a week of each another in September 1780:

> September 5, I longed, in prayer tonight, to be more useful. Oh that God would do somewhat by me! Nor is this, I trust, from ambition; but from a pure desire of working for God, and the benefit of my fellow sinners.

> September 12, . . . I think, of late, I cannot, in prayer, consider myself as a Christian, but as a sinner, casting myself at Christ's feet for mercy.[125]

Fuller's emotions as well as his outlook regarding relationship with God fluctuated often in his time at Soham.[126]

Aside from praying and meditating on Prov 3:6, two prayers that define Fuller's time at Soham are "O for an unerring guide" and "Into thy hands I commit my spirit."[127] Both expressions represent Fuller's deep commitment to the Lord's will and desire to submit to his will through prayer. Fuller's private life in prayer was consumed with pursuing the will of God, especially with regard to his station at Soham and the decision to remain or go to Kettering. On April 2, 1781, he wrote in his diary:

> Affected in prayer. Oh for an unerring guide! Oh that I knew the Lord's will! Verily, if I know mine own heart, I would do it. I had rather, I think, much rather, walk all my days in the most

---

124. Ryland, *Work of Faith*, 44.

125. Fuller, *Complete Works: Diary*, 1:14.

126. For a more in-depth analysis regarding Fuller's inner struggles as revealed in his diary, see Morden, *Life and Thought of Andrew Fuller*, 103–9. Morden interprets Fuller's disparaging outlook to be a reflection of his lingering high-Calvinist spirituality. He states that "it is true by the mid-1780s he had broken with high Calvinistic theology . . . Yet . . . it was the spirituality associated with it that he found hardest to shake off." See Morden, *Life and Thought of Andrew Fuller*, 109.

127. For Fuller's prayer for an unerring guide, see April 2 and May 14, 1781 in Fuller, *Complete Works: Diary*, 1:27, 30. For Fuller's prayer of committal, see November 19, 1780 and May 22, 1781 in Fuller, *Complete Works: Diary*, 1:19, 30.

miserable condition, than offend the Lord, by trying to get out of it.[128]

Nearly a week later, again in his diary, he wrote, "The thoughts of my situation now return and over power me. Tonight, I was exceedingly affected in prayer, earnestly longing that I might know the will of God." Eight days later, with his decision made to go to Kettering, Fuller wrote, "Earnest outgoings to God, in prayer. Tomorrow seems a day of great importance. Then I must give my reasons to the church, for what I have intimated concerning my removal. The Lord guide and bless them and me!"[129] Fuller, always one of a tender pastoral heart, was burdened greatly by the decision to stay or go.

Pastorate at Kettering (1782–1815)

In October 1782, Fuller finally removed to Kettering, where he was ordained as their pastor the following year, October 1783.[130] Morris described his move to Kettering as "the commencement of a distinct era in his public life."[131] Indeed, two years after praying for greater usefulness, Fuller's prayer seems to have been answered with his removal to Kettering.[132] The move brought him into closer proximity with other ministers within the association. These connections within the association developed into deep spiritual friendships and were a hallmark of Fuller's spirituality.

In May 1784, Fuller began "fasting and prayer, in conjunction with several other ministers, who have agreed thus to spend the second Tuesday in every month, to seek the revival of real religion, and the extension of Christ's kingdom in the world."[133] The appointed day for prayer for ministers soon turned to "monthly prayer meetings . . . in their respective

128. Fuller, *Complete Works: Diary*, 1:27.

129. Fuller, *Complete Works: Diary*, 1:27.

130. Fuller, *Works*, 1:32.

131. Morris, *Memoirs*, 32.

132. See Fuller's prayer on September 5, 1780 in Fuller, *Complete Works: Diary*, 1:14. Also see Fuller's letter to Wallis at Kettering. Fuller wrote, "Truly, sir, nothing but the thoughts of an open door for greater usefulness in Christ's cause, . . . and my having been so engaged to pray for the coming of Christ's kingdom, could have kept me from dropping all opposition, and yielding to the church's desire," that is Soham's desire for Fuller to remain their pastor. Fuller, *Works*, 1:30.

133. Ryland, *Work of Faith*, 96.

congregations, with the same revival focus."[134] This movement became known as "The Prayer Call of 1784."[135]

Fuller's role in the call to prayer was manifest most clearly in his preaching and writing. Fuller's sermon, *The Nature and Importance of Walking by Faith*, proved to be a catalytic event for the association's efforts in prayer. Fuller exhorted the association:

> Let this be attended with *earnest* and *united prayer* to him by whom Jacob must arise. A life of faith will ever be a life of prayer. O brethren, let us pray much for an outpouring of God's Spirit upon our ministers and churches, and not upon those only of our own connexion and denomination, but upon "all that in every place call upon the name of Jesus Christ our Lord, both theirs and ours!"[136]

Building upon his sermon, Fuller added *A Few Persuasives to a General Union in Prayer for the Revival of Real Religion*. Fuller made seven appeals within his short appendix:

1. Consider Christ's readiness to hear and answer prayer, especially on these subjects.

2. Consider what the Lord has done in times past, and that in answer to prayer.

3. Let the present religious state of the world be considered to this end.

4. Consider what God has promised to do for his church in times to come.

5. If we have any regard to the welfare of our countrymen, connexions, and friends, let this stimulate us in this work.

6. Consider, what is requested is so very small.

7. It will not be vain, whatever be the immediate and apparent issue of it.[137]

"This address," according to Morris, "operated as a powerful stimulant, and produced effects which in reality contained the germ of the future

---

134. Fuller, *Complete Works: Diary*, 1:47; Morden, *Life and Thought of Andrew Fuller*, 75.

135. Haykin devotes an entire chapter to describing the movement, its primary influencers, and general response of the movement. See Haykin, *One Heart and One Soul*, 153–71.

136. Fuller, *Works*, 1:131.

137. Fuller, *Persuasives*, 42–47.

mission."[138] For those at the association meeting at Nottingham in 1784, Fuller's sermon stirred their hearts to see the critical correlation between prayer and the life of faith, prayer and the outpouring of the Spirit, and not just within the Baptist interest. Fuller knew that the pouring out of God's Spirit was not only key to the spiritual awakening that was to come. The pouring out of the Spirit was directly tied to the prayers of God's people.[139]

The prayer call extended beyond the Baptist interest. Fuller addressed in the *Persuasives* "all who love and long for the coming of Christ's blessed kingdom, and whose hearts may be inclined to unite in seeking its welfare."[140] The call was given to consider more than one's own denominational interests. Fuller called readers to consider the interests of the world—"surely it is high time for us to awake out of sleep, and to send our united cries to heaven in [sic] of our fellow-creatures!"[141] "This last sentence," and Suctliff's own appeal to united prayer, according to Elwyn, point to an expanded vision of the church's work prior to the publication of Carey's *Enquiry*.[142]

The theme of praying for the expansion of Christ's kingdom around the world through the pouring out of God's Spirit continued for Fuller in his preaching. Seven years after preaching the association sermon that helped launch the Prayer Call of 1784, Fuller preached before a gathering of ministers at Clipstone, April 27, 1791.[143] The title of his sermon was *Instances, Evil, and Tendency of Delay, in the Concerns of Religion.* Fuller pleaded with the ministers that it was not enough to "pray for the conversion and salvation of the world, and yet neglect the ordinary means by which those ends have been used to be accomplished."[144] Fuller knew that prayer and the pouring out of the Spirit were essential to the expansion of Christ's Kingdom, but these things were not contrary to human efforts in the "propagation of the gospel."[145] Fuller's public exhortations to prayer and practice of prayer seemed to produce great effects extending to his own circle of friends, church, association, and beyond these connections. Meanwhile, Fuller's diary indicates that while preaching and writing on prayer

138. Morris, *Memoirs*, 80.

139. See Fuller's seventh persuasive in Fuller, *Persuasives*, 46.

140. Fuller, *Persuasives*, 42.

141. See Fuller's third persuasive in Fuller, *Persuasives*, 44.

142. Elwyn, *Northamptonshire Association*, 17.

143. Fuller, *Works*, 1:145.

144. Fuller, *Works*, 1:147–48.

145. Fuller, *Works*, 1:148.

achieved much to the satisfaction of others, his own prayer life and interest in kingdom matters suffered.[146]

Fuller's diary regularly points to struggles within his interest in prayer, whether public or private. For example, only a few months after the prayer call was issued, October 18, 1784, Fuller wrote in his diary, "Much depressed in spirit tonight on account of my little spirituality. Prayed at the evening meeting with tenderness of spirit—sensibly felt my entire dependence on the Spirit of God for the carrying on of the work of grace as well as for the beginning of it."[147] Early in the next year, January 3, 1785, Fuller wrote, "Felt very sensibly tonight at our monthly meeting for prayer, how far off a Christian life I live—how little real fellowship with Christ! How little of holy boldness can I use in prayer! Surely, if I were more to frequent the throne of grace in private it would be better with me!"[148]

The greatest time of dissatisfaction and distance from God came after the death of his daughter, Sally. On October 3, 1789, Fuller wrote:

> For upwards of a year & a half I have wrote nothing . . . Two or three years ago my heart began wretchedly to degenerate from God. Soon after my child Sally died I sunk into a sad state of carnality; . . . I feel at times some longing after the lost joys of God's salvation, but cannot recover them. I have backslidden from God; and yet I may rather be said to be habitually dejected on account of it than earnestly to repent for it.[149]

The next year he scarcely made any entries in his diary. One entry on March 27, 1790, still points to a struggle in satisfaction with his own private prayer: "Some weeks ago, I thought I felt to gain ground by closet prayer; but have lately relapsed again too much into indifference."[150]

---

146. Morden, *Life and Thought of Andrew Fuller*, 105. Morden offers a prudent caution "that his diary does not necessarily give a totally rounded picture of his spiritual life." Fuller's diary-keeping likely followed the Puritan practice of using a diary for self-examination. Morden referenced Bruce Hindmarsh's work on John Newton and proposed that "the same is probably true for Fuller . . . Most likely the Kettering pastor's state of mind was sometimes brighter than the extracts above, and others like them, would lead one to believe." Nonetheless, Morden states, "There seems little reason to doubt that in the years 1782–92, whilst his public ministry flourished, Fuller was often struggling in his Christian faith. Furthermore, from the middle of 1786 for three years he experienced spiritual depression, a 'dark night of the soul.' The evidence also indicates he was suffering from some form of clinical depression during this three year period." Morden, *Life and Thought of Andrew Fuller*, 105.

147. Fuller, *Complete Works: Diary*, 1:83.

148. Fuller, *Complete Works: Diary*, 1:101.

149. Fuller, *Complete Works: Diary*, 1:176.

150. Fuller, *Complete Works: Diary*, 1:179.

A positive turn in both Fuller's private and public prayer life came from the spiritual interest of five or six young people in his congregation. Fuller first mentioned these young people in his diary early in 1791.[151] They met weekly for conversation and prayer. Regarding these meetings, Fuller stated, "I hope that has been of use to both me and them."[152] The following year, 1792, the religious interest among the congregation's youth seemed to hold steady. They continued to meet weekly for reading, prayer, and conversation.[153] Fuller, now with more confidence, stated, "[I] have found it good both to them and me."[154] Sadly, the same year, Fuller would be sunk low again by the death of his wife and newborn daughter. The letter Fuller wrote to his father-in-law tells of the painful circumstances leading up to and shortly after the death of his first wife, Sarah Gardiner.[155]

On October 2, 1792, with barely a season to mourn the passing of both his wife and daughter, Fuller helped to found the BMS.[156] Fuller was elected the society's first secretary. His preaching, writing, and constant correspondence with missionaries on the field, especially William Carey, proved critical for the society's sustainment.[157] The added responsibilities, in addition to his pastoral duties at Kettering, perhaps led to the decline in his diary entries. Even still, prior to 1792 Fuller's diary contains repeated years of intermittent silence starting in 1786.[158] The lack of diary entries, especially ones regarding prayer, after 1792 leave an incomplete picture of Fuller's practice of prayer both in public and private arenas. "Of course it would be foolish to conclude, in light of this," Morden states rightly, "that Fuller did not give time to these things."[159] A decrease in diary entries does not necessitate a decrease in devotional life, prayer, and the like. "Nevertheless," Morden states, "we have to conclude that as his work increased to unmanageable proportions and as his health grew worse, he found regular private prayer and Bible reading increasingly more difficult."[160]

---

151. Fuller, *Complete Works: Diary*, 1:181–82.

152. Fuller, *Complete Works: Diary*, 1:181.

153. The prior entry in 1791 did not mention reading, which is why the aforementioned did not include reading along with the activities of conversing and praying.

154. Fuller, *Complete Works: Diary*, 1:183.

155. Ryland included the letter in his memoirs of Fuller. The letter is dated August 25, 1792, in Ryland, *Work of Faith*, 286–91.

156. Morden, *Life and Thought of Andrew Fuller*, 120.

157. Morden, *Life and Thought of Andrew Fuller*, 120; Haykin, *One Heart and One Soul*, 264–66.

158. McMullen and Whelan, "Introduction," xiii.

159. Morden, *Offering Christ to the World*, 174.

160. Morden, *Offering Christ to the World*, 174, 175.

The depiction left by Fuller's biographers was that of a man dying a "martyr to the mission" but without wavering in personal devotion.[161] Ryland recorded the moment right before Fuller's death:

> Soon after, his daughter Mary entering the room . . . he said, "Come, Mary, come and help me." He was then raised up in bed, and, for the last half-hour, appeared to be engaged in prayer. His children surrounded his bed, listening attentively, to catch, if possible, the last words of their dying parent; but nothing could be distinctly heard, but "Help me!" which words were repeated several times. Then, with his hands clasped, and his eyes fixed upwards, as in the attitude of prayer, he sunk back, sighed three times, and expired.[162]

One is left to wonder whether the prayer that guided Fuller through his first trial after his baptism, the start of two marriages, and the start of two pastorates was the same prayer that ushered him before the presence of Christ, this time not "through a glass, darkly." *In all thy ways acknowledge him, and he shall direct thy paths.*

Other Considerations

Scripture and Prayer

Beginning in 1780, the highs and lows of his life and ministry were borne out in the prayers of his diary. In his first entry, dated January 10, 1780, Fuller wrote out a "renewal of covenant with God" in his diary.[163] Fuller's prayer reveals his high view of Scripture and sets out his method of true spirituality in the Christian life. First, he asked God to give him "a determination to take up no principle at second-hand; but to search for every thing [sic] at the pure fountain of *thy word*."[164] In the next paragraph, he prayed "O Lord, never let me, under the specious pretence [sic] of preaching *holiness*, neglect to promulgate the truths of thy word; for this day I see, and have all along found, that holy practice has a necessary dependence on sacred *principle*."[165] True spirituality in the Christian life is built upon the sacred principles of

---

161. Morris, *Memoirs*, 49.

162. Ryland, *Work of Faith*, 358–59.

163. Fuller, *Works*, 1:19–20.

164. Fuller, *Works*, 1:20.

165. Fuller, *Works*, 1:20.

God's Word. The pure fountain of God's Word was the wellspring for all aspects of Fuller's spirituality, prayer not excluded.

From the early days of his ministry at Soham, prayer and the word were nearly inseparable in Fuller's practice and thinking.[166] Scripture not only guided the matter and manner of prayer, as evidenced by his exposition of the Lord's Prayer, but Scripture also saturated the language in Fuller's prayers.[167] Two examples suffice to show how Scripture guided and saturated Fuller's practice of prayer. On September 23, 1780, Fuller wrote in his diary, "O blessed by God, he has appeared once again. Tonight, while I prayed to him, how sweet was Colossians 1:19 to me . . . O for some heavenly clue, to guide me to the fullness of Christ! O for an overcoming faith!"[168] On November 9, 1780, he wrote, "Found a heart to pray today—Into thine hands I commit my spirit. Enlighten my judgement, guide my choice, direct my conscience, and keep it tender. Found my heart disposed to ask counsel of God, and leave him to guide me in his own way."[169] One of the final accounts of Fuller's practice of prayer attests to the longevity of this practice, despite his numerous seasons of struggling with personal devotion. Fuller's son, A.G. Fuller, recorded an account from April 9, 1815: "I have been importuning the Lord that whether I live it may be to him, or whether I die it may be to him. Flesh and heart fail; but God is the strength of my heart, and my portion for ever [sic]."[170] Two days later, he prayed:

> Into thy hands I commit my spirit, my family, and my charge; I have done a little for God; but all that I have done needs forgiveness. I trust alone in the sovereign grace and mercy. I could be glad to be favoured with some lively hopes before I depart hence. God, my supporter and my hope I would say, "Not my will but thine be done!"—"God is my soul's eternal rock, The

---

166. Brewster states, "As Fuller saw it, constant engagement in prayer and immersion in the Word of God was a *sine qua non* for the pastor-theologian." Brewster, "Model Baptist Pastor-Theologian," 64. Nearly all of his diary entries on the Lord's Day make reference to both preaching and praying. See Appendix 1.

167. Numerous examples from Fuller's diary reflect that his practice of prayer aligned with what Ellis describes as "Scriptural Prayer." According to Ellis, "Attention to Scripture carries a devotional dimension in the worshiper's prizing of the Word of God." Ellis, *Gathering*, 122–23. Similar to the examples he explored, primarily from Bunyan's prayers, within Fuller's prayers "there is a profusion of scriptural phrases and ideas." See Ellis, *Gathering*, 113–22.

168. Fuller, *Complete Works: Diary*, 1:15.

169. Fuller, *Complete Works: Diary*, 1:19. Fuller prayed the same prayer nearly 35 years earlier, "Into thine hands I commit my spirit."

170. Fuller, *Works*, 1:101.

strength of every saint." I am a poor sinner; but my hope is in the Saviour of sinners.[171]

Friendships and Prayer

John Sutcliff and John Ryland Jr. were two of Fuller's most significant friendships. With particular reference to prayer, Edwards's *A Humble Attempt* left an indelible mark on Fuller's theology.[172] Sutcliff and Ryland were of particular importance in "strongly encouraging Fuller to read Edwards."[173] Sutcliff wrote the preface to an English republication in 1789.[174] The influence of Edwards on Fuller, Sutcliff, and Ryland is perhaps the most apparent from the admiration they all bore for Edwards.

Fuller specifically came under the influence of Edwards's works early on in ministry. On August 6, 1780, Fuller concluded the diary entry with these words: "Some savour today, in reading *Edwards on the Affections*."[175] About six months later, Fuller wrote on February 3, 1781:

> I think I have never entered into the true idea of the work of the ministry. If I had, surely I should be like Aaron, running between the dead and the living. I think I am by the ministry, as I was by my life as a Christian before I read *Edwards on the Affections*. I had never entered into the spirit of a great many important things. Oh for some such penetrating, edifying writer on this subject! Or, rather, oh that the Holy Spirit would open my eyes, and let me into the things that I have never yet seen![176]

---

171. Fuller, *Works*, 1:101.

172. For an introduction to the influence of Edwards on Fuller, Sutcliff, and Ryland Jr., see Haykin, *One Heart and One Soul*, 139–43; Morden, *Life and Thought of Andrew Fuller*, 57–65. For an introduction to the influence of Edwards on the Prayer Call of 1784, see Haykin, *One Heart and One Soul*, 153–71. For a more in-depth look at Edwards's influence, specifically on Fuller's theological formation, see Nettles, "Influence of Edwards on Fuller"; Chun, "Sense of the Heart," 117–34; Chun, *Legacy of Edwards in the Theology of Fuller*.

173. Haykin, *One Heart and One Soul*, 140. For more on the significance of spiritual friendships in Fuller's spirituality and specifically Fuller's friendship with Ryland, see Haykin, *Armies of the Lamb*, 42–46.

174. Edwards, *Humble Attempt*, 2:278–312.

175. Fuller, *Complete Works: Diary*, 1:12.

176. Fuller, *Works*, 1:5; Fuller, *Complete Works: Diary*, 1:24.

The prevalence of Edwards's influence on Fuller's spiritual life is evidenced by numerous diary entries similar to the above quotation.[177]

Further testament to the high regard for Edwards among these three friends—Fuller, Sutcliff, and Ryland—came just before Fuller's death in 1815. The men were criticized by some stating that "if Sutcliff and some others had preached more of Christ, and less of Jonathan Edwards, they would have been more useful." Fuller responded in a letter to Ryland that "if those who talk thus, preached Christ half as much as Jonathan Edwards did, and were half as useful as he was, their usefulness would be doubled what it is. It is very singular that the Mission to the east should have originated with men of these principles."[178]

One final friendship deserves mention, Samuel Pearce. Although addressed here, Pearce could have been mentioned under Fuller's significant works. Upon Pearce's death, Fuller penned the *Memoirs of the Rev. Samuel Pearce*.[179] Morris praised the work as "one of the best specimens of Christian biography, and, perhaps, . . . the most useful of all Mr. Fuller's writings."[180] According to Haykin, "Fuller's portrait of Samuel Pearce was thus by far his most published literary work and it helped crystallize a form of Baptist piety well-fitted for the expansion that the Baptists experienced in the British Isles and North America during the first three decades of the nineteenth century."[181] Pearce was not the first friend to be remembered through one of Fuller's spiritual biographies, although *Memoirs of the Rev. Samuel Pearce* was unique in its length and perhaps is the best exemplification of what Haykin describes as "Fuller's high view of friendship."[182] "It is highly significant," as Haykin states, "that Fuller had the . . . poignant words of David that bore witness to one of the greatest friendships of the Bible placed on the title page of his *Memoirs* of Pearce"—'Oh Jonathan, thou slain upon thy high places. I am distressed for thee, my brother Jonathan!'"[183] In life, perhaps

---

177. Fuller, *Complete Works: Diary*, 251.

178. Quoted from Haykin, *One Heart and One Soul*, 350.

179. Haykin, "Editor's Introduction," 1. For more on the life and spirituality of Samuel Pearce, see Haykin, *Joy Unspeakable*; Dees, "The Way to True to Excellence."

180. Morris, *Memoirs*, 182.

181. Haykin, "Editor's Introduction," 1.

182. Haykin, "Editor's Introduction," 26. Fuller also wrote "small memoirs for a number of his friends who predeceased him as a mark of his love for them: Robert Hall, Sr.; Beeby Wallis (d.1792), a valued deacon at Fuller's Kettering church; and his close friend John Sutcliff (1752–1814)." Haykin, "Editor's Introduction," 26.

183. Haykin, "Editor's Introduction," 31. For a facsimile of the title page, see Fuller, *Complete Works: Samuel Pearce*, xv.

no other person had so deep an impact on Fuller's understanding of true Christian friendship and spirituality.

In death, Pearce's influence continued into Fuller's own spiritual theology. The way in which Fuller articulated and understood spirituality was shaped by his portrayal of Pearce's spirituality in the *Memoirs*. Pearce was such a formative influence on Fuller's faith that he wrote in a letter to Sutcliff, "Let the God of Samuel Pearce be my God."[184] The biography positions Pearce as "a model of spirituality to emulate."[185] According to Haykin, "Fuller firmly believed that Christian biography was a vital means that God used to sanctify his ministers and his people."[186] Considering these reasons for Fuller's spiritual theology being impacted by Pearce, the greatest evidence comes from the concluding reflections. In the final section of the *Memoirs*, Fuller stated:

> The great ends of Christian biography are instruction and example. By faithfully describing the lives of men eminent for godliness, we not only embalm their memory, but furnish ourselves with fresh materials and motives for a holy life . . . There can be no reasonable doubt that the life of Mr. Pearce ought to be considered as one of these examples. May that same divine Spirit who had manifestly so great a hand in forming his character, teach us to derive from both instruction and edification![187]

Fuller must have felt a solidarity with Pearce on seeing one whom he admired both struggle and persevere in the practice of private prayer. Pearce wrote in a letter to a friend, "There is nothing that grieves me so much, or brings so much darkness on my soul, as my little spirituality, and frequently wanderings in secret prayer."[188] Pearce was at times distressed regarding the inconsistency of his feelings when in "the house of God" versus in his closet. He feared that he was more stirred by the presence of the people than the "presence of God."[189] In those moments, Pearce reminded himself of advice he was given: "If you did not plough in your closet, you would not reap in the pulpit."[190] When considering Fuller's advice to a young minister—that one ought to study first as a Christian rather than as a pastor searching for

---

184. Fuller, "Letter to John Sutcliff, September 1, 1801," quoted in Haykin, "Acknowledgements," ix.

185. Haykin, "Editor's Introduction," 29.

186. Haykin, "Editor's Introduction," 29.

187. Fuller, *Complete Works: Samuel Pearce*, 4:143.

188. Fuller, *Complete Works: Samuel Pearce*, 4:47.

189. Fuller, *Complete Works: Samuel Pearce*, 4:47.

190. Fuller, *Complete Works: Samuel Pearce*, 4:47.

something to say on Sunday—the kindred spirit between Fuller and Pearce is plain to see.[191]

191. Fuller, *Works*, 1:714.

2

The Father and Prayer

I need not say to you that just views of the Divine character lie at the
foundation of all true religion. Without them, it is impossible, in the
nature of things, to love God, or to perceive the fitness of our being
required to love him, or the evil of not loving him, or the necessity of such
a Saviour and such a salvation as the gospel reveals.[1]

—ANDREW FULLER, *LETTERS ON SYSTEMATIC DIVINITY*,
"THE PERFECTIONS OF GOD"

THE DOCTRINE OF GOD is a neglected subject in Fuller Studies.[2] Paul Brewster stated correctly that "Fuller's writings pertaining to the doctrine of God have generally been overlooked in the tendency to focus on his innovative

---

1. Fuller, *Works*, 1:705.

2. Paul Brewster acknowledges the inattention given to Fuller's doctrine of God in his doctoral study on Fuller as a consummate pastor-theologian. He has started to fill the lacuna with a recent article addressing Fuller's doctrine of God, especially as it related to his response to Deism and Thomas Paine's *Age of Reason*. See Brewster, "Model Baptist Pastor-Theologian," 178; Brewster, "Fuller's Doctrine of God." An example of the neglect may be reflected in Peter Morden's decision to delimit his study from closely examining Fuller's *Gospel Its Own Witness*, see Morden, *Life and Thought of Andrew Fuller*, 8. *The Gospel Its Own Witness* was Fuller's chief response to Deism and was one of his most sought-after works during his lifetime. According to Morris, the book was praised as useful by men inside and outside of the Baptist denomination, such as William Wilberforce, John Newton, and Robert Hall. See Morris, *Memoirs of Andrew Fuller*, 241.

and influential contributions to Baptist soteriology and missiology."[3] Another reason for the neglect is that "many areas of Fuller's doctrine of God were never fleshed out in his published works."[4] However, "his doctrine of the knowledge of God is an exception."[5] Fuller held special revelation to be at the heart of a correct knowledge of God. From special revelation, one's knowledge of God expands to love the glory of the divine character and the harmony of God's moral government.[6] These two aspects of Fuller's doctrine of the knowledge of God—the glory of the divine character and the harmony of God's moral government—demonstrate reciprocity with Fuller's theology of prayer.

The present chapter—and all remaining chapters—will proceed in a methodical manner to explore the reciprocity of Fuller's theology of prayer with his doctrine of God.[7] Each chapter will consist of four sections. The first section presents a brief explanation of the major aspects of the doctrine, especially as the said doctrine correlates to Fuller's theology of prayer. The second section considers the implications for Fuller's theology of prayer based on his expressed understanding of the said doctrine. The third section describes either an example of Fuller's practice of prayer or a prescribed practice of prayer that correlates with the said doctrine. The fourth section considers the implications for the said doctrine based on Fuller's theology of prayer. The conclusion will make summary observations regarding ways in which Fuller's said doctrine affects his theology of prayer as well as the ways in which Fuller's theology of prayer affects the said doctrine.

Explanation of the Doctrine

The Knowledge of God

The two chief principles regarding Fuller's doctrine of the knowledge of God "were the presupposition of the existence of God and the indispensable need for special revelation in knowing God."[8] The whole of Fuller's theologi-

---

3. Brewster, "Fuller's Doctrine of God," 22.

4. Brewster, "Fuller's Doctrine of God," 23.

5. Brewster, "Fuller's Doctrine of God," 23.

6. Since the Fuller's defense of the divinity of Christ is a prominent piece of Fuller's promotion of an orthodox doctrine of the Trinity, the doctrine of the Trinity will be treated in the following chapter. See chapter 3, "The Son and Prayer."

7. The researcher provided a more thorough introduction to the order of exploration here in order to relieve subsequent chapters of redundant introductions.

8. Brewster, "Fuller's Doctrine of God," 23.

cal system centers on what he called "the doctrine of the cross."⁹ "The whole
of the Christian system," Fuller stated, "appears to be *presupposed by* it, *included in* it, or to *arise from* it."¹⁰ Fuller's presupposition of God's existence
is *presupposed by* his doctrine of the cross.¹¹ Fuller stated, "To undertake
to prove his existence seems to be almost as unnecessary as to go about to
prove our own. The Scriptures at their outset take it for granted; he that calls
it in question is not so much to be reasoned with as to be reproved."¹² And
while the Scriptures take the existence of God for granted, Fuller stated, "It
would be improper . . . to rest the being of God on Scripture testimony; seeing the whole weight of that testimony must depend upon the supposition
that he is, and that the sacred Scriptures were written by holy men inspired
by him."¹³ Nonetheless, "In the way that the works of nature imply a Divine
First Cause, so does the work of revelation. Men were as morally unable
to write such a book as they were naturally unable to create the heavens
and the earth. In this way the sacred Scriptures prove the being of God."¹⁴
Fuller's doctrine of God begins with a presupposition of God's existence,
but revelation through nature and Scripture stand as proofs of his existence
and inform humanity with particular knowledge of God's nature and works.

Regarding the knowledge of God, Fuller held that special revelation
was of absolute necessity and should be prioritized over natural revelation.
In his sermon *The Nature and Importance of an Intimate Knowledge of Divine Truth*, Fuller made this principle clear:

> All Divine knowledge is to be derived from the oracles of God.
> It is a proper term by which the sacred Scriptures are here de-
> nominated, strongly expressive of their Divine inspiration and
> infallibility: in them God speaks; and to them it becomes us to
> hearken. We may learn other things from other quarters; and
> things, too, that may subserve the knowledge of God; but the
> knowledge of God itself must here be sought, for here only it
> can be found.¹⁵

9. Fuller, *Works*, 1:690 and 692.

10. Fuller, *Works*, 1:690.

11. Brewster, "Fuller's Doctrine of God," 23.

12. Fuller, *Works*, 1:692–93.

13. Fuller, *Works*, 1:695.

14. Fuller, *Works*, 1:695.

15. Fuller, *Works*, 1:160–61. One can clearly see that Fuller's priority to special revelation does not diminish the usefulness of natural revelation. While natural revelation
does not lead to salvation by faith in Christ, special revelation ought not to be elevated
at the expense of natural revelation. Fuller stated, "The word of God is not to be exalted
at the expense of his works. The evidence which is afforded of the being and perfections

Eighteen years later, Fuller's views respecting the knowledge of God remain the same. In his *Letters on Systematic Divinity*, specifically "The Necessity of a Divine Revelation," Fuller prioritized special revelation above natural revelation for two reasons. First, Fuller stated that human reasoning is insufficient "to obtain from the mere light of nature a competent knowledge of God, and his will concerning us."[16] Second, natural revelation is insufficient to be the foundation for faith:

> Supposing mankind to be in a guilty and perishing condition, and that "God so loved the world as to give his only begotten Son, that whosoever believeth in him should not perish, but have everlasting life," a revelation from heaven was necessary as the ground of faith. "Faith cometh by hearing, and hearing by the word of God": without revelation, therefore, there would be no faith, and so no salvation.[17]

Special revelation is of absolute necessity for knowledge of God unto salvation. One can clearly see the connectedness of Fuller's priority of special revelation with what he saw as the center of the Christian system, the doctrine of the cross. Special revelation, in addition to being *presupposed by* the doctrine of the cross, revealed the glory of the divine character and the harmony of God's moral government.[18]

The Glory of the Divine Character

God has revealed, in nature and especially in Scripture, "the glory of the Divine character."[19] The divine character is of utmost importance in Fuller's theological system. In the opening lines of Letter 8, "The Perfections of God," Fuller stated:

> I need not say to you that just views of the Divine character lie at the foundation of all true religion. Without them, it is impossible, in the nature of things, to love God, or to perceive the

---

of God by the creation which surrounds us, and of which we ourselves are a part, is no more superseded by revelation than the law is rendered void by faith." Fuller, *Works*, 1:696. Brewster was also prudent to make this observation in his article. "Taking his cue from the *Second London Confession*, Fuller was careful to give general revelation its due without allowing it to eclipse Scripture." Brewster, "Fuller's Doctrine of God," 39.

16. Fuller, *Works*, 1:696.

17. Fuller, *Works*, 1:698.

18. See also Fuller's confession of faith, esp. articles 1–4, in Fuller, "Confession of Faith, October 7, 1783," 346–48; or Fuller, "Confession of Faith," 273–82.

19. Fuller, *Works*, 1:705.

fitness of our being required to love him, or the evil of not loving him, or the necessity of such a Saviour and such a salvation as the gospel reveals.[20]

In both "The Perfections of God" and *The Gospel Its Own Witness*, Fuller argued that "just views of the Divine character" precipitate from a proper understanding of the perfections of God, that is, a proper division of his perfections. Fuller divided the perfections of God into two categories, his natural and moral perfections.[21] "The former," Fuller stated, "respect his greatness, the latter his goodness; or, more particularly, the one refers to his infinite understanding, his almighty power, his eternity, immensity, omnipresence, immutability, &c.; the other, to his purity, justice, faithfulness, goodness, or, in one word, to his holiness."[22] Fuller argued at the onset of *The Gospel Its Own Witness* that this critical division was the watershed for a proper knowledge of God and right living before God.[23] Fuller stated:

> If we bear a sincere regard to moral excellence, . . . and if we consider the Divine Being as possessing it supremely, and as the source of it to all other beings, it will be natural for us to love him supremely, and all other beings in subserviency to him. And if we love him supremely on account of his moral character, it will be no less natural to take pleasure in contemplating him under that character.[24]

Fuller believed that the glory of the divine character, especially God's moral perfections, provide the basis for humanity's affection, love, and worship of God. A proper distinction and acknowledgment of both God's natural and moral perfections is necessary for a proper understanding of the glory of the divine character.

20. Fuller, *Works*, 1:705. All quotations retain Fuller's capitalization style.

21. Fuller, *Works*, 1:705; 2:9.

22. Fuller, *Works*, 1:705.

23. For a summary and analysis of *The Gospel Its Own Witness* from a contemporary of Fuller's, see Morris, *Memoirs*, 238–41. For a recent summary and analysis, see Ballitch, "An Analysis of Fuller's The Gospel Its Own Witness." The work is divided into two parts. The first part argues for the superior morality of Christianity over that of the immoral tendencies of Deism. The second part argues for the harmony of the Christian Scripture as evidence of it being from God.

24. Fuller, *Works*, 2:10.

The Harmony of God's Moral Government

God's moral perfections are also seen in what Fuller called God's moral government. Fuller used the phrase "moral government" in at least two different ways in his writings. Fuller used moral government terminology with reference to both his doctrine of divine providence and doctrine of the atonement. The latter use features prominently in a contested issue in Fuller Studies, namely, the influence of New England's New Divinity theologians and Fuller's use of governmental language with reference to substitution and imputation within his doctrine of the atonement.[25] The former use has received little scholarly attention, but fits well within the parlance of doctrine of God in Fuller's day. For example, in *A Complete Body of Doctrinal and Practical Divinity*, John Gill states:

> Providence may be considered as real and moral: real, is what concerns things, and the essence of them, by which they are sustained and preserved. *Moral providence, or what is commonly called God's moral government of the world*, respects rational creatures, angels and men, to whom God has given a law, as the rule of their actions, which consists of precepts and prohibitions, the sanctions of which are promises and threatenings; and it is explained and enforced by instructions, persuasions, admonitions, &c., and according to which reasonable law, a reasonable service is required of reasonable creatures.[26]

God's moral government as Gill and Fuller used the terminology referred to God's ordering of the world according to his will and purposes with respect to intelligent beings.

Jeremy Pittsley observes that Fuller's confession of faith in 1783 employed "moral government terminology . . . relatively early" in his ministry to refer to God's purposes in creation and his will concerning humanity.[27] Near the end of Fuller's ministry, when writing his *Letters on*

---

25. For an introduction to the influence of New Divinity theology on Fuller and his use of governmental language, see Morden, *Life and Thought of Andrew Fuller*, 124–49, esp. 139–46. The use of moral government language in relation to Fuller's doctrine of the atonement has been a contested subject in Fuller Studies. George Ella accuses Fuller of completely abandoning a penal substitution view of the atonement in favor of the moral government theory of the atonement; see Ella, *Law and Gospel*. For a defense of Fuller's view of the atonement as according with penal substitution and traditional Calvinism, see Nettles, "On the Road Again," 55–77. For a full appraisal of Fuller's doctrine of the atonement, see Box, "The Atonement."

26. Gill, *A Complete Body of Divinity*, 1:407. Emphasis mine.

27. Pittsley, "Christ's Absolute Determination to Save," 144; Fuller, "Confession of Faith," 273–82.

Systematic Divinity, Fuller clearly used moral government terminology with reference to divine providence: "The natural perfections of God are principally manifested in the creation and providential government of the world; his moral perfections in the creation, moral government, and salvation of intelligent beings."[28] Two things can be observed here. First, Fuller saw God's moral government as integral to manifesting the moral perfections of God. The two are closely connected because the latter reflects the former. Second, while Fuller implemented moral government language with reference to the atonement, he continued to apply moral government language with reference to divine providence. Even near the end of his ministry, his adaptation of moral government language to refer to the atonement did not eclipse his use of the terminology and understanding of moral government as a subheading of divine providence.

Implications for Prayer

Fuller's doctrine of the knowledge of God provided a strong foundation for Fuller's theology of prayer. Fuller believed that a proper motivation to pray was a vital implication flowing from the glory of the divine character. Fuller also believed that the duty of all men to pray was an implication of his understanding of God's moral government. Additionally, God's moral government dictated how one should pray. In summary, Fuller's doctrine of God has implications respecting basic questions of one's theology of prayer. Why should one pray? Who should pray? And how should one pray? The latter two questions are addressed under the subheading "Problem(s) of Prayer" because they were disputed questions in Fuller's day.

The Foundation of Prayer: "The Glory of the Divine Character"

Why should one pray? Fuller's doctrine of God, with respect to his understanding of the divine character, provided an enduring motive for prayer.

28. See Fuller's "Letter 3: Plan Proposed to Be Pursued," and "Letter 8: The Perfections of God," in Fuller, *Works*, 1:690 and 705. In Letter 3, Fuller stated, "The greatest number proceed on the analytical plan, beginning with the being and attributes of God, the creation of the world, moral government, the fall of angels and man, and so proceed to redemption by Jesus Christ, and the benefits and obligations resulting from it." In Letter 8, Fuller stated, "The natural perfections of God are principally manifested in the creation and providential government of the world; his moral perfections in the creation, moral government, and salvation of intelligent beings."

Fuller stated that "just views of the Divine character lie at the foundation of all true religion."[29] One derives a proper knowledge of the divine character from Scripture. Fuller stated:

> The true character of God, as revealed in the Scriptures, must be taken into the account, in determining whether our love to God be genuine or not. We may clothe the Divine Being with such attributes, and such only, as will suit our depraved taste; and then it will be no difficult thing to fall down and worship him: but this is not the love of God, but of an idol of our own creating.[30]

Indeed, the divine character as revealed in Scripture provided a solid foundation for Fuller's theology of prayer. Quite simply, Fuller stated, "If there is a God he ought to be worshiped."[31] If they love God, "they would delight in worshipping him; for love cannot be inoperative, and the only possible way for it to operate towards and infinitely glorious and all-perfect Being is by worshipping his name and obeying his will."[32] Thus in answering why one should pray, Fuller believed prayer, or any form of worship, to be the natural response of delight in the glory of the divine character.

The Problem(s) of Prayer

Whether it be the duty of all men to pray was a disputed question within the Baptist tradition dating back at least to the mid-to-late seventeenth century.[33] The answer, whether affirmative or negative, was implied from at least two doctrinal loci: the doctrine of God and doctrine of humanity. Particular Baptists who answered this question negatively based the exemption of the duty to pray on the basis of the divine decrees and, or, man's inability.[34] The same doctrinal principles were the basis of what Fuller called a self-justifying neglect of God's commands.[35] According to Fuller, "The common

---

29. Fuller, *Works*, 1:705.

30. Fuller, *Works*, 2:153–54.

31. Fuller, *Works*, 2:11.

32. Fuller, *Works*, 2:14.

33. For a more complete discussion regarding the history of this question in the Baptist tradition, see "A Proto-'Modern Question': Is it the Duty of All Men to Pray?" in chapter 5.

34. The subject of human inability will be explored in chapter 5, "Humanity and Prayer."

35. Ryland, *Work of Faith*, 218.

language of such persons is, 'Such a thing cannot be our duty: *that* is God's work.'"[36]

In Fuller's more immediate context, the widespread high-Calvinist and antinomian preoccupations with the secret will of God and the divine decrees accentuated this problem of prayer. Fuller addressed the question, "Ought a wicked man to pray?" directly in a small track entitled, *The Prayer of the Wicked*.[37] On first analysis, Fuller stated, "I suppose, would be thought very evangelical" to answer the question in the negative.[38] However, Fuller stated—much like a number of his eminent Particular Baptist forbearers— that to answer the question negatively "will be found subversive of the first principles of the gospel."[39] The harmony of God's moral government does not establish "two sorts of requirements, or two standards of obedience, one for good men, and the other for wicked men; the revealed will of God is one and the same, however differently creatures may stand affected toward it."[40] Fuller contended that "the same things which are required of the righteous, as repentance, faith, love, prayer, and praise, are required of the wicked."[41] An affirmative answer was a necessary implication in Fuller's understanding of God's moral government. In answering the question who ought to pray, Fuller's answer was all men ought to pray.[42]

Another problem of prayer developed as a result of focusing on the secret rather than the revealed will of God. Fuller developed a particular concern regarding God's moral government. Fuller's concern was based on what E. F. Clipsham calls "the popular high-Calvinist interpretation of the decrees."[43] In Fuller's system, the divine decrees and election both fall within the scope of God's moral government, a government that he argued to be in complete harmony with all other doctrines revealed in Scripture. Clipsham states:

> It was a commonly accepted *inference from the doctrine of the divine decrees*, that it was wrong for Christians to pray for the salvation of their neighbours, ministers for that of their hearers,

36. Ryland, *Work of Faith*, 219.

37. Fuller, *Works*, 3:772–73.

38. Fuller, *Works*, 3:773.

39. Fuller, *Works*, 3:773. Emphasis original.

40. Fuller, *Works*, 3:772.

41. Fuller, *Works*, 3:772.

42. On this point Fuller is in complete continuity with the *SLC*'s statement regarding prayer: "Prayer with thanksgiving, being one special part of natural worship, is by *God* required of all men." See *SLC* 22.3 in McGlothlin, *Baptist Confessions*, 260.

43. Clipsham, "Andrew Fuller and Fullerism," 102.

or parents for that of their children, lest they should prove to be not of the elect, since salvation was intended only for the elect.[44]

Clipsham acknowledged that both John Brine and John Gill, two prominent Particular Baptists, warned against such spiritually damaging extremes.[45] Both Brine and Gill, according to Clipsham, "distinguished between God's *commanding will,* revealed in His Word, which is the rule of men's duty, and His *decreeing will,* which is the rule of His own actions."[46] Fuller did not overlook Brine and Gill's judicious distinction.

Fuller made the distinction between God's revealed and secret will central for harmonizing prayer for one's neighbors with the clear instruction to pray according to God's will. Fuller stated, "We must take the *revealed* and not the secret will of God for the rule of our duty."[47] Fuller acknowledged the distinction as a critical point of departure between himself and William Button in their published dialogue regarding *The Gospel Worthy of All Acceptation.*[48] Fuller perceived Button to "make the decrees of God rules of

44. Clipsham, "Andrew Fuller and Fullerism," 102. Emphasis original. Clipsham did not provide specific sources that prohibited praying for the salvation of one's neighbors. Nonetheless, Fuller acknowledged in his treatise *Antinomianism Contrasted with the Religion of the Holy Scriptures* that the error was common in his day. Fuller, *Works,* 2:737–62. Although Clipsham did not cite Fuller's treatise as his source for the "popular high-Calvinist interpretation," his phrasing is nearly a direct quote from Fuller: "To what is owing, but to the substituting of the *secret will for the revealed will of God,* that Christians should be afraid to pray for the salvation of their neighbors, ministers for that of their hearers, and parents for that of their children, lest they should not prove to be of the elect?" Clipsham, "Andrew Fuller and Fullerism (1)," 102. The prohibition of praying for one's neighbors, hearers, children, and so forth is identified properly as belonging to hyper-Calvinism. The evidence that this teaching goes well beyond Calvin's belief is borne out clearly in Calvin's commentary on 1 Tim 2:1, "In the *second* chapter, he enjoins that public prayers be offered to God for all men, and especially for princes and magistrates; and here, in passing, he likewise makes a remark on the advantage which the world derives from civil government. He then mentions the reason why we ought to pray for all men; namely, that God, by exhibiting to all the gospel and Christ the Mediator, shews that he wishes all men to be saved; and he likewise confirms this statement by his own apostleship, which was specially appointed to the Gentiles. Next, he invites all men, whatever may be their country or place of abode, to pray to God; and takes occasion for inculcating that modesty and subjection which females ought to maintain in the holy assembly." See Calvin, *Commentaries on the Epistles,* 14.

45. Clipsham, "Andrew Fuller and Fullerism," 102. Brine and Gill are often identified with John Skepp as progenitors of high-Calvinism among the Particular Baptists in Fuller's day. See McBeth, *Baptist Heritage,* 176.

46. Clipsham, "Andrew Fuller and Fullerism," 102. Emphasis original.

47. Fuller, *Works,* 2:453. Emphasis original.

48. For a brief introduction to William Button's life and ministry, See Ivimey, *HEB,* 4:335–37.

human action."[49] Thus Fuller stated, "Herein lies a considerable part of the difference between us. We believe the doctrine of Divine predestination as fully as he does, but dare not apply it to such purposes."[50] Rather than object to praying for neighbors on account not knowing if they be elect, Fuller suggested that the harmony of God's moral government entailed "that in all our prayers there should be a condition implied, namely, that what we ask is according to the will of God."[51] Fuller continued:

> But if, lest what we ask should not accord with the Divine pur-
> pose, we refrain from asking any thing [*sic*], our conduct will
> resemble that of the slothful servant, who, from certain notions
> which he entertained the Lord's character, concluded that there
> was no encouragement for him to do any thing [*sic*], and there-
> fore went and buried his Lord's talent in the earth. And why
> should we neglect to pray for our neighbours, our hearers, or
> our children only, lest they should not have been elected? Why
> not also on the same ground neglect to pray for *ourselves?* There
> must have been a time when we had no ground to conclude our-
> selves elected; and did we wait till we had obtained evidence of
> this before we began to pray for the salvation of our own souls?
> If we did not, and yet object on this account to pray for others,
> surely self-love must be the Alpha and Omega of our religion.[52]

For Fuller, substituting the revealed for the secret will of God as a rule for life not only led to the grievous error of prayerlessness for one's neighbors, hearers, children, and so forth, it also subverted the chief obligation of God's moral law—to love the Lord thy God with all thy heart. Thus Fuller's doc-trine of God supplies two abiding rules with respect to how one should pray. One ought to pray in a spirit of love for God and according to God's will.

Example of Fuller's Practice of Prayer: "What Profit Shall We Have if We Pray unto Him?"

Fuller's diary, far from revealing the life of one who had mastered the disci-pline of prayer, reflects a journey of emotional highs and lows. Fuller's sense of affection toward God fluctuated with a dullness of heart. For example, on June 19, 1784, Fuller wrote, "Tender in prayer again this morning—but

49. Fuller, *Works*, 2:453.
50. Fuller, *Works*, 2:453.
51. Fuller, *Works*, 2:760.
52. Fuller, *Works*, 2:760.

O what a poor, carnal, stupid wretch nearly throughout the day. Some little fervor tonight in meditation on Christ's mercy."[53] The next week, on the Lord's Day, he expressed a similar frustrating level of inconsistency: "A tenderish forenoon on *waiting* upon God—but a poor cold heart this afternoon even though commemorating the Lord's death!"[54] The former entry reflects his experience in his private practice of prayer. The latter reflects his experience in his public practice of prayer. Both of these entries come on the heels of the 1784 Association meeting in Nottingham. This is the meeting from which the Prayer Call of 1784 was issued. In the face of such fluctuating feelings, dark and painful circumstances, the death of congregants, friends, and family, Fuller would learn to trust in the goodness of God through prayer.

On August 1, 1785, Fuller wrote:

> Some very tender feelings and outgoings of heart in prayer tonight at the monthly prayer meeting. Surely *Unbelief* damps our near addresses to God—and something of that spawn "What profit shall we have if we pray unto him?" lies at the bottom of our indifference to this duty.[55]

Little did Fuller know the depth to which he would explore this question through the loss of his daughter Sally and the subsequent three years of "spiritual depression," as Morden describes it, "a dark night of the soul."[56]

Sally died on May 30, 1786.[57] Fuller laid in his bed crippled by his own sickness as he heard of her passing from the other room. He recalled in his diary, "I enquired . . . and all were silent!—but all is well! I feel reconciled to God! I called my family round my bed—I sat up & prayed as well as I could. I bowed my head &worshipped, and blessed a taking as well as a giving God."[58] Fuller's identification with Job is palpable. All was not well.

What remains of Fuller's diary after Sally's death until October 3, 1789 are but a few entries in June 1786. In October, Fuller wrote, "For upwards of a year & a half I have wrote nothing . . . Two or three years ago my heart began wretchedly to degenerate from God. Soon after my child Sally died I sunk into a sad state of carnality; . . . I feel at times some longing after the

---

53. Fuller, *Complete Works: Diary*, 1:56.
54. Fuller, *Complete Works: Diary*, 1:58.
55. Fuller, *Works*, 1:145. Emphasis original.
56. Morden, *Life and Thought of Andrew Fuller*, 105.
57. Fuller, *Complete Works: Diary*, 1:172.
58. Fuller, *Complete Works: Diary*, 1:172.

lost joys of God's salvation, but cannot recover them."[59] In the same entry, Fuller continued:

> During this summer I have sometimes thought what *Joy* Christians might possess in this world were they but to improve their opportunities & advantages . . . I have preached two or three times upon this subject . . . Once from John 15:11, . . . Another time from Nehemiah 8:10, . . . And again from Mark 11:24, Whatsoever things ye desire when ye pray, believe ye shall receive them, & ye shall receive them. In which the chief sentiment on which I insisted was how *confidence in God's goodness was necessary to our success in prayer.*[60]

Through his painful suffering and a season of straying from God, Fuller was challenged with regard to his "confidence in God's goodness."[61] His confidence in God's goodness was tested. Still in the entry from October 3, Fuller wrote:

> Some time ago I set apart a day for fasting & prayer; and seemed to get some strength in pleading with God. The very next day, as I remember, I found my heart so wretchedly strayed away, such a load of guilt contracted, that I was frightened at my own prayer the preceding day—and I have not set apart a day to fast and pray since. But surely this was one of Satan's devices by which I have been befooled. Perhaps also I trusted too much to my fasting & praying, and did not on that account follow it with watchfulness.[62]

One may infer that Fuller's prayer life was stifled by a lack of confidence in the goodness of God, a blow to the heart of knowing and loving the glory of the divine character. Fuller's diary entries from 1789 to 1792 resort to large summary entries recounting either the whole year or preceding months.[63] From the few details given, his diary still recounted a fluctuating

---

59. Fuller, *Complete Works: Diary*, 1:176–77.

60. Fuller, *Complete Works: Diary*, 1:177. Emphasis original.

61. Fuller, *Complete Works: Diary*, 1:177.

62. Fuller, *Complete Works: Diary*, 1:176–77. Fuller's theme of a lack of watchfulness as lending one to be in a state of spiritual decline or backslidden is an area for further research. Fuller mentioned watchfulness in his 1785 circular letter; however, the priority of watchfulness seems to increase in his later publication, *The Backslider* (1801). For his circular letter, "Causes of Declension in Religion, and Means of Revival," see Fuller, *Works*, 3:318–24. Cf. with *The Backslider* in Fuller, *Works*, 3:635–59. Perhaps this moment marks the genesis of Fuller's conviction regarding the need to pair both prayer and watchfulness.

63. Fuller, *Complete Works: Diary*, 1:176–85.

outlook on his own spiritual life, yet the end of 1789 seems to mark a change for the better.[64] Recounting the last quarter of 1789, Fuller stated, "I seem to have gained some ground in spiritual things."[65] In addition to reading some of Jonathan Edwards's sermons, Fuller stated, "[I] have attended more constantly than heretofore to private prayer, and feel a little renewed strength. Sometimes also I have been much affected in public prayer."[66] While 1789 may mark a change in Fuller's overall spiritual outlook, in 1792 Fuller faced his darkest night. Struggling with the failing mental health of his wife in the middle of her pregnancy, Fuller prayed, July 25, 1792:

> O my God, my soul is cast down within me! The afflictions in my family seem too heavy for me. O Lord I am oppressed, undertake for me! My thoughts are broken off and all my prospects seem to be perished! I feel however some support from such Scriptures as these—All things shall work together for good &c. God, even our own God, shall bless us. It is of the Lord's mercy that I am not consumed. One of my friends observed yesterday, that it was a difficulty in many cases to know wherefore God contended with us? But I thought that was no difficulty with me![67]

While Fuller saw the trial as the Lord contending with him, he also held fast to the divine moral character. He clung to the revealed will of God: "All things shall work together for good &c." His wife died on August 23, 1792. Shortly over a week later, Fuller's diary maintained a ray of hope. September 2, 1792, Fuller wrote, "New scenes seem to be opening before me—new trials—O that I may glorify God in every stage!"[68] And, it would seem, God answered Fuller's prayer. The following month, October 2, 1792 the Baptist Missionary Society was formed at the meeting in Kettering. Two years later, Fuller—to the glory of God—wrote, "Within the last two years I have experienced perhaps as much peace and calmness of mind as at any former

---

64. See entries on February 16, 1790 and March 27, 1790 in Fuller, *Complete Works: Diary*, 1:179.

65. Fuller, *Complete Works: Diary*, 1:178.

66. Fuller, *Complete Works: Diary*, 1:178.

67. Fuller, *Works*, 1:184. A penetrating and personal account of Sarah (Gardiner's) death can be read from Fuller's own hand in a letter to his father-in-law, see Ryland, *Work of Faith*, 286–91.

68. Fuller, *Complete Works: Diary*, 1:185.

period."[69] It was this confidence in God's goodness that Fuller preached as "necessary to our success in prayer."[70]

Implications for Doctrine

The Lord's Prayer

Fuller's exposition of the Lord's Prayer clearly connected a right understanding of the divine character with a proper motivation to come before God in prayer and a proper order to it. The character of God, rightly understood, reveals that one's prayers may be offered on neither the case of "presumption [nor] despair . . . the two dangerous extremes to which mankind are prone in religious concerns."[71] Fuller explicitly connects right understanding of God's character with our posture in coming before him in prayer. In his exposition of the Lord's Prayer, he stated with respect to the invocation, "Our Father, who art *in heaven*":

> As the endearing character of the father inspires us with confidence, this must have no less tendency to excite our reverence; and both together are necessary to acceptable worship . . . Fear without hope would sink us into despair; and hope without fear would raise us to presumption; but united together, they constitute the beauty of holiness. It is not, however, for the purpose of inspiring reverence only that God is said to be in heaven, but to encourage us to confide in his absolute supremacy and almighty power.[72]

Several observations should be made regarding the above quotation. First, *both together are necessary*, that is, both hope and fear are necessary dispositions of the heart for proper worship. Fuller believed that proper worship was not only tied to the object of prayer—that is, the Triune God—but also, contingent on a proper internal disposition of the heart toward God through knowledge of his divine character. In his letter on "The Perfections of God," Fuller stated, "The Divine character lie at the foundation of all true religion." Why is God's character at the foundation of true religion? Fuller

---

69. Fuller, *Complete Works: Diary*, 1:187.

70. Fuller, *Complete Works: Diary*, 1:177; Morden, *Life and Thought of Andrew Fuller*, 99.

71. Fuller, *Works*, 2:121. Fuller is quoting from Robert Robertson's note in Jean Claude's work on the composition of a sermon. See Claude, *Composition of a Sermon*, 364. For more on Robinson, see *Baptist Encyclopaedia*, s.v. "Robinson, Robert."

72. Fuller, *Works*, 1:578.

knew that one cannot love that which he does not know.[73] "Without them," that is, without just views of the divine character, "it is impossible, in the nature of things to love God, or to perceive the fitness of our being required to love him, or the evil of not loving him, or the necessity of such a Saviour and such a salvation as the gospel reveals."[74] Knowledge of the divine character is antecedent to the love of God and thus antecedent to a proper disposition of the heart necessary for motivation to pray. Whereas a proper foundation for prayer is rooted in proper knowledge of God's character, likewise the proper knowledge of God's character, particularly his moral character, is revealed in Scripture. Thus, Scripture is inherently tied to developing a pure motivation for prayer.[75] Hence, Fuller stated, "the glory of God's character, and the coming of his kingdom, stand first in all his works, and therefore must have the precedence in all our prayers."[76] Why should one pray? One is obliged to pray out of a love for God and the glory of his divine character.

Next, Fuller stated, "It is not, however, for the purpose of inspiring reverence only that God is said to be in heaven, but to encourage us to confide in his absolute supremacy and almighty power."[77] While Fuller prioritized God's moral character and perfections as revealed in Scripture, the natural perfections of God also tend to motivate one to pray. Fuller stated, "He is above all our enemies, and has the direction and control of all events. What can be more consoling than the thought of having the Lord of the universe for our Father!"[78] Thus one ought to bring their needs before God based on his divine character and sovereignty over all events. Yet on the basis of the divine character, the proper order of prayer is to place the glory of the divine character first in one's prayers. Fuller called this disinterested love of God in prayer:

> That which some have denominated "disinterested love," or the love of God for what he is in himself, as far as I can understand it, is no other than hallowing his name, which is essential to true religion . . . To embrace the gospel as first glorifying God, and then giving peace on earth; and to seek our own interest

73. This was a major point in Fuller's sermon preached June 29, 1800, at Maze Pond, London, "Paul's Prayer for the Philippians," in Fuller, *Works*, 1:358.

74. Fuller, *Works*, 1:705.

75. A number of scholars have observed the inseparable link between Scripture and prayer in Fuller's spirituality. See Morden, *Offering Christ to the World*, 172–75; Brewster, "Model Baptist Pastor-Theologian," 62–64.

76. Fuller, *Works*, 1:579.

77. Fuller, *Works*, 1:578.

78. Fuller, *Works*, 1:578–79.

as bound up with the honour of his name, and as tending to promote it.[79]

Fuller's priority of love for God and the glory of God in prayer was also borne out in other sermons preached on the prayers of Scripture.

Paul's Prayer for the Philippians

Fuller preached from Phil 1:9–11 on June 29, 1800, at Maze Pond, London. The title of the sermon, whether titled by Fuller or the editor, is "Paul's Prayer for the Philippians." Fuller's sermon highlighted Paul's prayer for the Philippians to increase in love, knowledge, and judgment. "The end to which they were directed," according to Fuller, was "to the praise and glory or [sic] God."[80] There are at least two implications of Paul's prayer on one's doctrine of God, namely—prayer stokes the heart to love God and is one of the means whereby one increases in knowledge of God.

First, prayer stokes the heart to love God. Fuller distinguished between Christian love and other things that may go under the name of love, such as "natural affection" or "party attachment."[81] Christian love has its object in what is holy, "for it is the love of that in the Divine character."[82] "Love is one of the first principles of all religion," according to Fuller," and it is "the first thing that the apostle holds up as an object of desire."[83] Since love is a first principle of all religion, also it must be a first desire in prayer. However, Paul knew that if love was to increase, knowledge must also increase. The two are integrally tied together in this prayer and have apparent implications for a proper doctrine of God.

Second, prayer is one of the means whereby one increases in the knowledge of God. Fuller preached, "Knowledge of Divine truth is that to the mind which food is to the body; it nourishes it and keeps it alive. We cannot love an unknown being; we cannot love an unknown gospel."[84] So how does one increase in such love and knowledge of God? Fuller stated, "It is necessary . . . that we read and pray, and hear and labour, to cultivate the knowledge of God."[85] Prayer is one of the means for increased

79. Fuller, *Works*, 1:580.
80. Fuller, *Works*, 1:357.
81. Fuller, *Works*, 1:357.
82. Fuller, *Works*, 1:357.
83. Fuller, *Works*, 1:357.
84. Fuller, *Works*, 1:358.
85. Fuller, *Works*, 1:358.

knowledge of God experientially. Fuller's belief regarding the integral role of prayer in an experiential knowledge of God was explicitly borne out in his recommendation to a young pastor: "To understand the Scriptures in such a manner as profitably to expound them, it is necessary to be conversant with them in private; and to mix, not only faith, but the prayer of faith, with what we read."[86] Fuller stated that herein lay "the great difference between reading the Scriptures *as a student*, in order to find something to say to the people, and reading them *as a Christian*, with a view to get good from them to one's soul."[87] Fuller warned the young pastor, "That which we communicate will freeze upon our lips, unless we have first applied it to ourselves; or to use the language of Scripture, 'tasted, felt, and handled the word of life.'"[88] Fuller understood prayer to be an integral part of one's experiential knowledge of God, one's tasting, feeling, and handling the word of life.

Conclusion

Doctrine's Influence on Prayer

Fuller's doctrine of God and theology of prayer demonstrated identifiable areas of reciprocity. The researcher observed the most significant areas of correlation to be within Fuller's doctrine of the knowledge of God. Fuller's doctrine of the knowledge of God bore implications for answering three questions related to Fuller's theology of prayer:

> *Why should one pray?*—The glory of the divine character provides enduring motivation for all worship and prayer.
>
> *Who should pray?*—The harmony of God's moral government obligates all humans to pray.
>
> *How should one pray?*—Each person ought to pray out of a spirit of love for God according to the will of God.

Prayer's Influence on Doctrine

Fuller's theology of prayer prioritized the practice of prayer as one of the divinely appointed means for gaining a proper love for and knowledge of

---

86. Fuller, *Works*, 1:713–14.
87. Fuller, *Works*, 1:714. Emphasis original.
88. Fuller, *Works*, 1:714.

God. Fuller's doctrinal sermon, *The Nature and Importance of an Intimate Knowledge of Divine Truth*, explicates the point well:

> *We must learn truth immediately from the oracles of God.* Many religious people appear to be contented with seeing truth in the light in which some great and good man has placed it; but if ever we enter into the gospel to purpose [*sic*], it must be by reading the word of God for ourselves, and by praying and meditating upon its sacred contents. It is "in God's light that we must see light." By conversing with the sacred writers, we shall gradually imbibe their sentiments, and be insensibly assimilated into the same spirit.[89]

Fuller's theology of prayer prioritizes prayer as necessary for a proper knowledge of God; that is, prayer is essential for an experiential knowledge of God as one who has "tasted, felt, and handled the word of life."[90]

---

89. Fuller, *Works*, 1:714. Emphasis original.

90. Fuller, *Works*, 1:714. Fuller was not alone in the Particular Baptist milieu concerning his view of prayer being vital for true knowledge of God. Consider Wheeler's analysis regarding the widespread belief among Particular Baptists regarding the need for prayer to acquire divine knowledge as distinct from human knowledge. Wheeler stated, "Human, or natural knowledge, included information derived from academic disciplines such as, the liberal arts, biblical languages, history, logic, apologetics, and even extra biblical writings of Christians. But as useful as these were as a supplement to the studying the Scriptures, they were less important than divine knowledge. Divine knowledge was the 'knowledge of God and his will, of Christ and the way of salvation by him . . . ' and was acquired mainly through prayer, Bible study, and meditation on Scripture." Wheeler, "Eminent Spirituality and Eminent Usefulness," 132. Fuller was no exception to this Particular Baptist norm articulated through Wheeler's analysis of Particular Baptist ordination sermons. See also, Fuller, *Works*, 136.

3

The Son and Prayer

The *doctrine* we teach must be that of Jesus Christ and him crucified.
The person and work of Christ have ever been the corner-stone of the
Christian fabric: take away his Divinity and atonement, and all will go to
ruins.[1]

—Andrew Fuller, "God's Approbation of Our Labours
Necessary to the Hope of Success"

Two aspects of Fuller's Christology surface as bearing the most apparent
corollary relationship with Fuller's theology of prayer, namely, the deity of
Christ and the work of Christ as mediator and intercessor. No other branch
of theology is closer to Fuller's theological center than his Christology. All
things doctrinal and practical hinged on the doctrine of the cross.[2] Fuller
wrote to Ryland in his *Letters on Systematic Divinity*, "Error concerning the
person and work of Christ is of such importance as frequently to become
death to the party. We may err on other subjects and survive, though
it be in a maimed state; but to err in this is to contract a disease in the

---

1. Fuller, *Works*, 1:190.

2. In his *Letters on Systematic Divinity,* Fuller wrote to Ryland, "I do not know how it
may prove on trial, but I wish to begin with the centre [*sic*] of Christianity—*the doctrine
of the cross*, and to work round it; or with what may be called the heart of Christianity,
and to trace it through its principal veins or relations, both in doctrine and practice."
Fuller, *Works*, 1:690.

vitals, the ordinary effect of which is death."[3] Fuller took a prominent role among Baptists in defending Trinitarian orthodoxy against the increasingly prevalent Socinian heresy among dissenters.[4] Socinians denied the most vital of Christian doctrines, rejecting both the Trinity and deity of Christ. The rejection of Christ's deity also undercut the work of Christ. Much of what Fuller wrote with respect to the person and work of Christ came in response to the Socinian heresy, especially with reference to the implications these had on his theology of prayer.

Explanation of the Doctrine

The Trinity

The vital doctrine of the Trinity was solidified early in Fuller's ministry.[5] The greatest implication for the doctrine, according to Fuller, is "its affecting our views of the doctrine of the person and work of Christ."[6] In "Letter 9: The Trinity," Fuller stated that the doctrine of the Trinity "is a subject of pure revelation."[7] Likewise, in his sermon *The Nature and Importance of an Intimate Knowledge of Divine Truth*, Fuller stated, "On this ground," that is, the ground of special revelation, "we believe that 'there are three who bear record in heaven, the Father, the Word, and the Holy Spirit; and that these three are one.'"[8]

3. Fuller, *Works*, 1:691.

4. Michael Haykin describes Socinianism as "the leading form of heterodoxy within English Dissent in the last quarter of the eighteenth century." Haykin, "A Socinian and Calvinist Compared," 196.

5. Early in ministry, Fuller was introduced to questions regarding the preexistence of Christ's human soul and the eternal sonship of Christ. These questions helped him in the later writings that he undertook against Socinianism. See Ryland, *Work of Faith*, 38–39; Haykin, "A Socinian and Calvinist Compared," 190.

6. Fuller, *Works*, 1:708.

7. Fuller, *Works*, 1:708.

8. Fuller, *Works*, 1:163. The quotation beginning with "we believe" may allude to a commonly known confession. Exploring Baptist confessions, the quotation could be traced to "Propositions and Conclusions concerning True Christian Religion, containing a Confession of Faith of certain English people, living at Amsterdam," believed to be authored chiefly by John Smyth. The confession was assembled after his death in 1612 and before 1614. See Article 43 in McGlothlin, *Baptist Confessions*, 66–85. A more likely origin would be "A Declaration of Faith of English People Remaining at Amsterdam in Holland," since the opening article of Helwys's confession begins with a similar phrase. See Article 1 in McGlothlin, *Baptist Confessions*, 85–93. Other Baptist confessions, which preceded Fuller's day, included a similar phrase in their confessions. See "The Standard Confession" (1660), Article 7; and "Orthodox Creed" (1678), Article

Some may contest rightly that the treatment of Fuller's doctrine of the Trinity belongs in the prior chapter. While the doctrine of the Trinity properly falls under the doctrine of God, treatment of the doctrine of the Trinity with respect to Fuller's Christology is equally as suitable. Fuller's defense of the doctrine of the Trinity centers on his defense of the deity of Christ. Additionally, his doctrines of the Trinity and the deity of Christ bore significant implications for Fuller's understanding of the proper object of prayer. His doctrines of the Trinity and deity of Christ helped him answer a vexing theological question of his day, whether Christ ought to be the object of prayer.

Eternal Sonship of Christ

Fuller's doctrine of the deity of Christ and work of Christ were linked to his belief regarding the eternal sonship of Christ. In a treatise *On the Sonship of Christ*, Fuller considered at least three lines of connection. First, "The proper Deity of Christ precedes his office of Mediator, or High Priest of our profession, and renders it an exercise of *condescension*. But the same is true of his sonship."[9] Second, "The proper Deity of Christ . . . gives *dignity* to his office as Mediator; but this dignity is ascribed to his being the 'Son of God.' We have a *great* High Priest, Jesus the *Son of God*." Third, "The proper Diety of Christ . . . gives *efficacy* to his sufferings: 'by *himself* he purges our sins.' But this efficacy is ascribed to his being the 'Son of God': 'The blood of Jesus Christ, *his Son*, cleanseth us from all sin.'"[10] On all three connections, Fuller concluded, "His being the Son of God, therefore, amounts to the same thing as his being a Divine person."[11] Fuller's view respecting the eternal sonship of Christ was essential for a proper Christology. As the eternal sonship was essential to the deity of Christ, so the deity of Christ was foundational to his views regarding the work of Christ. "The incarnation, resurrection, and exaltation of Christ," all elements the work of Christ, "did not *constitute*, him the Son of God; nor did any of his offices."[12] Fuller stated, "God *sent* his Son into the world. This implies that he was his Son antecedently to his

---

3. McGlothlin, *Baptist Confessions*, 114 and 126. Even still, the most likely source is the *Comma Johanneum*, 1 John 5:7–8, a common Trinitarian proof-text within the Authorized Version still used in Fuller's day. Cross and Livingstone, "Johannine Comma." For more on the *Comma Johanneum*, see Metzger and Ehrman, *Text of New Testament*, 146–48.

9. Fuller, *Works*, 3:706. Emphasis original.

10. Fuller, *Works*, 3:706. Emphasis original.

11. Fuller, *Works*, 3:706.

12. Fuller, *Works*, 1:710.

being sent."[13] The Sonship, and likewise deity of Christ, antecedent to his being sent is essential for "when the value, virtue, or efficacy of what he did and suffered are touched upon, they are never ascribed either to the Father or the Spirit, but to himself."[14] Thus the nature of the second person of the Trinity as the eternal Son of God was a lynchpin for the value, virtue, and efficacy of the work of Christ. If Jesus is not Divine, then the atonement and thus "our calling on his name" would be of no effect.[15]

Implications for Prayer

The Object of Prayer: "Three Divine Persons in One Essence"

With the rise of Socinianism particularly among the General Baptists in the latter part of the seventeenth century and eighteenth centuries, the proper object of prayer was a critical question with respect to one's doctrine of God, especially as with respect to the person of Christ.[16] In *The Calvinistic and Socinian Systems Examined and Compared*, Fuller described a dispute between Francis Davides (1510–1579) and Faustus Socinus (1539–1604). Fuller used the dispute to illustrate the importance of harmony between belief and practice regarding the Trinity and prayer. According to Fuller, Socinus imprisoned Davides for invoking Christ in his prayers. Fuller stated, "They both held Christ to be a mere man. The former, however was for praying to him; which the latter, *with much greater consistency*, disapproved."[17] Although both parties were wrong, Fuller assessed Socinus as more internally consistent with respect to the coherence of his errant doctrine of God and theology of prayer. If Jesus is not God, then he ought not to be invoked in prayer. By reversing Fuller's logic, one could infer that if Jesus is God, then he ought to be invoked in prayer.[18] But with Fuller, one is not left only with inference.

---

13. Fuller, *Works*, 1:710. Emphasis original.

14. Fuller, *Works*, 1:710–11.

15. For Fuller's "The Deity of Christ Essential to the Atonement" and "The Deity of Christ Essential to Our Calling on His Name and Trusting in Him for Salvation," see, respectively, Fuller, *Works*, 3:693–95; and Fuller, *Works*, 3:695–97.

16. See Ivimey, *HEB*, 2:447; McBeth, *Baptist Heritage*, 155–58; Garrett, *Baptist Theology*, 44–46.

17. Fuller, *Works*, 2:165. Emphasis added.

18. It is worth noting that this account dates the question of the proper object of prayer within Protestant circles to as early as the mid-sixteenth century.

Joseph Priestley, a principal proponent of Socinianism in the early eighteenth century, accused those who prayed to Christ as detracting from the "essential glory of the Father."[19] Fuller countered Priestley by stating:

> It ought to be considered that, in worshipping the Son of God, we worship him not on account of that wherein he differs from the Father, but on account of those perfections which we believe him to possess in common with him. This, with the consideration that we worship him not to the exclusion of the Father, any more than the Father to the exclusion of him, but as one with him, removes all apprehensions from our minds that, in ascribing glory to the one, we detract from that of the other.[20]

Because the Son is God, he is the proper object of prayer.[21] One cannot pray to the Son to the exclusion of the Father, just as one cannot pray to the Father to the exclusion of the Son. Fuller unambiguously defended the practice of praying to Christ as a necessary implication of his doctrine of the Trinity. Opposing contemporary Socinian denials of the deity of Christ, Fuller articulated that Christ is the proper object of prayer, a distinct yet inseparable person of the Trinity.

Fuller reiterated his position regarding the appropriateness of prayer addressed to Christ in a letter to Henry Davis.[22] Fuller stated:

> But "something like this," he thinks, "is the case when the three persons are separately addressed in prayer." Did not the primitive Christians call on the name of Christ? Did not Stephen call upon the Lord Jesus to receive his spirit? And was not this praying to him as distinct, though not as "separate," from the Father? Yet I suppose Stephen will not be accused of making "a division in Deity."[23]

19. Fuller, *Works*, 2:160. For an introduction to Joseph Priestley and his Socinian views respecting prayer, see Haykin, "A Socinian and Calvinist Compared," 178–87.

20. Fuller, *Works*, 2:161.

21. Fuller, *Works*, 2:180; Haykin, "A Socinian and Calvinist Compared," 191.

22. The letter in Fuller's *Works* is entitled "Defence [*sic*] of the Deity of Christ." Fuller, *Works*, 3:697–99. Henry Davis was an Independent minister in Leicestershiere and wrote a small piece against the Socinian heresy, "A Caution against Socinianism, in reply to Dr. Priestley." While Fuller, according to John Morris, "made no direct reply to this performance, . . . he saw in it a tendency to betray the cause which it pretended to defend." Fuller, *Miscellaneous Pieces*, 100–101. Davis, according to Morris, "stated his belief to be, 'that God is so united to the derived nature of Christ, and does so dwell in it, that by virtue of this union, Christ my properly be called God; and that *such regards* become due to him as are not due to any created nature, or mere creature, be it in itself so excellent.'" Fuller, *Miscellaneous Pieces*, 100.

23. Fuller, *Works*, 3:698.

Fuller's doctrine of the Trinity does not comprehend such a division in the Godhead as to pray to one to the exclusion of the other. As Fuller stated in his tract titled *The Doctrine of the Trinity*, "No sober Trinitarian would take upon him to say precisely to what degree the distinctions in the Godhead extend."[24] However, it does not follow that one cannot "decide upon the precise kind and degree of *union* which is necessary to denominate the great Creator of the world."[25] "The obvious conclusion," according to Fuller, "is that these three are one God, and that the Scripture doctrine of unity is of more persons than one in the Godhead."[26] The implication from Fuller's doctrine of the Trinity for prayer is that the object of prayer may be distinguishable with respect to the Father, Son, and Spirit, yet indivisible with respect to the Godhead. Prayer addressed to the Father cannot be offered at the exclusion of either the Son or the Spirit for "these three are one God."[27] Hence, Fuller defended prayer addressed to Christ as a theologically coherent implication of his doctrines of the Trinity and the deity of Christ.[28]

The Work of Christ: "The Great and Gracious Intercessor"[29]

Fuller's understanding of the work of Christ bore implications for the attitude in which one approaches God in prayer. In the second edition of *The Gospel Worthy of All Acceptation*, Fuller rejected a view of the atonement that understood Christ's death to be the "literal payment of a debt."[30] Such a view, according to Fuller, "Might, for aught I know, be inconsistent with indefinite invitations. But it would be equally inconsistent with the free *forgiveness* of sin, and with sinners being directed to apply for mercy as *supplicants*, rather than as claimants."[31] In Fuller's understanding, the limited nature of the atonement is in "the sovereignty of its application," rather than

24. Fuller, *Works*, 3:707.

25. Fuller, *Works*, 3:707.

26. Fuller, *Works*, 3:707.

27. Fuller, *Works*, 3:707.

28. In this light, one may infer the same to be true of invoking the Holy Spirit in prayer; however, Fuller is silent regarding the appropriateness of prayers directed to the Spirit as a distinct, albeit not separate, member of the Godhead. Chapter 4 will consider implications for "The Spirit and Prayer."

29. Fuller, *Works*, 1:272. The quotation in the title is taken from a phrase in Fuller's sermon, "The Reception of Christ the Turning Point of Salvation." Fuller, *Works*, 1:266–75.

30. Fuller, *Works*, 2:373.

31. Fuller, *Works*, 2:373. Emphasis original.

"in its insufficiency to save more than are saved."[32] While Fuller's views with respect to the extent of the atonement have been debated, the focus here is the implication of his doctrine of the atonement with respect to prayer.[33] The important aspect to notice is Fuller's position that one's approach to God for mercy properly comes as a supplicant and not as a claimant. One prays for mercy with an attitude of humility rather than a spirit of entitlement.

In his *Antinomianism Contrasted with the Religion Taught and Exemplified in the Holy Scriptures*, Fuller articulated a similar concern for consistency with respect to one's approach to God in prayer as a supplicant rather than a claimant.[34] Fuller stated, "But if salvation were so obtained by the propitiation of Christ as that the bestowment of it should be required by essential justice, it had not been an object of *intercession* on his part, nor of *prayer* on ours."[35] The intercession of Christ and prayer of humanity entreating God for mercy, according to Fuller, is rendered superfluous in a strictly commercial understanding of the atonement.[36] According to Fuller, "That which essential justice requires is not of grace, but of debt, and admits of the language of appeal rather than of prayer."[37] The implications that Fuller cautions against are not simply hypothetical. Fuller stated, "These consequences have been actually drawn: the intercession of Christ in heaven has been considered as possessing the nature of a *demand*."[38] Some took the implications even farther, omitting "to pray for the forgiveness of sin" altogether.[39] In Fuller's understanding, a strictly commercial view of the atonement, at its best, undermined the proper attitude of one approaching God in a spirit of humility. At its worst, the commercial view made prayer altogether superfluous.

---

32. Fuller, *Works*, 3:374.

33. The point is unchanged whether one concedes Fuller to hold to a particular or universal extent of the atonement. For a contemporary example of this varied interpretation, cf. Tom Nettles and David Allen's perspectives, respectively, in Nettles, "Contributions of Andrew Fuller," 68–77; Allen, *Extent of the Atonement*, 477–97.

34. The work was published posthumously. Fuller, *Antinomianism Contrasted*, v–vi; Fuller, *Works*, 2:737–62.

35. Fuller, *Works*, 2:756. Emphasis original.

36. Fuller, *Works*, 2:756. See Fuller's use of the expression "essential justice" and "moral justice" in *Antinomianism Contrasted* and *The Gospel Worthy of All Acceptation*. Fuller juxtaposed commercial understanding with his own sovereign design view by associating the expression "essential justice" with a literal payment of a debt and "moral justice" with his own view. Fuller, *Works*, 2:756 and 374.

37. Fuller, *Works*, 2:756.

38. Fuller, *Works*, 2:756.

39. Fuller, *Works*, 2:756.

Example of Fuller's Practice of Prayer

Fuller's diary left only one explicit example of him praying to Christ. On June 26, 1780, while at his first pastorate in Soham, Fuller recorded in his diary, "Dull and unaffected. How soon do I sink from the spirit of the gospel! I have need of thine intercession, O Lord Jesus, that my faith fail not."[40] Fuller's prayer comported with his principle that Christ is a proper object of prayer as a distinct but not separate person of the Trinity. Additionally, Fuller's prayer articulated his dependence on the continuing work of Christ as intercessor. The single entry from his diary at a minimum demonstrates that Fuller's future theological disputes over the correctness of praying to Christ were more than theological conjecture.

According to Haykin, "Both Priestley and his theological opponents were agreed that prayer was a formal act of worship, and if offered to Christ, was tantamount to confession of his deity."[41] Fuller was no exception. He was an adamant opponent concerning Priestley's claim that Christ was not God and thus neither a proper object of worship nor of prayer. Though they were opponents, Fuller agreed with Priestley on at least two points. First, if Jesus is God, then he ought to be worshipped and prayed to, considering prayer a proper aspect of worship.[42] Second, Fuller also agreed that those who worship Jesus as God and those who reject the deity of Christ ought to worship separately.[43]

Fuller's belief respecting the person and work of Christ pervaded his exposition of the Lord's Prayer, especially the invocation, "Our Father." Fuller's stated, "It is no small proof that the privilege of approaching God as Father has respect to the mediation of Christ."[44] Priestley's rejection of the deity of Christ not only led him to ere respecting Christ as a proper object of prayer, but it also led him to deny the ongoing work of Christ as intercessor. Priestley stated:

> The intercession of Christ with God for us is needless. We are to address our prayer to God himself immediately; and

40. Fuller, *Complete Works: Diary*, 1:4.

41. Haykin, "A Socinian and Calvinist Compared," 186.

42. Haykin, "A Socinian and Calvinist Compared," 186. Fuller stated, "Now as a rejection of the Divinity of Christ renders it idolatry to worship him . . . If there were no objection on the part of Trinitarians there ought to be on the part of Arians and Socinians, to render their conduct consistent. If we be guilty of idolatry, they ought to come out from amongst us, and be separate, as the Scriptures command Christians to do with respect to idolaters." Fuller, *Works*, 3:696–97.

43. Haykin, "A Socinian and Calvinist Compared," 196.

44. Fuller, *Works*, 1:578.

his affection for us in such as will always induce him to grant whatever is proper for us, without the intercession or mediation, of any being whatever for us.[45]

The Socinians were not alone in their tendency to vitiate the work of Christ as mediator and intercessor. Fuller felt that Antinomians had a tendency to make the same error. He stated, "I am far from thinking that every one [sic] who has pleaded for salvation as a matter required by essential justice is an Antinomian; but such may be the tendency of the principle notwithstanding."[46] A few paragraphs later, Fuller stated:

> *Substitutionary* atonement, or atonement made for the sin of
> *another*, whether it be by slain beasts, or by any other means,
> in nowise interferes with grace. In *pecuniary* satisfactions, if the
> creditor be but paid, whether it be by the debtor, or by a surety
> on his behalf, *he has received his due*, and no room is left for re-
> mission or for grace; but it is not so here. In cases of *crime*, noth-
> ing can render deliverance a matter of claim, but the criminal
> himself having suffered the full penalty of the law. Deliverance
> by the interposition of a mediator, though it may answer the
> great ends of justice, and so be *consistent with it*, yet can never be
> *required by it*, nor be any other than an act of grace. This truth,
> while it repels the objections of Socinianism, corrects the abuses
> of Antinomianism.[47]

Fuller addressed the errors of Socinians and Antinomians with his govern-mental nuance of substitutionary atonement.[48] His perspective respecting

45. Priestley, *Notes on All the Books of Scripture*, 3:469; Haykin, "A Socinian and Calvinist Compared," 185. Priestley was commenting on John 16:27. On John 16:23, Priestley stated, "We see here that Christ is not to be the object of worship or prayer in any respect, notwithstanding any thing [sic] he may have to do in the government of the church, from the time of his ascension into heaven to his second coming, concerning which we are intirely [sic] ignorant." Priestley, *Notes on All the Books of Scripture*, 3:469.

46. Fuller, *Works*, 2:756.

47. Fuller, *Works*, 2:757. Emphasis original.

48. According to Bart Box's in-depth study of Fuller's doctrine of the atonement, "Fuller found the governmental scheme useful in confronting theological systems that promoted immorality or licentiousness on the basis of a commercial view of the atone-ment. In the place of debt and credit, Fuller advanced the notion that the atonement proceeded more along the lines of crime. Thus, the governmental system held an attrac-tion for Fuller as an apologetic against morally deficient representations of Christian-ity . . . To conclude: over the course of his ministry Fuller modified and added to his position on the atonement . . . However, the words 'modification and 'addition' should not obscure the fact that many of Fuller's beliefs concerning the atonement remained consistent throughout his ministry." With respect to substitutionary atonement, Bart states, "He never waivered in his affirmation of substitutionary atonement, even if his

the work of Christ not only renders prayer a needed exercise on the part of humanity pleading for mercy but also respects the ongoing role of Christ as intercessor and mediator before the Father.

Implications for Doctrine

The Prayer of Stephen

Certain prayers in Scripture featured prominently in the disputes regarding the deity of Christ and whether he is a proper object of prayer. One such prayer was Stephen's in Acts 7. Fuller saw this text as a key proof supporting the practice of addressing Christ in prayer.

In *Socinianism Indefensible on the Ground of Its Moral Tendency*, Fuller replied to Joshua Toulmin's (1740–1815) *The Practical Efficacy of the Unitarian Doctrine Considered*. Toulmin subtitled the work *Proved and Illustrated from the Acts of the Apostles, and the Epistle of Paul to Timothy and Titus*.[49] Fuller took Toulmin to task for his discriminatory avoidance of Stephen's prayer. Fuller stated, "Dr. Toulmin finds Stephen before the council, but makes no mention of his death, in which he is described as praying to Christ, saying, 'Lord Jesus, receive my spirit'—'Lord, lay not this sin to their charge.'"[50]

The Practice of Primitive Christians

For Fuller, Stephen's prayer coupled with the New Testament's equating "calling on the name of the Lord Jesus . . . with believing in him," was a strong testament to the deity of Christ and suitability of praying to Christ. These two pieces of evidence went hand-in-hand in Fuller's writings. For example, Fuller paired these two New Testament evidences in his letter to Davis on "Remarks on the Indwelling Scheme":

> Excuse me if I inquire further, Will your scheme allow you to *worship* Christ, I do not say "separately," but distinctly from the Father, as the martyr Stephen worshipped him, and prayed to

---

terminology obscured rather than clarified his ideas . . . Whether substitutionary atonement and governmental views of the atonement are harmonious in truth, one cannot doubt but that Fuller saw them as such." Box, "Atonement in the Thought of Andrew Fuller," 217–18.

49. Toulmin, *A Review of the Preaching of the Apostles.*

50. Fuller, *Works*, 2:260.

him in his dying moments; and as all the primitive Christians worshipped him, *calling upon his name?*[51]

Fuller paired the two pieces of evidence again in *The Calvinistic and Socinian Systems Examined and Compared.* He stated:

> The primitive Christians will be allowed to have loved God aright; yet they worshipped Jesus Christ. Not only did the martyr Stephen close his life by committing his departing spirit into the hands of Jesus, but it was the common practice, in primitive times, to invoke his name. "He hath authority," said Ananias concerning Saul, to bind "all that call on thy name."[52]

Loving, worshipping, and praying to Christ is not mutually exclusive to loving, worshipping, and praying to God because Jesus is God. Fuller understood Stephen's prayer and the practice of primitive Christians as explicitly sanctioning direct appeals to Christ and as supporting his doctrines of the Trinity and deity of Christ in particular.

In his sermon on *The Prayer of Faith, Exemplified in the Woman of Canaan*, Fuller stated that the Canaanite woman's prayer was "*the prayer of faith*" because "she *believed*, and confessed him to be the Messiah."[53] In another sermon, *Nature and Extent of True Conversion*, Fuller stated, "True conversion to Christ will be accompanied with the *worship* of him. Worship, as a religious exercise, is the homage of the heart, presented to God according to his revealed will. This homage being paid to the Messiah affords a proof of his proper Deity."[54] Thus the worship and prayer of the Canaanite woman provided further scriptural evidence respecting the deity of Christ. The implication from the prayer of the Canaanite woman is that Jesus is God.

Fuller applied the same reasoning to prayer of primitive Christians in the New Testament. In *The Calvinistic and Socinian Systems Examined*, Fuller stated:

> The primitive Christians are characterized by their "calling upon the name of the Lord Jesus." . . . That this is designed as a description of true Christians, will not be denied; but this description does not include Socinians, seeing they call not upon

---

51. Fuller, *Works*, 3:701.
52. Fuller, *Works*, 2:160.
53. Fuller, *Works*, 1:238. Emphasis original.
54. Fuller, *Works*, 1:552.

the name of Christ. The conclusion is, Socinians would not have been acknowledged, by the apostle Paul, as true Christians.[55]

Socinians, like Mr. Lindsey, according to Fuller, believed that the phrase "'called upon the name of Christ,' should be rendered, *called by the name, of Christ.*"[56] In commenting on 1 Cor 1:2, Priestley stated, "This ought to have been rendered, *who call themselves by the name of Christ*, that is, who are christians [sic]."[57] Priestley offers no comment on Romans 10:13. One is left to wonder what explanation Priestley could have provided. Fuller speculated on the matter with respect to Lindsey's rendering of the phrase "*called by the name, of Christ.*" Fuller stated:

> Mr. Lindsey's observation, . . . if applied to Rom. 10:13, would make the Scriptures promise salvation to every one [sic] that is called a Christian. Salvation is promised to all who *believe, love, fear,* and *call upon the name of the Lord*; but never are the possessors of it described by a mere accidental circumstance, in which they are not voluntary, and in which, if they were, there is no virtue.[58]

The suggested rendering by Lindsey and Priestley led, in Fuller's mind, to absurd conclusions.

Conclusion

Doctrine's Influence on Prayer

Fuller's doctrine of the Trinity and the deity of Christ affected his understanding of Christ as a proper object of prayer. Fuller's doctrine of the Trinity allowed for prayers to be offered to Christ as a distinct and not a separate person of the Trinity. Fuller's affirmation of Christ as a proper object of prayer was a theologically coherent implication of his doctrine of the Trinity and of the deity of Christ.

Fuller's doctrine of the work of Christ also bore implications for the attitude of one approaching God in prayer. Fuller believed that a strictly commercial view of the atonement bore negative implications for one's attitude in approaching God as a claimant rather than a supplicant for mercy. Fuller believed that the commercial view may even lead to a neglect of prayer

---

55. Fuller, *Works*, 2:180–81.

56. Fuller, *Works*, 2:181, note. Emphasis original.

57. Priestley, *Notes on All the Books of Scripture*, 4:83.

58. Fuller, *Works*, 2:181, note. Emphasis original.

altogether. The claimant, in the commercial view, has no need to pray because the debt is paid already regardless of one's entreating God for mercy. In Fuller's understanding, this rendered the intercession of the Son before the Father and the petitions of humanity as superfluous. Fuller sought for his position on the atonement to be consistent with Christ's ongoing work as intercessor and mediator before the Father. Such a concern was likely a safeguard against the radical implications of Socinians. For example, men like Priestley rejected any need for Christ's intercession. Fuller felt that his view of the atonement harmonized and implied an attitude of prayer that retained the posture of humility with respect to approaching God through Christ, the "great and gracious Intercessor."[59]

Prayer's Influence on Doctrine

The prayer of Stephen in Acts 7, the prayer of the Canaanite woman, and the practice of primitive Christians "calling upon the name of the Lord Jesus" clearly affected Fuller's Christology. These three pieces of evidence were not the sole foundation of his Christology; however, they were argumentative evidence reinforcing his position regarding the Trinity and deity of Christ. As a theologian, Fuller was committed not to take any principle at second hand. The importance of Scripture's testimony regarding examples of prayer to Christ cannot be understated. Fuller's understanding of Stephen and the Canaanite woman's prayer as worship to Christ coupled with the practice of primitive Christians "calling upon the name of the Lord Jesus" were solid scriptural supports for Fuller's own practice of praying to Christ as fully divine, eternally the Son of God.

59. Fuller, *Works*, 1:272.

4

The Spirit and Prayer

We must not live in the neglect of prayer at any time because we are un-
conscious of being under Divine influence, but rather, as our Lord directs,
pray *for* his Holy Spirit. It is *in* prayer that the Spirit of God ordinarily
assists us.[1]

—ANDREW FULLER, "PRINCIPLES AND PROSPECTS OF A SER-
VANT OF CHRIST"

Explanation of the Doctrine

The Person and Work of the Spirit

In Fuller's writings, the person and work of the Spirit are not as
prominently featured as the person and work of Christ. This is not to say
that his pneumatology was less significant than his Christology but simply
acknowledges that Fuller wrote less about the person and work of the Spirit
than the person and work of Christ. Less attention given to the Spirit may
be attributed to three things borne out in Fuller's letter on the Trinity in
Letters on Systematic Divinity. First, Fuller stated that the office of the
Spirit "is not the grand object of ministerial exhibition."[2] Fuller felt that

1. Fuller, *Works*, 1:343.
2. Fuller, *Works*, 1:711.

"the more sensible we are, both as ministers and Christians of our entire dependence on the Holy Spirit's influences, the better; but if we make them the grand theme of our ministry, we shall do that which he himself avoids, and so shall counteract his operations."[3] Albeit of no less importance, Fuller understood the person and work of the Spirit to be inconspicuous compared to the person and work of Christ. Second, Fuller stated, "As the father is allowed on all hands to be a Divine person, whatever proves the Divinity and personality of the Son proves a plurality of Divine persons in the Godhead. I need not adduce the evidences of this truth: the sacred Scriptures are full of them."[4] Later in the same letter, he argued that many of the faulty arguments "to prove the inferiority and posteriority of Christ as the Son of God; namely, reasoning from things human to things Divine," are used "to reduce the Holy Spirit to a mere property, or *energy*, of the Deity."[5] Fuller seemed to think that if one successfully established the testimony of Scripture regarding the deity of Christ, then the deity of the Spirit followed suit. In the face of Socinian and Unitarian heterodoxies, Fuller understood that the deity of the Spirit would be a moot point if the one would not accept the deity of Christ.[6] Third, "Much less is said in the sacred Scriptures on the Divinity and personality of the Holy Spirit."[7] Fuller, being faithful to derive

3. Fuller, *Works*, 1:711.

4. Fuller, *Works*, 1:710.

5. Fuller, *Works*, 1:711.

6. It is interesting to note how the early church confessions progressed along these same lines of doctrinal development. The early Christological formulations were developed in response to Arians, Nestorians, Apollinarians, Sabellians, and so forth. Fuller, like many early defenders of orthodoxy, was forced to defend and put into writing that which was most contested in his day. The same reason could be given for Fuller's writing on the work of the Spirit outweighing his writing on the deity of the Spirit. Fuller's "epoch-making book," *The Gospel of Christ Worthy of All Acceptation* (1785), devoted a section to "the Spirit's work of regeneration." Fuller's book received criticism and responses from both Arminian and Hyper-Calvinist camps. Michael Haykin observed an unexpected area of agreement between Fuller's opponents who openly disagreed with him regarding the work of the Spirit. Both Arminians and Hyper-Calvinists argued that "if God commands sinners to do something then they must be able to accomplish it without the Spirit's power. For the Arminian, since faith is commanded of sinners by God, then they must be able to believe without the irresistible drawing of the Spirit. Similarly, the Hyper-Calvinist reasons that since faith is wrought by the Spirit it cannot be an act of obedience." Haykin, "The Honour of the Spirit's Work," 155. Thus, Fuller's attention to the work of the Spirit, as opposed to the deity of the Spirit, may once again be attributed to his being forced to put into writing that which was most contested by his interlocutors. Orthodox Arminians and Hyper-Calvinists alike were in agreement regarding the deity of the Spirit. The work of the Spirit proved to be a point of division between Fuller's opponents and the evangelical Calvinism that he espoused.

7. Fuller, *Works*, 1:711.

principles from the "pure fountain" of God's word, seemingly acquiesced to the proportion that Scripture speaks regarding the person and work of the Spirit.

The Doctrine of Divine Influence

Fuller's writing on the work of the Spirit, what he called "the doctrine of *Divine influence*," far outweighed his writing on the deity of the Spirit.[8] Fuller believed that the work of the Spirit was one of the most vital doctrines of the Christian faith. In *Letters on Systematic Divinity, Letter 2: Importance of a True System*, he stated that "*the influence of the Holy Spirit*" is one of "three of the leading doctrines of the gospel."[9] The other two were the doctrine of election and the atonement. As with each of these vital doctrines, Fuller held that "if the doctrine of *Divine influence* be considered in its Scriptural connexions, it will be of essential importance in the Christian life; but if these be lost sight of, it will become injurious."[10] The "Divine influence" is so vital in the Christian life because, as Fuller stated, it "is that by which sinners are renewed and sanctified."[11] In both the renewal and sanctification of sinners, Fuller never wavered with respect to these being entirely a work of God, "wholly of grace."[12]

Sinners Renewed

Fuller included a section titled, "Of the Work of the Holy Spirit" in *The Gospel Worthy of All Acceptation* (1801).[13] In the first sentence of the section, Fuller stated, "The Scriptures clearly ascribe both repentance and faith wherever they exist to Divine influence."[14] Some had concluded that since repentance and faith are works of God that in order to make appeals to sinners "from the pulpit to repent and believe," the pastor must accept one of two false lines of reasoning. Fuller understood the dilemma as either "'faith and conversion, seeing they are acts of obedience, cannot be wrought of God'; or, . . . that seeing they are wrought of God, they cannot be acts of

8. Fuller, *Works*, 1:688. Emphasis original.
9. Fuller, *Works*, 1:685; Sheehan, "Great and Sovereign Grace," 87.
10. Fuller, *Works*, 1:688.
11. Fuller, *Works*, 1:688
12. Fuller, *Works*, 1:284.
13. Fuller, *Works*, 2:379–80.
14. Fuller, *Works*, 2:379.

obedience."[15] Fuller found the either-or-dilemma to be completely unscriptural. Fuller believed that divine influence and human obligation were not mutually exclusive. He stated, "If we need the influence of the Holy Spirit *to enable us to do our duty*, both of these methods of reasoning fall to the ground."[16] Fuller maintained that the influence of the Spirit was consistent with gospel invitations and the duty of all humans to believe in Christ.

Fuller upheld the same line of reasoning in his correspondence with Dan Taylor in *The Reality and Efficacy of Divine Grace*.[17] He stated, "I maintain that it is owing to Divine agency, and to that *alone*, that one sinner, rather than another, believes in Christ."[18] Fuller continued, "I conceive that men become active, when the Spirit operates upon their minds, though they were passive *in* that operation . . . That the mind, in receiving Christ, is active, I allow; but this is in no way inconsistent with the Holy Spirit being the proper, sole, efficient cause of such activity."[19] Though humans are passive in the regenerating work of the Spirit, the "immediate effect may be activity."[20] Thus, Fuller saw the work of the Spirit to be in no way inconsistent with the human obligation to believe in Christ. Likewise, the obligation as such in no way diminished the role of the Spirit as the "proper *cause* of our believing."[21]

Sinners Sanctified

The work of the Spirit is every bit as vital in the sanctification of individual humans as in their renewal. In Fuller's sermon on Paul's prayer for the Ephesians, Fuller stated, "Nothing good is found in fallen man: . . . If any thing [sic] holy be found there, it must be produced by the Spirit of God,

15. Fuller, *Works*, 2:379–80. Fuller identified the first option as typical of an Arminian or Socinian position. The second position likely represents what Fuller understood as the high Calvinist or Antinomian position because of the insistence that faith is neither an obligation nor duty. According to Peter Morden, "The prevailing High Calvinist definition of faith . . . Understood faith as being analogous to a person having an 'inner persuasion' of their 'interest' in Christ, something given to them by the Holy Spirit." Thus without "a so-called 'warrant of faith,'" there can be no obligation. Morden, *Offering Christ to the World*, 24.

16. Fuller, *Works*, 2:380. Emphasis original.

17. The collection of thirteen letters was published together under the above title. Initially, Fuller responded under the pseudonym Agnostos. Fuller, *Works*, 2:512–60. For a full discussion on the debate between Fuller and Taylor regarding the Spirit see Haykin, "Honour of the Spirit's Work."

18. Fuller, *Works*, 2:515. Emphasis original.

19. Fuller, *Works*, 2:516.

20. Fuller, *Works*, 2:516.

21. Fuller, *Works*, 2:516.

who worketh in us to will and to do of his good pleasure. Nor is Divine influence less necessary in carrying on the good work after it is begun."[22] Fuller rightly stated, "What encouragement is here for prayer!"[23] That is, because God gives inner strength "'according to the riches of his glory,' . . . let us ask much, and we shall have much."[24] The strengthening of the Spirit in sanctification is tied directly with one's activity in prayer. The same "*sole, efficient*, and proper *cause* of our believing" is likewise the sole, efficient, and proper cause of one's sanctification.[25]

Implications for Prayer

A Question of Regeneration: "To What Purpose Was It to Pray?"

If regeneration is a work entirely of God, wrought by the work of the Spirit prior to one's coming to Christ, then one may ask, "To what purpose was it to *pray* for what they already had?"[26] Fuller's conviction that the Spirit was the sole, efficient, and proper cause of one's belief did not make prayer obsolete. On the contrary, Fuller believed that prayer was a vital implication tied to the Spirit's work. Fuller was stimulated to pray because he believed the work of the Spirit to be in complete harmony with the examples of prayers and promises of Scripture regarding the outpouring of the Spirit.

Fuller interpreted the prayers of the apostles in Acts and the prayers of "primitive ministers" as correlating directly with the outpouring of God's Spirit in the early church.[27] Fuller stated, "The *prayers* of the apos-

22. Fuller's treatment of the second prayer is from a sermon, "Paul's Prayer for the Ephesians." The sermon dealt with Eph 3:14–16, a text not referenced in *The Gospel Worthy of All Acceptation*. Fuller, *Works*, 1:429.

23. Fuller, *Works*, 1:432.

24. Fuller, *Works*, 1:432.

25. Fuller, *Works*, 2:516. Emphasis original. Interestingly, Eph 1:13–14 and 17–18 was also a point of discussion in Fuller's reply to both William Button and Dan Taylor. Fuller, *Works*, 2:449 and 468–69, respectively. Haykin offers a brief discussion of Fuller's interpretation of Eph 1:13–14 and 17 in response to Taylor. See Haykin, "Honour of the Spirit's Work," 159. Perhaps there is room for more work regarding Fuller's interpretation of Ephesians 1 as a critical passage for understanding the work of the Spirit.

26. Fuller, *Works*, 2:464. Emphasis original. This was a question addressed by Fuller in his "Reply to Philanthropos," under the section, "Whether Regeneration is Prior to Our Coming to Christ." Fuller, *Works*, 2:462–71. Fuller's answer to whether regeneration preceded faith in Christ "affirmed the Calvinist position that regeneration both precedes faith and is its cause." Owens, "Fuller's Reply to Philanthropos," 20.

27. Fuller, *Works*, 2:464.

tles and primitive ministers show that their hope of success did not arise
from the pliableness of men's tempers, or the suitableness of the gospel to
their dispositions, but from the power of Almighty God attending their
ministrations."[28] Far from stifling the prayers of the apostles, their belief that
salvation is wholly a work of God precipitated by "*outpourings of the Spirit of
God*" motivated them to pray.[29] Thus, Fuller stated:

> "The weapons of their warfare," however fitted for the purpose,
> "were *mighty* through God to the pulling down of strong holds."
> To God they sent up their earnest and united petitions before
> they opened their commission. Meeting in an upper room,
> "they continued with one accord in prayer and supplication."
> And, afterwards, we find the apostle Paul requesting his Thessa-
> lonian brethren to pray for him and his associates in the work of
> the ministry, "that the word of the Lord might have free course
> and be glorified."[30]

Fuller observed that the "hope of success" for the "apostles and primitive
ministers" in their proclamation of the gospel was in direct correlation with
their prayers for the outpouring of God's Spirit. As such, Fuller believed that
the apostles and primitive ministers' hope of success was consistent with
their own hope of success and labors in prayer for outpourings of God's
Spirit. Perhaps this explains why Fuller felt such conviction regarding a
single verse in Acts 6.[31] After expounding the chapter that Sunday, Fuller
recorded in his diary, "One verse in particular carries in it conviction to
me, *That we may give ourselves wholly to prayer and ministry of the Word!*"[32]

The promises of Scripture regarding "the great accessions to the
church of God in the *latter days*," according to Fuller, "are ascribed to the
same cause"; that is, the outpouring of God's Spirit.[33] Similar to prayers exemplified in Scripture, these promises provided a strong motive for prayer.
Fuller held that if the outpouring of God's Spirit was not the cause, then
the promises of Scripture—regardless of "however strongly they speak of
the latter-day glory"—were nothing more than "mere predictions of what

28. Fuller, *Works*, 2:464.

29. Fuller, *Works*, 2:463. Emphasis original.

30. Fuller, *Works*, 2:464.

31. Wheeler cited Acts 6:1–7 as a critical passage for Particular Baptist practice of
ministers presiding over ordination services. Wheeler, "Eminent Spirituality and Eminent Usefulness," 84 and 127. Fuller's emphasis on verse four likely indicates that he
was reflecting on the priorities of prayer and the word in his own calling as a minister.

32. See Fuller's diary entry from Sunday, January 9, 1785. Fuller, *Complete Works:
Diary*, 1:102. Emphasis original.

33. Fuller, *Works*, 2:464. Emphasis original.

will be, rather than promises of what *shall* be."[34] The certainty of Scripture's promises undergirded Fuller's confidence in praying for the outpouring of God's Spirit. Otherwise, Fuller stated:

> Might not the apostles have expected some such answer to their prayers as was given to Dives?[35] "They have Moses and the prophets," yea, Christ and the apostles, "let them hear them"; I have given them grace sufficient already; I shall do nothing more in order to their conversion [*sic*], nothing at all, until they have believed.[36]

Fuller articulated the same points in his *Few Persuasives to a General Union in Prayer for the Revival of Real Religion*. One ought to consider what God has done in the past and promised to do in the future "and that in answer to prayer."[37] The prayers and promises of Scripture regarding the outpouring of God's Spirit motivated Fuller to pray and to invite others to unite in prayer for the outpouring of God's Spirit.

Prayer and the Use of Means

Fuller's belief regarding the work of the Spirit did not give license for men and women only to pray for the outpouring of the Spirit and salvation of souls, neglecting other God-ordained means for gospel witness. Paul Brewster perhaps said it best:

> If Fuller was an innovator at the time in arguing for the fullest use of means in the Church's mission to seek out the lost, he nonetheless retained the highest regard for the absolute necessity of divine influences as well. *Thus, means and prayer were inseparably wed in Fuller's ministry.*[38]

Fervent prayer for sinners to repent and believe was an indispensable implication of Fuller's doctrine of the Spirit. Fervent prayer for the lost was

34. Fuller, *Works*, 2:464. Emphasis original.

35. Dives is the name often given to the rich man from the parable in Luke 16 regarding the rich man and Lazarus. The rich man is "often called Dives from the Latin for 'rich man.'" Wead, "Lazarus," 3:94.

36. Fuller, *Works*, 2:464–65.

37. Fuller, *Persuasives*, 42–45. *A Few Persuasives* is slightly abridged in Fuller, *Works*, 3:666–69. In all, Fuller wrote regarding seven persuasives to unite in prayer for revival. The call to remember what God has done is the second persuasive. The call to look to what God has promised is the fourth persuasive.

38. Brewster, "Model Baptist Pastor-Theologian," 144. Emphasis added.

intended to be added to, and not replace, the means for calling sinners to repent and believe in Christ.

Fuller understood prayer to be the means for humble dependence on the power of the Spirit of God in all human efforts. Brewster illustrated "how prayer held a vital place in Fuller's efforts to win souls to faith in Christ" by considering his circular letter, "The Promise of the Spirit the Grand Encouragement in Promoting the Gospel" (1810), and Fuller's own practice of keeping a journal of persons that he was praying for their salvation.[39] Fuller knew that any use of means must be united with prayer for there to be any effect. As Brewster stated, "Prayer . . . was a required complement to the use of means in successful evangelism."[40]

Fuller demonstrated remarkable consistency on this interrelationship between prayer and the work of the Spirit. In his second circular letter for the association, "Causes of Declension in Religion, and Means of Revival" (1785), Fuller wrote, "Let us not forget to intermingle *prayer* with all we do."[41] "Our need of God's Holy Spirit," Fuller continued, "to enable us to do anything, and every thing [sic], truly good, should excite us to this."[42] "This" in context clearly denotes the pursuit of the Spirit's aid through prayer.

Example of Fuller's Practice of Prayer

Fuller's practice of prayer was marked by humble dependence on the Spirit's presence and work. Fuller sought the presence and influence of the Spirit in his own life and the lives of others through prayer. Early in his ministry, Fuller's awareness of his need for "entire dependence on the Holy Spirit's influences" was borne out in his diary.[43] On January 10, 1780, Fuller prayed:

> O Lord, never let me, under the specious pretence [sic] of preaching *holiness*, neglect to promulge the truths of thy word; for this day I see, and have all along found, that holy practice has a necessary dependence on sacred *principle*. O Lord, if thou wilt open mine eyes to behold the wonders of thy word, and give me to feel their transforming tendency, then shall the Lord be my God; then let my tongue cleave to the roof of my mouth, if I

39. Brewster, "Model Baptist Pastor-Theologian," 144–46.
40. Brewster, "Model Baptist Pastor-Theologian," 146.
41. Fuller, *Works*, 3:324. Emphasis original.
42. Fuller, *Works*, 3:324.
43. Fuller, *Works*, 1:711.

shun to declare, to the best of my knowledge, the whole counsel of God.[44]

A year later, on February 3, 1781, Fuller prayed, "O that the Holy Spirit would open my eyes, and let me into the things that I have never yet seen!"[45] Fuller's prayer, clearly connected to his reading and interpretation of Scripture, falls in line with the Baptist belief and practice of the day. Haykin in "A Great Thirst for Reading," juxtaposed the "literary culture" of the Anglican establishment with that of Dissenters and Baptists. The Anglican establishment, according to Haykin, "was . . . primarily dependent upon the level of one's formal academic attainments such as a university degree."[46] Whereas Dissenters, and particularly Baptists, with less access and emphasis on formal education, relied on a "reading that was ultimately 'spiritual,' that is, made possible only by the Holy Spirit, and was intimately tied to the heart."[47] A few days later, on February 8, Fuller prayed, "O would the Lord the Spirit lead me into the nature and importance of the work of the ministry! Reading a wise spiritual author might be of use: yet, could I, by divine assistance, but penetrate the work myself, it would seek deeper, and be more durable."[48] Fuller's prayer for the Spirit's aid, far from reflecting a lack of intellectual ability, reflected consistency with his understanding of the work the Spirit in reading Scripture. Prayer was a necessary accompaniment that helped the reader enter into "a tender, humble, holy frame."[49] A frame of mind that, according to Fuller, was "of more importance to our entering into the mind of the Holy Spirit than all other means united. It is thus that, by 'an unction from the Holy One, we know all things.'"[50] In this respect, Brewster rightly identified prayer as a critical aspect of Fuller's theological method: "As Fuller saw it, constant engagement in prayer and immersion in the Word of God was a *sine qua non* for the pastor-theologian."[51]

On September 15, 1784, now the pastor of the Baptist Church in Kettering, Fuller wrote, "Nothing of any remarkable exercise for these two or

44. This prayer is a section of a larger entry identified by Fuller as "A solemn vow or renewal of covenant with God." Fuller, *Complete Works: Diary*, 1:1. Emphasis original.

45. Fuller, *Complete Works: Diary*, 1:24.

46. Haykin, "A Great Thirst for Reading," 6.

47. Haykin, "A Great Thirst for Reading," 6–7.

48. Fuller, *Complete Works: Diary*, 1:24.

49. Fuller, *Works*, 3:788.

50. Fuller, *Works*, 3:788. Fuller found reading Scripture prior to prayer to also be a useful practice. "To read a part of the Scriptures, previous to prayer," Fuller stated, "tends to collect the thoughts, to spiritualize the affections, and to furnish us with sentiments wherewith to plead at a throne of grace." Fuller, *Works*, 3:788.

51. Brewster, "Model Baptist Pastor-Theologian," 63–64.

three days except some little tenderness in prayer. Last Tuesday I found some heart to pray for God's *Holy Spirit* that it might not be taken from us, and on some seasons since then have felt that desire renewed."[52] Note how Fuller's dependence and the pursuit of the Spirit's influence were not always natural or easy. The quotation from his diary comes two years into what Peter Morden identifies as roughly ten years of ongoing and at times severe depression.[53] "Whilst his public ministry flourished," Morden states, "Fuller was often struggling in his Christian faith."[54] While Fuller maintained "that holy practice has a necessary dependence on sacred *principle*," a commitment to sacred principle does not make holy practice effortless.[55]

Late in 1791, Fuller recorded a year in review.[56] The entry captures a key landmark in Fuller's spiritual journey. After a long season of feeling distant from God, and in many respects avoiding prayer altogether, Fuller sought once again the presence of the Holy Spirit through prayer as the means for restoring the joy of salvation for himself and other believers. Fuller wrote:

> O to be spiritually alive amongst ourselves! One Monday evening meeting, I think in October, I told our friends of some things and prayed with them with more than usual affection—I was particularly encouraged by the promise of giving the Holy Spirit to them that ask. Surely if ever I wrestled with God in my life I did so then for *more grace*, for *forgiveness*, for the restoration of the joys of salvation; and that not only for myself, but for the generality of Christians amongst us, who I plainly perceived to be in a poor lukewarm state when compared with the primitive Christians.[57]

Fuller's wrestling with God—a euphemism for prayer or efforts that are intermingled with prayer—would continue even more in the years to follow with the founding of the BMS in 1792.

---

52. Fuller, *Complete Works: Diary*, 1:75–76. Emphasis original.

53. Morden, *Life and Thought of Andrew Fuller*, 105.

54. Morden, *Life and Thought of Andrew Fuller*, 105.

55. Fuller, *Complete Works: Diary*, 1:1.

56. By this time, Fuller departed from the practice of making daily or even weekly entries in his diary. For more on Fuller's diary keeping and extant copies of his diaries, see Fuller, *Complete Works: Diary*, 1:xiii.

57. Fuller, *Complete Works: Diary*, 1:181–82. Emphasis original. Interestingly, Fuller began expounding the Psalms this same year. The reinvigoration of his prayer life and the beginning of his exposition of the Psalms may be more than a serendipitous connection.

Implications for Doctrine

Wrestling with God: Prayer, the Spirit, and Use of Means

In 1792, William Carey published his *An Enquiry into the Obligations of Christians to Use Means for the Conversion of the Heathens*. With respect to the work of the Spirit and prayer, Carey stated, "The most glorious works of grace that have ever took place, have been in answer to prayer: and it is in this way, we have the greatest reason to suppose, that the glorious out-pouring of the Spirit, which we expect at last, will be bestowed."[58] Prayer precipitates, in Carey's view, the outpouring of the Spirit. Whereas some may have seen this as reason to pray only, Carey argued that "we must not be contented . . . with praying, without *exerting ourselves in the use of means* for obtaining of those things we pray for."[59] Fuller's sermon the year before pervades Carey's statement. At a meeting of ministers at Clipstone, April 27, 1792, Fuller stated:

> The truth is, if I am not mistaken, we wait for we know not what; we seem to think "the time is not come, the time for the Spirit to be poured down from on high." We *pray* for the conversion and salvation of the world, and yet *neglect the ordinary means* by which those ends have been used to be accomplished. It pleased God, heretofore, by the foolishness of preaching, to save them that believed; and there is reason to think it will still please God to work by that distinguished means.[60]

The ubiquity between Fuller and Carey just in comparing these two statements further supports the claim that "Fuller's theology was the mainspring behind the formation and early development of the Baptist Missionary Society . . . Fuller, though not so visible, was utterly vital to its genesis."[61]

The BMS was founded in 1792. Certainly, it is more than a coincidence that the origins of the society came nearly eight years after

58. Carey, *An Enquiry*, 79–80.

59. Carey, *An Enquiry*,81.

60. Fuller, *Works*, 1:147–48. Emphasis original. The sermon was titled *Instances, Evil, and Tendency of Delay in the Concerns of Religion*. Haykin observes that Fuller's contribution is often forgotten in light of Carey's fabled role as the first missionary of the BMS. Haykin and Weaver, *Dangerous Impact*, 7–10; Haykin, *One Heart and One Soul*, 11–14.

61. Haykin, "Review of *The Legacy of Jonathan Edwards*," 391. Bruce makes a similar observation, pointing to the decision by "the Evangelical Calvinists of the Northamptonshire Association" to pray for the advance of the gospel around the globe "well before William Carey's *Enquiry*." Bruce, "Grand Encouragement," 218.

the Northamptonshire Baptist Association committed to praying for the salvation of the world.[62] Even more certain is the timeliness of Fuller's sermon calling the association to do more than pray only. The time had long come for them to couple their prayers with the "ordinary means" for "the conversion and salvation of the world"; namely, "preaching."[63] Fuller proposed that efforts first be made by local ministers to preach to local villages within their vicinity. Carey took Fuller's charge to its logical conclusion. The time had come for members of their association to leave the continent and go preach to those the uttermost parts of the earth. The next year on October 2, 1792, a group of ministers gathered to form the BMS. According to Francis Cox, "The Rev. John Ryland, Reynold Hogg, William Carey, John Sutcliff, and Andrew Fuller, were constituted a committee; Reynold Hogg, being appointed Treasurer, and Andrew Fuller, Secretary."[64]

Prayer, for Fuller, was vital to one's wrestling with God. Prayer was the connection between the use of means and absolute dependence on God for success in the BMS's efforts. In 1801, Fuller stated in his sermon *Desire for the Success of God's Cause*, "As we must never confide in God to the neglect of means; so we must never engage in the use of means without a sense of our dependence on God."[65] No wonder in his circular letter "The Promise of the Spirit the Grand Encouragement in Promoting the Gospel" (1810), Fuller stated that prayer "is the natural consequence of the doctrine."[66] He continued:

> If all our help be in God, to him it becomes us to look for success. It was from a prayer-meeting, held in an upper room, that the first Christians descended, and commenced that notable attack on Satan's kingdom in which three thousand fell before them. When Peter was imprisoned, prayer was made without ceasing of the church unto God for him. When liberated by the

62. Elwyn, *Northamptonshire Association*, 17–18; Payne, "Prayer Call of 1784," 19. Payne, partly quoting F.A. Cox, stated the case most directly, "'The primary cause of the missionary excitement in Carey's mind, and its diffusion among the Northamptonshire ministers,' finds it in the Call to Prayer issued in 1784 by the Northampton Association, . . . and all those who have written understandingly of the origins of the modern missionary movement, have recognized the fundamental and determining influence of the concerted prayer which resulted from that call." Payne, "Prayer Call of 1784," 19.

63. Fuller, *Works*, 1:148. Fuller led the way in the initiative to do more than pray for the lost in his own vicinity.

64. Cox, *History of the English Baptist Missionary Society*, 18.

65. Fuller, *Works*, 1:416.

66. Fuller, *Works*, 3:362.

angel, in the dead of night, he found his brethren engaged in this exercise.[67]

Fuller saw from the examples in Scripture that prayer and dependence on the Holy Spirit persist in a corollary relationship. Prayer was the natural consequence of a right understanding of one's dependence on the work of the Spirit. Likewise, Fuller saw from his own experience of the principal events preceding and surrounding the founding of the BMS that prayer was the precipitating activity of their association's missionary efforts. As Fuller stated:

> It was in prayer that the late undertakings for spreading the gospel among the heathen originated. We have seen success enough attend them to encourage us to go forward; and probably if we had been more sensible of our dependence on the Holy Spirit, and more importunate in our prayers, we should have seen much more. The prayer of faith falls not to the ground. If "we have not," it is "because we ask not"; or, if "we ask and receive not," it is "because we ask amiss."[68]

Prayer was the vital activity that preceded the missionary activism of the BMS originating from within the Northamptonshire Baptist Association.[69]

67. Fuller, *Works*, 3:362.

68. Fuller, *Works*, 3:362.

69. There is room here for further exploration of the role that prayer played within evangelicalism as a catalyst for and sustainment of activism. Activism, here, is used with reference to David Bebbington's quadrilateral. Activism, as defined by Bebbington, is "the expression of the gospel in effort." Bebbington, *Evangelicalism in Modern Britain*, 2. In his section introducing activism, Bebbington stated that this characteristic within evangelicalism brought about "a transformation in the role of a minister of religion." Bebbington, *Evangelicalism in Modern Britain*, 10. Bebbington illustrates the rise of activism among evangelicals with a quotation from R.W. Dale. Dale states, "The Evangelical saint to-day . . . is not a man who spends his nights and days in fasting and prayer, but a man who is a zealous Sunday-school teacher, holds mission services among the poor, and attends innumerable committee meetings. 'Work' has taken its place side by side with prayer." Bebbington, *Evangelicalism in Modern Britain*, 10. Edwards in *A Treatise Concerning Religious Affections*, nearly 150 years prior stated something of the same spirit as Dale. Edwards stated, "And although self-examination be a duty of great use and importance, and by no means to be neglected; yet it is not the *principal* means, by which the saints do get satisfaction of their good estate. Assurance is not to be obtained so much by *self-examination*, as by *action*." Edwards, *Works of Jonathan Edwards*, 1:263. The extent to which Particular Baptists went through a transformation of pastoral theology has been explored by both Keith Grant and Nigel Wheeler. Wheeler, "Eminent Spirituality and Eminent Usefulness"; Grant, *Andrew Fuller*. Both researchers use Andrew Fuller as their principal subject of exploration and present differing perspectives. While Grant understood Fuller's pastoral theology to be an innovation of evangelical characteristics within his own denomination, Wheeler "does not argue

Among the most, if not the most, influential persons in affecting the concerted effort in prayer among the Northamptonshire Particular Baptists was John Sutcliff. "It was on *his* [Sutcliff's] motion," Fuller recalled in the funeral sermon for his dear friend, "that the Association at Nottingham, in the spring of 1784, agreed to set apart an hour on the evening of the first Monday in every month for social prayer for the success of the gospel, and to invite Christians of other denominations to unite with them in it."[70] The minutes from the 1784 association meeting evidence that the origins of the local and global missionary movement sought the revival of religion and conversion of the lost through the outpouring of God's Spirit. These ministers held that the outpouring of the Holy Spirit would come in response to the prayers of His people.[71] The minutes recorded a unanimous decision of the ministers who encouraged "meetings for prayer to bewail the low estate of religion, and earnestly implore a revival of our churches, . . . and for that end to wrestle with God for the effusion of his Holy Spirit, which alone can produce the blessed effect."[72] Evidencing the belief that the Spirit would come in response to their prayers, the minutes recorded that "the grand object in prayer is to be, that the Holy Spirit may be poured down on our ministers and churches that sinners may be converted, . . . the interest of religion revived, and the name of God glorified."[73] The minutes also demonstrate that the ministers gathered in 1784 already had a vision for the outpouring of God's Spirit beyond the boundaries of their Particular Baptist interests: "At the same time remember, we trust you will not confine your requests to your own societies, or to our own immediate connection, let . . . the spread of the gospel to the most distant parts of the habitable globe be the object of your most fervent requests."[74]

---

in favour of a radical redefinition of pastoral theology transformed by the so-called rise of evangelicalism." Wheeler, "Eminent Spirituality and Eminent Usefulness," 239. Rather, Wheeler understood Fuller's pastoral theology to be primarily in continuity with his late-seventeenth and early-eighteenth-century Particular Baptist predecessors. Thus evangelical innovations in pastoral theology among eighteenth-century Particular Baptists, according to Wheeler, should be understood more in terms of a "return to the evangelical priorities of their seventeenth century [*sic*] Baptist forerunners . . . rather than a radical pastoral theological revamping." Wheeler, "Eminent Spirituality and Eminent Usefulness," 240.

70. Fuller, *Works*, 1:350.

71. Ryland, *Circular Letter 1784*, 12.

72. Ryland, *Circular Letter 1784*, 12.

73. Ryland, *Circular Letter 1784*, 12.

74. Ryland, *Circular Letter 1784*, 12.

Sutcliff's Funeral Sermon, "Praying in the Holy Spirit"[75]

In addition to recognizing Sutcliff's principal role in the Prayer Call of 1784, Fuller's sermon explored the meaning of *"praying in the Holy Spirit."*[76] One of the primary points made by Fuller was "that religion which has its foundation in the faith of Christ will increase by *"praying in the Holy Spirit.* As there is no true practical religion without faith in Christ, so there is no true prayer but 'in the Holy Spirit.'"[77] One cannot pray without the aid of the Spirit. Far from giving license to neglect the duty of prayer, Fuller stated, "the Holy Spirit works that in us which God as the Governor of the world requires of us."[78] Fuller acknowledged that one is not "always sensible" of the Spirit's aid but this does not give license to neglect prayer. "But rather," Fuller stated, "as our Lord directs, pray *for* his Holy Spirit."[79] Of vital importance is to notice Fuller's next sentence. "It is *in* prayer," Fuller stated, "that the Spirit of God ordinarily assists us."[80] One's energy, effort, and time in prayer—specifically, prayer in the Spirit—had, in Fuller's estimation, a direct correlation to one's joy and effectiveness in the Christian life.

Fuller's encouragement to pray *for* and *in* the Spirit was illustrated by the desire of their departed pastor. Fuller stated, "One of the last sentences uttered by your deceased pastor, when drawing near his end, was, 'I wish I had prayed more.'"[81] Responding to Sutcliff's statement, Fuller in a vulnerable moment of reflection shared with the congregation his own desire to have

75. For another treatment of this same sermon see Haykin, *One Heart and One Soul*, 341–44.

76. Fuller, *Works*, 1:343. Emphasis original. He preached from Jude 20–21, a text that explicitly called for "praying in the Holy Spirit."

77. Fuller, *Works*, 1:343. Emphasis original. Haykin rightly observes, "This had long been affirmed by Calvinistic Baptist spirituality." Haykin, *One Heart and One Soul*, 341. Haykin offers John Bunyan as an example of Calvinistic Baptist spirituality and praying in the Spirit. For a lengthier treatment of prayer in Baptist spirituality, see Ellis, "From the Heart," 103–24. Ellis quotes Bunyan predominantly. For another example of a Calvinistic Baptist interpreting praying in the Spirit as the only true means of prayer, see Gill, *Exposition of the New Testament*, 3:679. Gill states, "Particularly by *praying in the Holy Ghost*; which is a special means of increase and establishment in the doctrine of faith: the Holy Ghost is the author and editor of prayer, and an assister in it; without him saints cannot call God their father, nor pray with faith and fervency, or with freedom and liberty." Gill, *Exposition of the New Testament*, 3:679. See also his discussion on "praying in the Holy Ghost" in his section treating "Of Public Prayer," in Gill, *Body of Divinity*, 2:690.

78. Fuller, *Works*, 1:343.

79. Fuller, *Works*, 1:343. Emphasis original.

80. Fuller, *Works*, 1:343. Emphasis original.

81. Fuller, *Works*, 1:344.

prayed more. Fuller expressed a desire for more prayer in four areas. First, Fuller wished that he "*had prayed more . . . for the success of the Gospel.*"[82] For, Fuller stated, if "I had prayed more, I might have seen more."[83] Second, Fuller wished that he "had prayed more . . . *for the salvation of those about me.*"[84] For, Fuller stated, "have I not by this guilty negligence been accessory to the destruction of some that are dear to me?"[85] Third, Fuller wished that he "had prayed more . . . *for my own soul.*"[86] For, Fuller stated, "I might then have enjoyed much more communion with God."[87] Fourth, Fuller wished that he "had prayed more . . . *in all my undertakings.*"[88] For, Fuller stated, "I might then have had my steps more directed by God, and attended with fewer deviations from his will."[89] The brief section from Fuller's sermon eulogizing the pious regret of Sutcliff, to include his own regret, is perhaps the most powerful expression in all of his works with respect to Fuller's high regard for prayer.[90]

Prayer was, in Fuller's thinking, the ordinary and vital means "to keep alive this sacred flame," that is, the love of God, "amidst the temptations of this world."[91] To remain in prayer is to remain in communion with God. As Fuller stated, "There is no intercourse with God without prayer. It is thus that we walk with God, and have our conversation in heaven."[92] Thus Fuller could conclude that keeping one's love for God "by means of building on our most holy faith, and praying in the Holy Spirit," is "in a manner the sum of the Christian life."[93]

82. Fuller, *Works*, 1:344. Emphasis original.
83. Fuller, *Works*, 1:344.
84. Fuller, *Works*, 1:344. Emphasis original.
85. Fuller, *Works*, 1:344.
86. Fuller, *Works*, 1:344. Emphasis original.
87. Fuller, *Works*, 1:344.
88. Fuller, *Works*, 1:344. Emphasis original.
89. Fuller, *Works*, 1:344.
90. The influence of Fuller's sermon on other ministers' prioritization of prayer, even among those outside of the Baptist denomination, may be evidenced by Thomas Binney's inclusion of the section on praying in the Spirit within his preface to *The Closet and the Church*. Binney, *Closet and the Church*, viii–xi. For more on Binney, see Hooper, *Story of English Congregationalism*, 115.
91. Fuller, *Works*, 1:344.
92. Fuller, *Works*, 1:344.
93. Fuller, *Works*, 1:344.

Conclusion

Doctrine's Influence on Prayer

The doctrine of the work of the Spirit ought to, perhaps more than any other doctrine, excite one to prayer. Nowhere is this seen more clearly than in the close of Fuller's circular letter, "Causes of Declension in Religion, and Means of Revival" (1785). These were Fuller's final words before expressing a prayer for his readers:

> Without his blessing all means are without efficacy, and every effort for revival will be in vain. Constantly and earnestly, therefore, let us approach his throne. Take all occasions especially for *closet prayer;* here, if any where [sic], we shall get fresh strength, and maintain a life of communion with God. Our Lord Jesus used [sic] frequently to retire into a mountain alone for prayer: he, therefore, that is a *follower* of Christ, must follow him in this important duty.[94]

Since the renewal of the sinner comes only through the Spirit, "constantly and earnestly . . . let us approach his throne." Since efficacy in all efforts and means comes only through the Spirit's presence and influence, "constantly and earnestly . . . let us approach his throne."

Prayer's Influence on Doctrine

While one may believe in the necessity of the work of the Spirit for the renewal and sanctification of sinners, the Spirit's renewing and sanctifying work ordinarily is not experienced apart from prayer. As seen especially in Fuller's sermon *Desire for the Success of God's Cause*, prayer is the vital connection between the use of means and utter dependence on the Spirit for any effect to come from human efforts. In his funeral sermon for Sutcliff, Fuller's understanding of the essential relationship between prayer and the work of the Spirit was described clearly. Fuller believed wholly that if he had prayed more for the Spirit's influences, then he would have seen greater effects for the cause of the gospel within his own soul, associations, and the nations. To build on Carey's famous phrase—"Let us *expect* great things. Let us *attempt* great things"—prayer is the place where great expectations are borne and kept alive as we attempt great things for God in the power of the Spirit.[95]

94. Fuller, *Works*, 3:324.

95. The phrase comes from the two divisions in Carey's association sermon. Haykin,

5

Humanity and Prayer

The very exercise of prayer carries in it an implication that *our help must come from above;* a truth which, in all cases, it is highly necessary for us to know, and with which, in this case especially, we cannot be too deeply impressed.[1]

—ANDREW FULLER, *THE BACKSLIDER*

Explanation of the Doctrine

Two aspects of Fuller's doctrine of humanity surface as bearing the most apparent reciprocity with his theology of prayer, namely, total depravity and human accountability. According to Thomas Nettles, "Fuller places the doctrine of total depravity in the position of a *sine qua non* in theology."[2] The subject of human accountability also held a prominent place in Fuller's theological system. "Fuller," as stated by Thomas Ascol, "is unembarrassed to align his own views of salvation by grace with those of Reformed theologians who preceded him."[3] As such, Fuller worked hard to maintain "two theological tenets which are endemic to Reformed thought: the sovereignty

---

One Heart and One Soul, 217.

1. Fuller, *Works*, 3:655.
2. Nettles, "Contributions of Andrew Fuller," 58.
3. Ascol, "Doctrine of Grace," 261.

of God and the responsibility of man."[4] Fuller, like the evangelically-minded seventeenth-century Particular Baptists before him, affirmed both total depravity and the accountability of man.[5] In doing so, maintaining prayer to be the duty of all became a central point of concern for a number of Particular Baptists in the seventeenth and eighteenth century, to include Andrew Fuller.

"The Total Depravity of Human Nature"[6]

Total depravity was a centerpiece of Fuller's *Dialogues between Crispus and Gaius* in the *Evangelical Magazine* from 1793–1795.[7] The emphasis on total depravity in a number of Fuller's works, much like his emphasis on the deity of Christ, came in response to various heterodoxies which originated with the undermining of the doctrine of human depravity.[8] In "Dialogue 8, Human Depravity," Fuller stated, "I never knew a person verge toward Arminian, the Arian, the Socinian, or the Antinomian schemes, without first entertaining diminutive notions of human depravity, or blameworthiness."[9] A compromised view of human depravity, in Fuller's thought, led to a compromised view of the diety of Christ. A robust doctrine of humanity is tantamount to central doctrines of the Christian faith. Fuller stated, "Perhaps there is no one truth in the Scriptures of a more fundamental nature with respect to the gospel way of salvation" than the doctrine of total depravity.[10] To compromise the doctrine of human depravity, for Fuller, was to compromise a central aspect of the gospel—that is, salvation wholly of grace.[11]

4. Ascol, "Doctrine of Grace," 256.

5. See below, "A Proto-'Modern Question': Is it the Duty of All Men to Pray?" under the section "Implications for Prayer."

6. The subheading title comes from "Dialogue 9, The Total Depravity of Human Nature." Fuller, *Works*, 2:664.

7. Ryland, *Work of Faith*, 230. In Fuller's *Works*, the title is *Dialogues and Letters*. *Dialogues and Letters* is composed of nine dialogues and five letters. Two dialogues and three letters explicitly addressed the doctrine of depravity. Two additional letters discussed the consequences of total depravity. All the dialogues and letters can be found in Fuller, *Works*, 2:647–80.

8. Fuller, *Works*, 2:662.

9. Fuller, *Works*, 2:662. The author first observes the quotation by Nettles: "According to Fuller, all divergences from orthodox Protestantism have as their root some relinquishment of this doctrine." Nettles, "The Contributions of Andrew Fuller," 58.

10. Fuller, *Works*, 2:662.

11. Fuller stated, "This was manifestly the doctrine generally embraced at the Reformation, and which has been maintained by the advocates for salvation by sovereign grace in every age." Fuller, *Works*, 2:662.

Fuller argued the doctrine of total depravity "may be drawn from the four following sources; Scripture testimony, history, observation, and experience."[12] He described the nature of human depravity as that which is diametric to the "Divine law."[13] Since "the sum of the Divine law is love; the essence of depravity then must consist in the want of love to God and our neighbor; or in setting up some other object, or objects, to the exclusion of them."[14] "All the objects set up in competition with God and our neighbor," according to Fuller, "may be reduced to one, and that is *self*."[15] If then the nature of human depravity is the love of self usurping the love of God, the doctrine of total depravity maintains that "the human heart is by nature totally destitute of love to God, or love to man as the creature of God, and consequently is destitute of all true virtue."[16] For Fuller, the pervasive effects of human depravity cannot be understated.

Whereas the doctrine ought not to be understated, Fuller acknowledged that some following in the tradition of the "English Reformers" seem to have "carried things rather to an extreme."[17] According to Fuller, some argued that "if all the actions of unregenerate men be in their own nature sinful, surely there can be no ground for a ministerial address, no motive by which to exhort them to cease from evil and do good."[18] Fuller replied:

> If you mean to say that ministers, on this account, can entertain no well-founded hope of success from the pliability of men's hearts, I fully grant it. Our expectations must rest upon the power and promise of God, and these alone, or we shall be disappointed. But if you mean to suggest that therefore all addresses to unregenerate sinners, exhorting them to do good, are unreasonable, this is more than can be admitted. If a *total* depravity would take away all ground for a rational address, a *partial* one would take it away in part; and then, in proportion as we see men disinclined to goodness, we are to cease warning and expostulating with them! But this is self-evident absurdity. The truth is, while men are rational beings they are accountable for all they do, whatever be the inclination of their hearts; and

12. Fuller, *Works*, 2:662–63.

13. Fuller, *Works*, 2:662.

14. Fuller, *Works*, 2:662.

15. "Hence," Fuller maintained, "the first and grand lesson in the Christian school is—to *deny ourselves*." Fuller, *Works*, 2:662. Emphasis original.

16. Fuller, *Works*, 2:662.

17. Fuller, *Works*, 2:665.

18. Fuller, *Works*, 2:667.

so long as they are not consigned to hopeless perdition, they are the subjects of a gospel address.[19]

The totality of human depravity does not, in Fuller's understanding, eliminate rationality. As such, human accountability is not mitigated on account of depravity.[20]

Human Accountability

Fuller's appropriation of Edwards's theology was vital for his understanding of human accountability.[21] In particular, Edwards's distinction between

19. Fuller, *Works*, 2:672. In his reappraisal of *The Gospel Worthy of All Acceptation*, Gerald Priest claimed that Fuller and his theological mentor, Jonathan Edwards, tacitly verged on a partial depravity through their distinction of natural and moral ability. Regarding Fuller, Priest stated, "It is the doctrine of imputation that is so crucial to understanding man's culpability and his inability to respond to the gospel. And Fuller fails to adequately treat this. He instead falls back on moral inability and defines total depravity only in those terms, which leaves him open to the criticism of teaching partial depravity." Priest, "Andrew Fuller's Response to the 'Modern Question,'" 66–67. If Priest is referring only to Fuller's treatment of total depravity in *The Gospel Worthy*, then perhaps there is warrant for his concern. However, as the present section has demonstrated, Fuller defined total depravity in terms of opposition to God's law by "nature" and inability. While opposition to God's law, the absence of love by nature, does not address explicitly the doctrine of imputation or original sin, Fuller's language does implicitly adopt the consequence of the imputation of Adam's sin, namely, a fallen nature. With regard to the imputation of Adam's sin, Ascol states, "During the last fifteen years of his life, Fuller modifies his opinion considerably." Ascol, "Doctrine of Grace," 166. For a summary of the doctrine of imputation imbibed by Gill and early Fuller and the transformation Fuller underwent, see Ascol, "Doctrine of Grace," 164–170.

20. Much of the discussion surrounding human accountability often jumps to consider Fuller's appropriation of Jonathan Edwards's distinction between natural and moral ability. However, the focus on Fuller's adoption of Edwards's distinction perhaps overshadows Fuller's doctrine of total depravity in dichotomy with "that which constitutes the essence of genuine morality, namely, the love of God and man." Fuller, *Works*, 2:677. Central to Fuller's understanding of depravity, the absence of love for God or neighbor, was the belief that "all our actions are, in some mode or other, *the expressions of love*, or *they are not*." Fuller, *Works*, 2:677. Emphasis original. Fuller's understanding of sin being "the absence of benevolence" is a theme that surfaces also in *The Gospel Worthy of All Acceptation*. Priest, "Fuller's Response to the 'Modern Question,'" 64. There is room here for further study regarding human obligation being seated first in the moral character of God, rightly deserving and commanding the affections of humanity through the revelation of "the law and the gospel." See Fuller's section, "On the Divine, the Social, and the Personal Virtues," especially "Love to God," in his *Reply to Mr. Kentish's Sermon, &c.* in Fuller, *Works*, 2:270–72.

21. For the most thorough scholarly treatment of Edwards's influence on Fuller, see Chun, *Edwards in the Theology of Fuller*. Nathan Finn rightly described the work as a "signal contribution to the literature" of Fuller Studies. Finn, "Review of *The Legacy of*

natural and moral inability was vital for Fuller. According to Nettles, "This distinction is one of the clear guiding principles of Fuller's *Confession of Faith* presented to the church in Kettering upon his call there in 1783."[22] Fuller stated:

> I believe it is the duty of every minister of Christ plainly and faithfully to preach the gospel to all who will hear it; and as I believe the inability of men to spiritual things to be wholly of the *moral*, and therefore of the *criminal* kind—and that it is their duty to love the Lord Jesus Christ and trust in him for salvation though they do not; I therefore believe free and solemn addresses, invitations, calls and warnings to them, to be not only *consistent*, but directly *adapted*, as means in the hand of the Spirit of God, to bring them to Christ.[23]

For Fuller, the moral inability to keep the divine law did not negate one's obligation to keep the law. In *The Gospel Worthy of All Acceptation* (1801) Fuller stated, "No man is reproved for not doing that which is naturally impossible; but sinners are reproved for not believing, and given to understand that it is solely owing to their criminal ignorance, pride, dishonesty of heart, and aversion from God."[24] All humans, therefore, regardless of their being elect or non-elect, are reproved for they possess a natural ability to respond to the law of God. As Fuller stated in his essay, "Moral Inability," "Men have the same natural powers to love Christ as to hate him, to believe as to disbelieve; and this it is which constitutes their accountableness."[25] Thus, Fuller can seat the universal obligation of faith, for both the elect and non-elect, on the proclamation of the Divine law.

Implications for Prayer

A Proto-"Modern Question": Is It the Duty of All Men to Pray?

"The Modern Question" was a "turning-point" in the theological landscape of the eighteenth-century Particular Baptists.[26] The question was concerned

---

Jonathan Edwards, 536–38.

22. Nettles, "The Influence of Edwards on Fuller," 106.

23. Manly, "Fuller's Confession of Faith," 346–48. Emphasis original.

24. Fuller, *Works*, 2:335.

25. Fuller, *Works*, 3:768.

26. Nuttall, "Northamptonshire and 'The Modern Question.'" Hereafter, if the phrase, "The Modern Question," is in italics or quotation marks, then it is in reference

primarily with addressing whether or not it was the duty of unregenerate
man to repent and believe in Christ. As such, the Modern Question was
of great significance for Andrew Fuller and his theological development.[27]
Fuller's answer to the Modern Question was a definitive yes—effectively
turning the tide of Calvinism within the Particular Baptist denomination
out of the "trammels of Hyper-Calvinism," as phrased by Earnest Payne.[28]

In the introduction to the reprint of Fuller's collected works, Nettles
stated that "The Modern Question" was modern in its time because it was
"not until 1706 had the world even heard that such obligation could be
called into question."[29] And while the Modern Question with respect to
humanity's obligation to repent and believe in Christ may have its origin
in 1706, within the Baptist tradition a proto-Modern Question concerning
the duty of prayer preceded the question concerning the duty of faith. The
question originated in 1675, at least 30 years prior to what Nettles identified
as the advent of the Modern Question.[30]

---

to a particular work or quotation from a work. In all other occurrences, "The Modern
Question" will appear simply as the Modern Question without quotation marks to refer
generically to what Tom Nettles described as the following question: "Is unregenerate
man under spiritual obligation to repent of sin and believe in Christ upon hearing the
gospel?" Nettles, "Preface to the New Edition," v. This is essentially the same definition
given by Ivimey, *HEB*, 3:260.

27. Fuller, *Works*, 1:15. Although the Modern Question, as it came to be known,
did not originate with Abraham Taylor, Fuller's introduction to the Modern Question
seems to have been from Taylor's tract, *The Modern Question*. Other men preceding Taylor wrote concerning the same question, some answering in the affirmative
and some in the negative as to the duty of the unregenerate to believe. See Nuttall,
"Northamptonshire and 'The Modern Question.'"

28. Payne quoted in Nuttall, "Northamptonshire and 'The Modern Question,'" 101.

29. Nettles, "Preface to the New Edition," vi. Nettles traced the origin of the question
to Joseph Hussey (1660–1726), a Congregationalist minister of Cambridge. Nettles,
"Preface to the New Edition," vi. From Hussey, Ivimey traced the traditionally negative
answer of high Calvinists—that is, it is not the duty of the unregenerate to repent and
believe in Christ—among Particular Baptists to the likes of John Skepp, John Gill, and
John Brine. Ivimey, *HEB*, 3:259–60.

30. Ivimey, *HEB*, 3:260. In vol. 3, Ivimey explicitly connected the affirmative answer
to "The Modern Question" with a letter in 1675 addressing question of whether it be
the duty of all men to pray. The researcher discovered Ivimey's explicit connection between The Modern Question and the letter in question after recognizing the theological similarities between the two disputes in vol. 1. John Brine explicitly connected the
question of the duty to pray with the Modern Question in a letter to a friend refuting a
publication titled *The Modern Question*. In the letter, Brine stated, "A great number of
ill Consequences are drawn from that Opinion, in Answer to which, it is sufficient to
observe, that Sinners ought to pray, to read the Word of God, to hear it preached and
consider the dreadful Effects of Sin. That Ministers ought to set before them the Danger
of their State by Nature, and the Necessity of an Interest in Christ, and the Necessity

In 1675, a group of Particular Baptist ministers in London signed a letter responding to a question originating from Andrew Gifford. He inquired whether or not it was the duty of all men to pray. Particularly, the question concerned itself with whether this be the duty of the unregenerate. The letter was addressed to Joseph Morton. Seemingly at the request of Gifford, Morton shared the letter with a number of Baptist ministers gathered in London who answered with an emphatic yes. The group of Baptist ministers argued for the duty of all men to pray regardless of whether they are regenerate. "This letter," according to Ivimey, "demands the attention of all persons, and especially of all ministers."[31]

The Baptist ministers, responding affirmatively to the question of whether it was the duty of all men to pray, felt that to answer the question negatively was to undermine central principles of the gospel. They wrote:

> Forasmuch as neither the want of the Spirit's immediate motions to, or its assistance in the duty, doth not take off the obligation to the duty. If it would, then also from every other duty; and consequently all religion be cashiered. If the obligations to this and other duties were suspended merely for want of such motions and assistance, then unconverted persons are so far from sinning in the omission of such duties, that it is their duty to omit them . . . And so every man is sinless, whatever sin be committed, or whatever duty be neglected, if the Spirit do not immediately hinder us from the one and move us to the other.[32]

Human inability did not diminish in their minds the obligation for of all humanity to pray.[33] If human inability renders man unobligated, then a

---

of Faith in him." Brine, *Refutation of Arminian Principles*, 44. Capitalization original.

31. Ivimey, *HEB*, 3:332. The entire response to Gifford's letter is included in vol. 1 of Ivimey's *History of the English Baptists*. See Ivimey, *HEB*, 1:416–20.

32. Ivimey, *HEB*, 1:418.

33. Notice the obvious address of this question in the *Second London Confession*. In the article concerning worship, SLC 22.3 recorded, "*Prayer* with thanksgiving, being one special part of natural worship *is by God required of all men*. But that it may be accepted, it is to be made in the Name of the Son by the help of the Spirit, according to his Will; with understanding, reverence, humility, fervency, faith, love, and perseverance; and when with others, in a known tongue." Emphasis mine. The confession would have been adopted just two years after the letter responding to Gifford's question. The importance of the question—whether it be the duty of all men to pray—in the Baptist milieu is evidenced by Robert Hall Sr. addressing the question in his influential work, *Help to Zion's Travellers*. Hall, *Help to Zion's Travellers*, 117. According to Hall, "It is shocking to think that any poor sinner should be taught to consider himself exempted from an acknowledgment to God for the mercies he enjoys, and likewise from an application to him for present or future favors. Besides, it is absurd to assert, that a person ought not to pray until he feels himself converted, for it is much the same as saying a man ought

central tenant of the gospel is undermined—that is, every human stands a sinner in need of forgiveness.

The Prayer of the Wicked

Over one hundred years later, in an essay titled *The Prayer of the Wicked*, Fuller offered a similar answer to the question of whether it be the duty of "a wicked man to pray."[34] Fuller, representing a possible retrieval of principles from his seventeenth-century Baptist forerunners, stated:

> If in a state of unregeneracy he were under no obligation to do any thing [sic] pleasing to God, and were so far rendered incapable of doing any thing [sic] to displease him, so far he must be sinless, and therefore stand in no need of a Saviour. Where there is no obligation, there can be no offence; and where there is no offence, there needs no forgiveness.[35]

The inability of humanity to do anything pleasing to God apart from the influences of the Spirit does not negate human obligation. If human obligation were negated, then human sin too would be negated. Where there is no duty there is no sin. Thus, Fuller believed that to concede that prayer is not the duty of all men meant conceding "there needs no forgiveness."

---

not to ask for guidance until he knows he is right, nor seek for a cure till he feels himself healed." Hall, *Help to Zion's Travellers*, 119. Haykin describes both Hall's *Help to Zion's Travellers* and Fuller's *Gospel Worthy of All Acceptation* as pivotal in bringing revival within the Baptist interests in England. Haykin acknowledges that "it was especially the latter work that brought home to Baptist pastors the need of presenting to all men the obligation of repentance and faith in Christ, an emphasis which had often been lacking in eighteenth-century Baptist preaching up until that point." Haykin, "The Oracles of God," n.p. Whereas Hall's work was not as influential of a work as Fuller's, the presence of the question in *Help to Zion's Travellers*, nonetheless, establishes that the concern for whether the unconverted ought to pray was more than a passing question in theological reflection among Particular Baptists in the seventeenth and eighteenth centuries. There is room here for further work considering whether one's answer to the question regarding man's duty to pray precipitates one's answer to the question regarding man's duty to repent and believe in Christ. Although there may be some who answer one in the affirmative and the other negative, my hypothesis is that most Particular Baptists answered both questions in the affirmative or both in the negative, rather than a split between the two.

34. Fuller, *Works*, 3:803.
35. Fuller, *Works*, 3:773.

Example of Fuller's Practice of Prayer

Themes of human depravity and prayer were interwoven in Fuller's diary, especially in 1780. On a number of occasions, Fuller's entries reflected prayers in response to his own depravity. For example, Fuller recorded on July 1, 1780,

> My soul has been dejected today, in thinking on the plague of the human heart; but I have been sweetly refreshed tonight, by a hymn of Dr. Watts, (85th, Second Book,) . . . This was my dear Brother Driver's funeral hymn. I had a sweet time in prayer, tonight. Through the glass of my depravity, I see, O I see the preciousness of that blood which flowed on Calvary! O that the ideas I have had tonight were written indelibly on my heart! But, alas! One hour of sin will, I fear, efface them all.[36]

The sweetness of Fuller's time in prayer seems to be, in some part, connected to his own understanding of "the preciousness of that blood which flowed on Calvary," as he said, "through the glass of my own depravity." Regretfully, the sweetness of prayer was eclipsed by the fearful effects of his own sin, perhaps even committed that day. Near the end of the same month, Fuller wrote, "Am I not a fool, and slow of heart to believe? Not withstanding all the Scripture says of my impotency, all the experience I have had of it, and all my settled and avowed principles, how hard is it for me to believe that I am *nothing*!"[37] At times Fuller was consumed with an awareness of his own depravity. Nevertheless, from the latter entry, it becomes apparent that he fluctuated with regard to acknowledging his own depravity. Fuller knew that to lose a sense of his own depravity was to open oneself up to increased opportunity for sin. As one entry recorded, also in July of 1780, "O wretched man that I am! . . . Oh may the remembrance of *this* make thee shrink back from sinning! Surely the renewal of a fresh conflict with old corruptions is not the trial I feared? Lead me not into temptation, but deliver me from evil, O Lord!"[38]

On other occasions, Fuller's diary entries considered the depravity of all humanity with respect to the implications this had on his ministry. On August 30, 1780, after reading an account of John Eliot, Fuller began

---

36. Fuller, *Complete Works: Diary*, 1:6. Five years later he reflected in his time in prayer was affected by reflecting on the depravity of human nature: July 24, 1785 "A pretty good forenoon on the above subject. Much solemn feeling in prayer on the ruined state of man by nature." Fuller, *Complete Works: Diary*, 1:143.

37. Fuller, *Complete Works: Diary*, 1:11. Emphasis original.

38. Fuller, *Complete Works: Diary*, 1:8. Emphasis original.

to ponder over the constraints placed on appeals to sinners to repent and believe.[39] He wrote:

> I found also suspicion, that we shackle ourselves too much in our addresses to sinners; that we have bewildered and lost ourselves, by taking the decrees of God as rules of action. Surely Peter and Paul never felt such scruples in their addresses, as we do. They addressed their hearers as *men*—fallen men; as we should warn and admonish persons who were blind, and on the brink of some dreadful precipice. Their work seemed plain before them. Oh that mine might be so before me![40]

September 3, 1780, four days later and on a Lord's Day, Fuller wrote, "Found a heart to pray for the conversion of the congregation."[41] The entry, perhaps, marks a watershed moment for Fuller's practice of prayer. His practice was being shaped by a burgeoning theological principle; namely, that it be the duty of all men to believe. From where did Fuller's heart for prayer arise? Perhaps concurrent with Fuller's shift in theological principle came a shift in holy practice.

Note the continuity of positing an observable shift in practice based on a shift in principle. Fuller acknowledged the reciprocal relationship of principle and practice earlier this same year, January 1780, in his covenant of renewal: "Holy practice has a necessary dependence on sacred *principle*."[42] This may be the clearest example of Fuller's practice of prayer developing on the heels of a transformation in Fuller's theological principle regarding gospel appeals to sinners. Within four years, Fuller penned his first publication, a published sermon, *The Nature and Importance of Walking by Faith . . . To Which are Added Persuasives to a General Union in Extraordinary Prayer for the Revival and Extent of Real Religion*.[43] Fuller's appeal for prayers to be offered for revival locally and globally was perhaps the most far-reaching appeal for prayer for the lost that the Baptist denomination had seen yet. Fuller's heart for praying for the lost swelled well beyond the banks of his own stream. The appeal for united prayer for the lost was given not just to "the *Leicestershire* and *Northamptonshire* association," but also, "to any who love and long for the coming of Christ's blessed kingdom."[44]

---

39. Fuller, *Complete Works: Diary*, 1:13.

40. Fuller, *Complete Works: Diary*, 1:13. Emphasis original.

41. Fuller, *Complete Works: Diary*, 1:13.

42. Fuller, *Works*, 1:20.

43. Morden, *Life and Thought of Andrew Fuller*, 77.

44. Fuller, *Persuasives*, 41. Fuller's appeal reflects the same "evangelical catholicity" imbibed in the prayer call originating from the association meeting about two months

Implications for Doctrine

The Backslider

Whereas Fuller maintained that "holy practice has a necessary dependence on sacred principle," he also stated that practices helped to sustain vital principles. In *The Backslider*, Fuller described the nature of some backsliding as "first appears *by a relinquishment of evangelical doctrine*."[45] Nonetheless, Fuller stated:

> If these departures from evangelical principles were closely examined, it would be found that they were preceded by a neglect of private prayer, watchfulness, self-diffidence, and walking humbly with God; and every one [sic] may perceive that they are followed with similar effects.[46]

Fuller acknowledged the reciprocal relationship of practice and principle. Thus a decline in holy practice precedes and proceeds from a decline in sacred principle. To illustrate his point, Fuller stated:

> It has been acknowledged, by some who have embraced the Socinian system, that since they entertained those views they had lost even the gift of prayer. Perhaps they might draw up and read *an address to the Deity*; but they could not pray. Where the principles of the gospel are abandoned, the spirit of prayer, and of all close walking with God, will go with it.[47]

In this specific example, Fuller highlighted the decline in prayer following an abandonment of central principles of the gospel. Even still, the neglect of prayer, as Fuller stated explicitly, precedes and proceeds a departure from sacred principle.

In the final section of *The Backslider*, considering "The Means of Recovery," Fuller proposed prayer as an indispensable means, perhaps the most vital of all means, to recovering from a backslidden state. Fuller offered eight means for recovery. Five of the eight means for recovery specifically address the practice of prayer. Although not stated, the other three,

---

prior. Haykin, *One Heart and One Soul*, 163–64.

45. Fuller, *Works*, 3:637. The full or alternate title of *The Backslider* is *The Backslider: Or an Inquiry into the Nature, Symptoms, and Effects of Religious Declension, with the Means of Recovery* in Fuller, *Works*, 3:635–59. The alternate or longer title is a summary of the four divisions within the work treating the nature, symptoms, effects of, and means for recovery from backsliding.

46. Fuller, *Works*, 3:637.

47. Fuller, *Works*, 3:637.

no doubt, include prayer since Fuller stated, "Prayer is a kind of religious exercise which is necessary to accompany all others."[48]

As the first means, Fuller encouraged reading Scripture included with prayer as frequently as possible. "Reading the word of God and prayer are duties which mutually assist each other: the one furnishes us with confessions, pleas, and arguments; while the other promotes solemnity and spirituality of mind, which," according to Fuller, "goes further towards understanding the Scriptures than a library of expositions."[49] Prayer is the essential means for deriving the full benefit of reading, understanding, and applying God's word. Here, prayer is the explicit dependence on the Spirit, but also, the implicit recognition of human inability. Hence, one's own reasoning, and even "a library of expositions," cannot replace the work of the Spirit nor diminish the human inability to recover oneself. "The very exercise of prayer," Fuller stated, "carries in it an implication that *our help must come from above*; a truth which, in all cases, it is highly necessary for us to know, and with it which, in this case especially, we cannot be too deeply impressed."[50] The recovery from a backslidden state, therefore, comes in tandem with a recovery of a proper view of one's depravity and inability. Thus, prayer is the active acknowledgment of one's true condition and need for God. Fuller stated:

> Solemn approaches to God are adapted to impress the mind with a sense of sin, and to inspire us with self abhorrence on account of it. It was by a view of the holiness of God that Isaiah felt himself to be "a man of unclean lips"; and by conversing with him that Job was brought to "abhor himself, and repent in dust and ashes."[51]

The clear implication is that to neglect prayer is to neglect the God-ordained means for sustaining a proper view of human depravity and inability. For Fuller, the God-ordained means for inviting the influences of the Spirit was the same means for exciting the human heart to a proper view of oneself before God. Thus, Fuller stated, "The more we are emptied of self-sufficiency, the more sensibly shall we feel our dependence, and the more importunately implore that the Lord would save us as it were from ourselves, and restore us '*for his name's sake*.'"[52]

---

48. Fuller, *Works*, 3:655.
49. Fuller, *Works*, 3:654.
50. Fuller, *Works*, 3:655.
51. Fuller, *Works*, 3:655.
52. Fuller, *Works*, 3:655. Emphasis original.

As the fifth means for recovery, Fuller proposed setting aside *"special times to humble yourself before God by fasting and prayer."*[53] "A day devoted to God in humiliation, fasting, and prayer, occasionally occupied with reading suitable parts of the Holy Scriptures," according to Fuller, "may, by the blessing of the Holy Spirit, contribute more to the subduing of sin, and the recovery of a right mind, than years spent in a sort of half-hearted exercises."[54] If done with the proper motivation and blessed by the Spirit, extraordinary efforts in prayer may bring about an extraordinary "subduing of sin, and the recovery of a right mind."

Fuller proposed as the sixth means of recovery, *"To prayer it is necessary to add watchfulness."*[55] When on the road to recovery, Fuller stated that one may grow complacent and become vulnerable "on account of having so lately been engaged in earnest devotion."[56] Thus, when temptation comes, "he has been surprised and overcome."[57] Fuller stated:

> The consequence, as might be expected, has been a future neglect of prayer, under the idea that it must have been mere hypocrisy before, and would now be adding sin to sin. Instead of depending upon spiritual frames for preservation, and especially when they are over, perhaps we ought to expect that our comforts should be succeeded by conflicts.[58]

Fuller knew from Scripture and experience that seasons of earnest seeking after God are often followed by attacks.

As the seventh means for recovery, Fuller stated, *"In your approaches to the Saviour, let it be under the character in which you first applied to him for mercy, that of a sinner."*[59] "If you attempt to approach the throne of grace as a good man who has backslidden from God," Fuller stated, "you may find it impossible to support that character." Instead, Fuller stated, "your approach, therefore, must not be as one that 'is washed, and needeth not save to wash his feet'; but as one who is defiled throughout, *whose hands and head*, and every part, need to be cleansed."[60] Once again, Fuller connected a proper

---

53. Fuller, *Works*, 3:658. Emphasis original.

54. Fuller, *Works*, 3:658. Once again the distinction between natural and moral inability can be seen here. The recovery is of right state of mind, a spiritual state of mind, not of rational capacity.

55. Fuller, *Works*, 3:658. Emphasis original.

56. Fuller, *Works*, 3:658.

57. Fuller, *Works*, 3:658.

58. Fuller, *Works*, 3:658–59.

59. Fuller, *Works*, 3:659. Emphasis original.

60. Fuller, *Works*, 3:659.

view of human depravity with prayer. "One thing is certain," Fuller stated, "you are a *sinner*, a poor, miserable, and perishing sinner: the door of mercy is wide open; and you are welcome to enter in. Let your past character then have been what it may, and let your conversion ever be so doubtful, if you can *from this time* relinquish all for Christ, eternal life is before you."[61]

As the eighth means for recovery, Fuller stated, "*In all your supplications, be contented with nothing short of a complete recovery.*"[62] Fuller did not want his readers to be contented with mere "ascendency over . . . evil propensities." Fuller stated:

> Sin is not to be opposed so much directly as indirectly; not by mere resistance, but by opposing other principles to it, which shall overcome it. It is not by contending with the fire, especially with combustible materials about us, that we shall be able to quench it; but by dealing plentifully with the opposite element. The pleasures of sense will not be effectually subdued by foregoing all enjoyment; but by imbibing other pleasures, the relish of which shall deaden the heart to what is opposite. It was thus that the apostle became "dead to the world by the cross of Christ." Do not, therefore, reckon thyself restored till thou hast recovered communion with God.[63]

Regular communion with God, for Fuller, meant regular prayer. Prayer is not just a primary means for gaining victory over sin. Prayer is also a primary means for regular communion with God.[64]

"The Harmony of Scripture Precepts, Prayers, and Promises"

On August 26, 1783, Fuller wrote a paper at the request of his friend, John Ryland Jr. The paper was titled, "The Harmony of Scripture Precepts, Prayers, and Promises."[65] Fuller developed the paper as a "key" for explaining a corresponding publication—which Ryland at the time could

61. Fuller, *Works*, 3:659. Emphasis original.

62. Fuller, *Works*, 3:659.

63. Fuller, *Works*, 3:659.

64. Recall Fuller's confession in Sutcliff's funeral sermon. He stated, "I wish I had prayed more than I have *for my own soul*: I might then have enjoyed much more communion with God." Fuller, *Works*, 1:344.

65. Fuller, "Harmony of Scripture," 213. Ryland published Fuller's paper in his memoirs of Fuller, *The Work of Faith*. See Ryland, *Work of Faith*, 218–21.

not locate—which arranged numerous Scriptures according to "*commands, petitions*, and *promises*."[66]

Fuller's paper confronted the tendency of those answering the Modern Question to respond to the commands of Scripture with one of two false extremes. "*One* is," according to Fuller, "an idea of *self-sufficiency* to obey God's commands; and the *other* is, a spirit of *self-justification* in neglecting them."[67] For Fuller neither the Arminian spirit of self-sufficiency nor the Antinomian spirit of self-justification were warranted in Scripture.[68] For with the commands, Scripture supplies also prayers and promises. Fuller stated:

> [Infer] the views which saints in old time had of these things, will appear, by the following collection of Scriptures, wherein we may observe,—*First*, God *commanding*: by this they understood his just authority over them, and their great obligations to him. But, *secondly*, conscious of their moral inability to obey his righteous requirements; or, in other words, of their propensity to neglect and disobey them, they return them, as it were, to heaven, accompanied with earnest prayer, that God, by his Holy Spirit, would work those very things in them, which, by his law, he required of them. Then, *thirdly*, we see the Lord mercifully sending down both precepts and prayers, accompanied with exceedingly great and precious *promises*, wherein, as the God of grace, he engages to bestow those very things which, as a lawgiver, he requires.[69]

Thus, Fuller saw obligation precipitating from God's commands, prayer precipitating from humanity's moral inability, and promises precipitating from the righteous lawgiver—the one "God who graciously *promises* that which he *commands*, and for which we *pray*."[70] As Fuller stated, "Here, in *one* part, you see the divine *authority* of the lawgiver; in *another*, the moral *insufficiency* of the creature; and, in the *other*, the *all-sufficiency* of the God of Grace."[71] Fuller understood the prayers of the saints in Scripture to be evidence of humanity's moral inability to keep the commands of God. One's prayers, thus, affirm what God affirms—he has all authority and all power.

66. Fuller, "Harmony of Scripture," 218. Emphasis original.

67. Fuller, "Harmony of Scripture," 218. Emphasis original.

68. The researcher infers Arminian and Antinomian extremes here because later in the paper Fuller refers to the two extremes as "*Arminian pride* and *Antinomian presumption*." Fuller, "Harmony of Scripture," 221. Emphasis original.

69. Fuller, "Harmony of Scripture," 220. Emphasis original.

70. Fuller, "Harmony of Scripture," 220.

71. Fuller, "Harmony of Scripture," 221. Emphasis original.

Thus, Fuller concluded that if one "will . . . cease from *self-sufficiency*, on the one hand, and *self-justification*, on the other . . . You will own your obligations, feel and mourn your defects, pray for what you want, praise for what has been granted, and trust Jehovah for what he has promised."[72] On this word, Fuller's paper concluded.

Conclusion

Doctrine's Influence on Prayer

Fuller's own response to the proto-Modern Question—whether it be the duty of the unregenerate to pray—reflected sensitivity guarding first principles of the gospel; namely the depravity of humanity.

Fuller's practice of prayer, particularly as represented in his diary entries from 1780, reflected what may be the most significant reciprocity with his doctrine of depravity. As Fuller's views with respect to humanity shifted regarding open appeals to repent and believe, so did his theology of prayer. Within four years of recording that he found a heart for prayer for the lost in his congregation, Fuller found a heart for prayer for the interest of the lost around the world.

Prayer's Influence on Doctrine

As reflected in *The Backslider*, Fuller's theology of prayer influenced his views respecting human depravity and inability. In *The Backslider*, Fuller addresses eight means of recovery for the backslider. Means two through four do not pertain to prayer, so they are not evaluated here. In the first means, Fuller believed prayer to be the God-ordained means for sustaining a proper view of one's inability and dependence on the power of God. In the fifth means, Fuller argued that special, set-aside times of prayer and fasting were highly effective in reawakening the heart to one's depraved condition before God. In the sixth means, Fuller reminded readers that one is prone to attack after such earnest efforts of devotion to God. False feelings of security often lead to a neglect of prayer leaving the person vulnerable to attack. To avoid such vulnerability, Fuller believed that watchfulness must be added to prayer. In the seventh means, Fuller proposed that the posture of one returning God in prayer is not one in partial need of cleansing, but one in complete need of cleansing. Indeed, an unembellished sense of one's

---

72. Fuller, "Harmony of Scripture," 221.

depravity ought to be sustained in prayer even after conversion. Finally, in the eighth means, Fuller encouraged continual efforts in prayer as to not be satisfied with the cessation of sin only. Prayer is the vital means for restoring full communion and peace with God.

Fuller's paper, "The Harmony of Scripture Precepts, Prayers, and Promises," also demonstrated reciprocity between his understanding of prayer and human inability. The prayers of saints in Scripture, reflecting "the moral *insufficiency* of the creature," were not license to neglect the commands or promises of Scripture.[73] Fuller understood all three components—prayers, commands, and promises—to be in harmony with each other. The example of saints turning precepts and promises into prayers for Fuller removed opportunity for either self-justification or self-sufficiency. The prayers signal one's obligation to keep the commands and one's total inability to keep them apart from "the *all-sufficiency* of the God of Grace."[74]

---

73. Fuller, "Harmony of Scripture," 221. Emphasis original.
74. Fuller, "Harmony of Scripture," 221. Emphasis original.

6

The Church and Prayer

So is God's will, through his wonderful grace, that the prayers of his saints should be one great and principal means of carrying on the designs of Christ's kingdom in the world. When God has something very great to accomplish for his church, it is his will that there should precede it the extraordinary prayers of his people.[1]

—JONATHAN EDWARDS, *SOME THOUGHTS CONCERNING THE PRESENT REVIVAL OF RELIGION*

FULLER UNDERSTOOD ENGLAND TO be divided into three ecclesial land-scapes: "Those who have disapproved of the *doctrine* of the National Church—those who approved of its doctrine, but were dissatisfied with the *degree of its Reformation*—and those who also approved of its doctrine, but disapproved not only of particular parts but of *the very principle of its constitution.*"[2] Presbyterians belong to the second; Baptists and Indepen-

1. Edwards, *Works*, 1:426.

2. Fuller, *Works*, 3:460. Emphasis original. Horton Davies describes the ecclesial landscape as being divided into two tracts in the prior century. According to Davies, the difference in set forms versus free forms of prayer in the seventeenth century typified the "two differing conceptions of the Church." More fully, Davies states, "If liturgical prayer adequately reflects what is held in common in its Creeds, its General Confession, its abstract Collects praying for graces required by all Christians, then free prayer meets individual's particular requirements. And, moreover, liturgical prayer does not demand that the minister should know the members of his congregation; whereas free prayer implies a smaller, more compact community all of whom, theoretically, are known to

dents belong to the latter swath of ecclesial territory. The way in which Fuller refuted the "principle" of the Church of England's formation revealed his understanding of the nature of the church and the mission that flows naturally from such an understanding.

Explanation of the Doctrine[3]

Nature of the Church

Fuller wrote a number of useful works touching on the ecclesiology of Dissenters and Baptists.[4] A chief principle of Fuller's ecclesiology was that the church is a gathered congregation of faithful men. In *A Brief Statement of the Principles of Dissent*, Fuller stated that the church's "being an ally, and as it were a branch of the state, and comprehending the body of the nation, good and bad, appeared to them," that is, to Independents and Baptists, "inconsistent with the nature of 'Christ's kingdom,' which 'is not of this world'; and of a Christian church, which in its own Articles is said to be 'a congregation of faithful men.'"[5] Fuller enlisted the language of their own *Thirty-Nine Articles* to reject the claim that the church should be "*considered as national.*"[6] In a *Vindication of Protestant Dissent*, Fuller conscripted the phrasing of Article 19 once again for his rebuttal to Thomas Robinson's pamphlet, "A Serious Call to a Constant and Devout Attendance on the Stated Services of the Church of England."[7] Once again, Fuller rejected the "grand principle" of the Church of England: "that is, its being *national*, and *established*, and

---

the minister." Davies, *Worship of the English Puritans*, 105.

3. Admittedly, ecclesiology is a broad cross-section of theological commitments. The chapter could have gone a number of different directions; however, the statements that Fuller made regarding the nature and mission of the church seemed to bear the most significant reciprocity with his theology of prayer. The chapter intentionally bracketed out a discussion on the structure of the church. For an interesting discussion regarding Baptist identity past and present, see, "Winding Quest for a Baptist Distinctive" in Ward, "Pure Worship," 1–10. Ward's provocative thesis is that pure worship was *the* priority of early English Particular Baptists. Ward, "Pure Worship," 252.

4. The majority of these works, which explicitly touch on ecclesiology, are contained under the section "Essays, Letters, Etc. on Ecclesiastical Polity," in Fuller, *Works*, 3:447–523.

5. Fuller, *Works*, 3:460. The edition utilized by the researcher was Burnet, *Thirty-Nine Articles of the Church of England*. See Article 19, "Of the Church." Burnet, *Thirty-Nine Articles of the Church of England*, 233.

6. Fuller, *Works*, 3:460. Emphasis original.

7. Fuller, *Works*, 3:463, note.

directed by civil authority."[8] According to Fuller, Robinson also argued "for the Church of England being 'apostolical.'"[9] To this claim, Fuller rebutted:

> It may appear singular to some that, in proving the Church of England to be apostolical, Mr. R. begins with the "order of her ministers," entirely passing over what the Church is *in itself*. A church, we are told in the Articles, is "a congregation of faithful men," &c. Why then did he not undertake to prove that such was the Church of England? That it was a *congregation* assembling together like that at Corinth, *in one place*; and a congregation of *faithful men*, gathered out of an unbelieving world, and sufficiently distinguished from it?[10]

The gathered church does not comprehend a nation's borders. The church, however, does comprehend all who call on the name of the Lord Jesus.

A Necessary Distinction

While one might be considered a Christian brother—that is, belonging to the kingdom of Christ—through a proper belief in the person and work of Christ, Fuller did not extend forbearance to the detriment of God's revealed will concerning the communion of "particular congregations."[11] Fuller's own confession of faith made the distinction clear:

> I believe, the ordinances which Christ, as King of Zion, has instituted for his church to be found in, throughout the gospel day, are especially two: namely, Baptism and the Lord's Supper. I believe the subjects of both to be those who profess repentance towards God, and faith towards our Lord Jesus Christ; and on such I consider them as incumbent duties. I believe that it is essential to Christian baptism, that it be by immersion, or burying the person in water, in the name of the Father, the Son, and the Holy Ghost. I likewise believe baptism as administered by the primitive church, to be prerequisite to church communion; hence I judge what is called strict communion to be consistent with the word of God.[12]

8. Fuller, *Works*, 3:463–64. Emphasis original.

9. Fuller, *Works*, 3:466.

10. Fuller, *Works*, 3:466.

11. See *SLC* 26.2, "Of the Church," in McGlothlin, *Baptist Confessions*, 264.

12. Manly, "Fuller's Confession of Faith," Article 26.

For Fuller, there is a necessary distinction between *"moral obligations* and *positive institutes."*[13] Believing in the person and work of Christ and calling on his name are moral obligations "binding on all mankind."[14] Positive institutions, like baptism and the Lord's Supper, are binding "to a part of mankind, usually described in the institutions themselves."[15] As Fuller stated:

> The one [moral obligations] being founded in our relation to God and one another, and approving themselves to the conscience, require neither precept nor precedent, but merely a general principle which shall comprehend them; the other [positive institutions], having their origin merely in the sovereign will of God, require a punctilious adherence to what is revealed concerning them.[16]

The positive institutions of baptism and the Lord's Supper are punctiliar commands of God for the New Testament church. By nature, these institutions separate and identify those who belong to the gathering of faithful men. The year before his death, Fuller still affirmed his position on the institution of baptism as an *"initiatory* ordinance of Christianity."[17] He illustrated the importance of baptism as tantamount to donning the soldiers' uniform after taking the oath of allegiance:

> The oath of allegiance does not, indeed, initiate a person into the army, as one may take that oath who is no soldier; but it is a prerequisite to being a soldier. Though all who take the oath are not soldiers, yet all soldiers take the oath. Now baptism is that Divine ordinance by which we are said *to put on Christ,* as the king's livery is put on by those who enter his service; and, by universal consent throughout the Christian world, is considered as the badge of a Christian. To admit a person into a Christian

---

13. Fuller, *Works,* 3:500.

14. Fuller, *Works,* 3:500.

15. Fuller, *Works,* 3:500.

16. Fuller, *Works,* 3:500. Bracketed additions are mine. Fuller also used this distinction of moral obligation and positive institution to argue for the use of music in worship as a positive institution and not a moral obligation. His explanation offers another nuance in the distinction between the two. Fuller stated, "That the vocal praising of God is a moral duty, I allow; but the use of instruments is not so. It is a practice which has every property of a positive institute, and not one, that I recollect, of moral obligation. That all duties, both moral and positive, are *commanded* of God, is true; but what is moral is commanded because it is right, and the motive by which it is enforced is not the mere will of the legislator; whereas that which is positive is right, because it is commanded." Fuller, *Works,* 3:516. Emphasis original.

17. Fuller, *Works,* 3:512.

church without it were equal to admitting one into a regiment
who scrupled to wear the soldier's uniform, or to take the oath
of allegiance.[18]

If the uniform is a suitable illustration for baptism, then perhaps calling on
the name of Christ is the suitable equivalent to the oath of allegiance. To call
on the name of Christ and not be baptized is like a soldier taking and yet
refusing the uniform. The two are incompatible.

The Mission of the Church[19]

Even with resolute convictions regarding baptism and closed communion,
Fuller's aim was not especially to grow the Baptist cause. He, like a number of his fellow Northamptonshire Baptist Association ministers—albeit
to varying degrees—exercised an "evangelical catholicity" with respect to
the mission of the church.[20] For example, two of Fuller's closest ministerial friends exercised open communion. Specifically speaking of John Sutcliff's position regarding open communion, Michael Haykin states, "Given
Sutcliff's evangelical catholicity, his position is not all surprising. What is
noteworthy is that Andrew Fuller, his close friend, was of a different opinion
regarding this issue, yet it obviously made no material difference in their
friendship."[21] One might also add, their difference in opinion obviously
made no material difference in their commitment to the expansion of the
kingdom of Christ as more important than purely expanding the Baptist
interests.[22] Similar to how "Sutcliff's commitment to Baptist distinctives

18. Fuller, *Works*, 3:512.

19. Utilizing Fuller as a historical point of departure, Paul Fiddes argues that "mission . . . is of the essence of the church." Fiddes, "Mission and Liberty," 273. For his
appropriation of Fuller, see Fiddes, "Mission and Liberty," 255–59.

20. Haykin, *One Heart and One Soul*, 83, 89, and esp. 165, 264, 292–94. Haykin
explains John Ryland Jr.'s "evangelical catholicity" as a conviction "which refused to
regard the Calvinistic Baptist cause as the only viable expression of the kingdom of
God." Haykin, *One Heart and One Soul*, 89. The researcher, here, co-opts Haykin's use
of the phrase "evangelical catholicity" and defines it as a theological commitment of
belief and praxis to emphasize the expansion of the kingdom of Christ as more important than purely expanding one's own denominational interests. Thus, when it came to
the church's mission, the researcher understands Fuller to exercise forbearance with
non-Baptists regarding differences in the positive institutions as long as they can agree
regarding the moral obligations to repent and believe in the deity and work of Christ
on the cross.

21. Haykin, *One Heart and One Soul*, 294.

22. Perhaps Fuller's theological commitments to both closed communion and evangelical catholicity are just as enigmatic as the eminent John Ryland Sr. Haykin describes

was mollified by his evangelical catholicity and his deep appreciation for evangelical paeodobaptist pastors and communities," Fuller's commitment to Baptist distinctives was not overshadowed by his commitment to Christ's kingdom. Thus, regarding the church's mission throughout the British Empire, Fuller argued that the goal was not "to convert them to *ourselves*" but, rather, "to convert them to *Christ*."[23] Defending the work of the BMS, Fuller stated:

> Our zeal has not been expended in making proselytes to a party, but in turning sinners to God through Jesus Christ. It was in pursuit of this object that we first engaged in missionary undertakings. We had no interest to serve but that of Christ. It was in our hearts to do something for his name among the heathen; and, if it might be, to enlarge the boundaries of his kingdom.[24]

Fuller saw the expansion of the boundaries of the kingdom of Christ to be the mission of the church, regardless of denominational sentiments.

Implications for Prayer

Family Worship

The distinction between positive institutions for the church and moral obligations for all humanity was significant for Fuller's endorsement of families gathering for worship within their own homes. Fuller stated that some "for want of attending to this plain distinction [had refused] to join in family worship, if any were present whom they accounted unbelievers."[25] Some evidently felt that such a gathering would carry the unintended consequence of giving unsaved family members false assurance of belonging to the covenant community on the merit of their worshiping together in the home. Others, such as "the Congregationalist," as Fuller referred to him in the letter, argued the opposite; that is, because you ought to gather in family worship, therefore, you ought also to include unsaved members in the positive institutions of baptism and the Lord's Supper.[26] Fuller maintained

---

Ryland Sr. as "a fascinating blend of theological positions: a High Calvinist who favoured the school of Brine and Gill, yet, because of his open communion stance, very catholic in his friendships." Haykin, *One Heart and One Soul*, 72.

23. Fuller, *Works*, 2:826.

24. Fuller, *Works*, 2:829.

25. Fuller, *Works*, 3:500.

26. Fuller, *Works*, 3:500. "The Congregationalist" is a reference to Samuel Newton, a Congregationalist minister who wrote a number of papers evidently arguing for infant

that the distinction between positive institutions and moral obligations safeguarded the practice of family worship from offering a false sense of belonging to the covenant community. Likewise, the distinction prohibited the "opposite extreme"; that is, "arguing from our joining in what is right for all men that we ought to join in what the Scriptures limit to certain characters."[27]

Fuller's "Letter 9: On Certain New Testament Practices," in *Strictures on Sandemanianism*, articulated both a theological and practical deficiency in those who prohibited family prayers. Theologically, Fuller found those who prohibited family prayers on the grounds of having unbelievers in the family to be rejecting the expressed will of God for all people.[28] Practically, Fuller asked, "Can a child be brought up in the nurture and admonition of the Lord when it never hears its parents pray for it?"[29] The theological and practical issues of neglecting the distinction between positive institutions and moral obligations also carried into broader areas of the church's activity and gatherings.

Church Worship

Returning to Fuller's response to Samuel Newton, Fuller stated that some, believing that public expressions of prayer are to be done only within the confines of the covenant community, "have gone as far as to refuse to engage in public prayer in a promiscuous assembly."[30] Fuller found this also to be theologically and practically deficient. The theological argument mirrors his response to those abstaining from family worship on these grounds.[31] Likewise, in the 1807 circular letter titled "On Moral and Positive Obedience," Fuller addressed the same issue related to the lack of a distinction between positive institutions and moral obligations. Fuller wrote:

> Others, on the same principle, have argued thus, or to this effect: "You withhold the unconverted from joining at the Lord's table, and *why not also from joining in family aud* [sic] *public prayer?*" Our answer is the same. The Lord's supper is the immediate

---

baptism and infant communion. Fuller, *Works*, 3:499. Newton's papers received responses from Dissenters and the Church of England. For a response from the Anglican perspective, see Wix, *An Affectionate Address*.

27. Fuller, *Works*, 3:500.

28. Fuller, *Works*, 2:625–26.

29. Fuller, *Works*, 2:625.

30. See Fuller, *Works*, 3:500.

31. Fuller, *Works*, 3:500.

duty of believers only; but prayer is binding on men in general, however far they may be from performing it in an acceptable manner. To join with unbelievers in what is not their immediate duty is to become partakers of their sin; but to allow them to join with us in what is the duty of every one is not so. We ought to pray for such things as both we and they stand in need of, and if they unite with us in desire it is well for them; if not, the guilt remains with themselves, and not with us.[32]

Since prayer is not a positive institution for the covenant community but a moral obligation for "binding on men in general," all men ought to pray. Since all men ought to pray, Fuller argued that the fear of praying in the presence of the lost was unfounded. The prayers of the covenant community ought to express the same desire as those who are lost or not yet members of the covenant community. As he preached in his sermon, *Instances, Evil, and Tendency of Delay, in the Concerns of Religion*, the invitation "to the heathen is still in force, '*Whosoever shall call upon the name of the Lord shall be saved.*'"[33]

Restricting public prayer for only those in the covenant community was also problematic practically. Returning to consider "Letter 9: On Certain New Testament Practices," Fuller stated, "The believer is not at liberty to join in the prayer of unbelief; but the unbeliever is at liberty, if he can, join in the prayer of faith. To deny him this were to deny him the right of becoming a believer, and of doing what every one [sic] ought to do."[34] In Fuller's sermon on the Lord's Prayer, he commented on the "*social* principle which invades prayer."[35] The social principle, as Fuller stated, did not include believers only. "Were this the case," Fuller stated, "we must restrain prayer in our congregations, and in our families."[36] He continued, "The worship of the primitive church had in it both prayer and singing, and that in a language that might be understood; yet it was open to unbelievers, or any person who chose to join in it."[37] Thus, according to Fuller, prayers in the home and church ought not to be restrained by the presence of unbelievers. Rather, by providing an opportunity for unbelievers to join in prayer in the home and church, believers would rightly ensure unbelievers have the opportunity to

32. Fuller, *Works*, 3:355.

33. Fuller, *Works*, 1:148. Emphasis original. The same theological argument is likewise repeated in "Letter 9: On Certain New Testament Practices," in *Strictures on Sandemanianism*. Fuller, *Works*, 2:625–26.

34. Fuller, *Works*, 2:626.

35. Fuller, *Works*, 1:579. Emphasis original.

36. Fuller, *Works*, 1:579.

37. Fuller, *Works*, 1:579.

pray as they ought—"The encouragement to the heathen is still in force, *"Whosoever shall call upon the name of the Lord shall be saved."*[38]

Example of Fuller's Practice of Prayer

Prayer in Fuller's Home

Consistent with his distinctions between positive institutions and moral obligations, Fuller prayed freely in the home and in the church. In the home, Fuller frequently prayed for the salvation of his children. Frequently, Fuller seized opportunities to pray with his family as a whole and privately with individual members. For example, Fuller wrote in a letter to fellow minister and friend, John Ryland Jr.:

> Sarah Fuller was born at Soham, Dec. 7, 1779. At the time of her birth, I committed her to God, as, I trust, I have done many times since. Once, in particular, viewing her as she lay smiling in the cradle, at the age of eight months, my heart was much affected: I took her up in my arms, retired, and, in that position, wrestled hard with God for a blessing; at the same time, offering her up, as it were, and solemnly presenting her to the Lord for acceptance. In this exercise I was greatly encouraged by the conduct of Christ towards those who brought little children in their arms to him, for his blessing.[39]

"With respect to [Fuller's] parental tenderness towards his daughter," Ryland stated, "I was an eye-witness of the uncommon degree in which it was manifested."[40] Fuller's tenderness as a father was demonstrated clearly in his sensitivity to both his daughter's physical and spiritual health during a painful season of sickness. Near or after her sixth birthday, his daughter, Sarah, became sick with the measles. Sarah's health fluctuated over the next year, but she never recovered. Sarah died on May 30, 1786. She was nearly seven years old.[41]

38. Fuller, *Works*, 1:148.

39. Ryland, *Work of Faith*, 270. Sarah was also the name of Fuller's first wife, Miss Sarah Gardiner (her maiden name). To distinguish between the two, Fuller sometimes referred to Sarah, his daughter, as Sally. For Mrs. Fuller's lineage, see Ryland, *Work of Faith*, 269.

40. Ryland, *Work of Faith*, 270.

41. Ryland, *Work of Faith*, 270. Sadly, Sarah was not the only child to precede Fuller in death. For more on Fuller's personal struggles, especially the bereavements of his immediate family, see Morden, *Life and Thought of Andrew Fuller*, 41–42, 97–109. According to Morden, Fuller's first marriage, while strong, "was marked by tragedy. They

Excerpts from letters and diary entries provide an insightful window into Fuller's private wrestling with God over the condition of his daughter's physical and spiritual state.[42] The letters and entries supplied by Ryland highlighted, among other things, Fuller's response of prayer for Sarah's physical healing and eternal salvation. Pleading for her physical healing, Fuller recounted, "As her death drew nigh, I was exceedingly affected, and very earnest in prayer for her soul, having now no hope of her life . . . About this time, I threw myself prostrate on the floor, and wept exceedingly, yet pleading with God for her."[43] Fuller's wrestling with God for his daughter's life caused him a great deal of physical pain, which, he said, "laid me quite aside for several days."[44] Although he was struck initially with severe emotional and physical pain, Fuller stated, "I then reflected, that I had sinned, in being so inordinately anxious. From this time, I felt a degree of calmness and resignation to God."[45] Nonetheless, still feeling the effects of his physical anguish, Fuller was confined to his bed in the adjoining room when he learned of Sarah's death. Fuller recounted that he called the family to his room and "attempted to bless a taking as well as a giving God; and to implore, that those of us who were left behind, might find grace in the wilderness."[46]

One particular account retold in a letter addressed to Ryland illustrates further the vital place of prayer in Fuller's relationship with his children. Once again, regarding Sarah's illness, Fuller wrote:

In March, I took her to Northampton, for the advice of Dr. Kerr. This cheered her spirits; as she loved Mr. and Mrs. Ryland, and wanted to go to see them. She stayed a fortnight, and her aunt with her. The doctor was very attentive and kind to her, and we still hoped she might recover. During this fortnight, I went two or three times to see her; and, one evening, being with her alone, she asked me to pray for her. "What do you wish me to pray for, my dear?" said I. She answered, "That God would bless me, and keep me, and save my soul." "Do you think, then, that you are a sinner?" "Yes, father." Fearing lest she did not understand what she said, I asked her, "What is sin, my dear?" She answered, "Telling a story." I comprehended this, and it went to my heart. "What, then, (I said,) you remember do you, my having corrected

had four children in the first four years of their marriage but three of them died very young." Morden, *Life and Thought of Andrew Fuller*, 42.

42. Ryland, *Work of Faith*, 270–85.
43. Ryland, *Work of Faith*, 274.
44. Ryland, *Work of Faith*, 274.
45. Ryland, *Work of Faith*, 274.
46. Ryland, *Work of Faith*, 274–75.

you once, for telling a story?" "Yes, father." I asked her, if she did
not try to pray herself. She answered, "I sometimes try, but I do
not know how to pray; I wish you would pray for me, till I can
pray for myself." As I continued to sit by her, she appeared much
dejected. I asked her the reason. She said, "I am afraid I should
go to hell." "My dear, (said I,) who told you so?" "Nobody, (said
she,) but I know, if I do not pray to the Lord, I must go to hell." I
then went to prayer with her, with many tears.[47]

In hindsight, Fuller looked back on this time with some consolation as it
appeared to be the beginning of Sarah's more earnest interest in her eternal
state and relationship with God. On June 1, 1786, Fuller wrote in his diary:

> I feel a solid pleasure in reflecting on our own conduct in her
> education: surely, we endeavoured to bring her up in the nurture
> and admonition of the Lord; and I trust our endeavours were
> not in vain. Surely, her visit to Northampton, too, was blessed
> for her good: she has certainly discovered, ever since, great ten-
> derness of conscience, and much of the fear of God; great regard
> for the worship of God, especially for the Lord's-day; and great
> delight in reading, especially the accounts of the conversion of
> some little children. But all is over now; and I am, in a good
> degree, satisfied.[48]

Indeed, the time in prayer with her father was quite affecting for her spiritual frame of mind. In addition to the prayers of her father, Sarah reflected
often on the verses of a hymn written for her by Ryland:

> Lord, teach a little child to pray,
> Thy grace betimes impart
> And grant, thy Holy Spirit may
> Renew my infant heart.

> A helpless creature I was born,
> And from the womb I stray'd;
> I must be wretched and forlorn
> Without thy mercy's aid.

> But Christ can all my sins forgive,
> And wash away their stain,
> And fit my soul with him to live,
> And in his kingdom reign.

> To him let little children come,

47. Ryland, *Work of Faith*, 272.
48. Ryland, *Work of Faith*, 284.

For he hath said they may;
His bosom then shall be their home,
Their tears he'll wipe away.

For all who early seek his face,
Shall surely taste his love;
Jesus will guide them by his grace,
To dwell with him above.[49]

At her request, Fuller, the tender father that he was, recited these verses over Sarah as they rode out in the field for fresh air. Conversing with Sarah, Fuller stated that "I asked her again, if she tried to pray herself: I found, by her answer, that she did, and was used to pray over the hymn which Mr. Ryland composed for her."[50] The hymn's lyrics were a fitting prayer for young Sarah. Additionally, the lyrics encapsulate the evangelical theology prized by both Ryland and Fuller.

Prayer in Fuller's Church

Much like in the home, the same "parental tenderness" manifest in his prayer for his family may be seen in Fuller's pastoral ministry. While Fuller went through seasons of great personal difficulty and long stretches of private prayerlessness between the years of 1782 and 1792, there is evidence to suggest that his public practice and affirmations of prayer's role in the church was codified early in his ministry with watershed instances in 1784 and 1785.[51] Consider these five examples:

First, note the prominence of prayer in Fuller's confession of faith before the congregation at Kettering. Haykin notes in his biography of John Sutcliff:

49. Ryland, *Work of Faith*, 273. Ryland's learning of Sarah's appreciation for his hymn must have been of some consolation to him. The affection Sarah had for both Mr. and Mrs. Ryland was certainly reciprocated. At Sarah's request, Ryland composed another hymn. He sent the hymn three days before Sarah's death. This hymn too was included in Ryland's memoirs of Fuller's life. See Ryland, *Work of Faith*, 280.

50. Ryland, *Work of Faith*, 273.

51. Morden, *Life and Thought of Andrew Fuller*, 98–109. Fuller's personal struggles have been alluded to already in chapter 4, pages 147–48. Morden cautioned readers from taking Fuller's diary as too literal of a representation of his spirituality because of the Puritan practice that Fuller seemed to be emulating. Nonetheless, "there seems little reason to doubt that in the years 1782–92, whilst his public ministry flourished, Fuller was often struggling in his Christian faith." Morden's conclusion, rather than contradicting, coheres with the proposal that Fuller's private prayer life fluctuated throughout this season of personal struggles, while his public practice and affirmations of prayer's role in the church resounded most clearly for his congregation and denomination.

In the statement of faith which Fuller gave at the time of his formal induction into the pastorate at Kettering in 1783, he firmly
declared that he believed that "The kingdom of Christ will be
gloriously extended, by the pouring out of God's Spirit upon the
ministry of the word," and that it was therefore incumbent upon
"all God's servants and churches most ardently to pray" for it.[52]

Prayer was of vital importance to the church's mission; namely, the expansion of Christ's kingdom. Fuller was not alone in his belief regarding the
importance of prayer.

Second, note the prominence of prayer for numerous other ministers
within the Northamptonshire Baptist Association. Fuller recorded in his
diary that several ministers around May of 1784 "agreed each at home by
himself to fast & pray the second Tuesday in every month for the revival of
real religion and the extending of Christ's Kingdom in the world."[53] The next
month, the association met at Nottingham for its annual meeting. It was
from this meeting in 1784 that the "famous prayer call was issued."[54] The
prayer call was issued to "all the *churches in our association*" appended to
that year's circular letter.[55] The churches were exhorted "to meet on the first
Monday evening" for one hour. If they were unable to join at that particular
hour or evening, the churches were encouraged to set apart a more suitable
time. Likewise, those who lived at a distance from the meeting houses in the
country were encouraged to "unite in *small societies*" at the same time.[56] Individuals who could not gather in small groups were encouraged nonetheless to keep the same day an hour "to unite the [breath] of prayer in private
with those who are thus engaged in a more public manner."[57]

Third, near the end of the June 1784 association meeting, the present
messengers and ministers requested that Fuller publish the sermon he delivered at the meeting, *The Nature and Importance of Walking by Faith*. Haykin
noted in his biography on John Sutcliff that "the very first item which Fuller
had published, . . . argued that 'A life of faith will ever be a life of prayer.'"[58]
Equally significant to note, Fuller appended to this very first publication a
series of "Persuasives to a General Union in Extraordinary Prayer, for the

---

52. Haykin, *One Heart and One Soul*, 157.

53. Fuller, *Complete Works: Diary*, 1:47.

54. Elwyn, *Northamptonshire Association*, 16.

55. Ryland, *Nature, Evidences, and Advantages*, 12.

56. Ryland, *Nature, Evidences, and Advantages*, 12.

57. Ryland, *Nature, Evidences, and Advantages*, 12.

58. Haykin, *One Heart and One Soul*, 157–58.

Revival and Extent of Real Religion."[59] Thornton Elwyn emphasized the significance of Fuller's persuasives as reflecting "the way some people's minds were working towards a wider view of the church's work."[60] Indeed, Fuller's "Persuasives" may be one of the best examples of the evangelical catholicity that was burgeoning from within certain circles of the Particular Baptists in the eighteenth century. For Fuller, prayer was a central point of unity for individual congregations and the broader kingdom of Christ, regardless of one's denomination. Note to whom Fuller addressed the persuasives, "To the churches in the *Leicestershire* and *Northamptonshire association*, and to any others who love and long for the coming of Christ's blessed kingdom, and whose hearts may be inclined to unite in seeking its welfare."[61] Whether divided by geography, throughout the Baptist associations, or divided on the application of divine institutions, throughout the globe, Fuller saw prayer for the expansion of Christ's kingdom, the mission of the church, as the great place of unity for Christ's kingdom. Fuller was not alone in developing his opinions regarding prayer for the expansion of Christ's kingdom beyond the denominational or national boundaries. Fuller's preaching at the association and the subsequent publication of his sermon provided further impetus for a burgeoning missionary movement within the Northamptonshire Baptist Association that would eventually spread to the breadth of the British Empire.

Fourth, on July 11 and 18, 1784, the following month, Fuller expounded Matt 6:1–8, "Alms-giving, and Prayer," and Matt 6:9–15, "The Lord's Prayer," respectively.[62] The following month, he expounded on Matt 7:7–12, an exposition titled "Prayer and Equity." With particular regard for corporate prayer, from Matt 6:1–8, Fuller cautioned, "If we have no freedom in private prayer, but live nearly if not entirely in the neglect of it, and at the

---

59. Fuller, *Persuasives*, 41–47.

60. Elwyn, *Northamptonshire Association*, 17. He particularly cites the third persuasive, "Let the present religious state of the world be considered to this end." He notes, "we must remember [these] were written before Cary's *Enquiry.*" Elwyn, *Northamptonshire Association*, 17.

61. Fuller, *Persuasives*, 41.

62. While Fuller's *Works* do not list the date of these expositions through Jesus's Sermon on the Mount in Matthew's Gospel, the date of each exposition may be determined with reasonable accuracy through a comparison of his *Works* and select passages from his *Diary*. Two in particular comment on his expounding from Matthew 5–7. First, July 11, 1784, Fuller stated, "Expounded the last part of the 5th chapter of Matthew this evening." Second, August 29, 1784, Fuller stated, "Expounded and finished Christ's Sermon on the Mount." Compare Fuller, *Works*, 1:561–92; Fuller, *Complete Works: Diary*. See Appendix 2 for a proposed timeline built on this comparison of Fuller's *Works* and the relevant entries from his *Diary*.

same time possess great zeal and fluency in our public exercises, we ought
surely to suspect that things are far from being right between God and our
souls."[63] To this caution, he added:

> In general, it is right to avoid long prayers, especially in the fam-
> ily, and in the church, which are not only wearisome to men, but
> offensive to God . . . It is not our Lord's design, however, to con-
> demn *all* long prayers, nor all repetitions. He himself, on some
> occasions, continued for a whole night; and in Gethsemane he
> three times repeated the same words. They are *vain* repetitions
> which he censures, and the hope of being heard *for* much speak-
> ing. It is observable, however, that whenever Christ or any of
> the apostles were long in prayer, it was in private. If many who
> pray for an hour or longer in public, and with tedious repeti-
> tions, were equally circuitous in the closet, whether we should
> commend their discretion or not, we might hope well of their
> sincerity. But where the reverse of this is true, it certainly has the
> appearance of the very spirit which it was our Saviour's inten-
> tion to condemn.[64]

Fuller's exposition of Matt 6:9–15 and 7:7–12, likewise, offers salient cautions and exhortations for proper motives and manners for praying in public. In his exposition of the Lord's Prayer, Fuller taught his congregation
the vital distinction between positive institutions for the church and moral
obligations for all of humanity. Fuller stated:

> The *social* principle which pervades the prayer.—"*Our* Father—
> forgive *us*," &c . . . taught not to confine our petitions to what
> respects ourselves, but to identify with our own cases those of
> our brethren. Nor is it necessary that they should be actually
> present to hear us, and join with us; the prayer of faith and love
> will embrace in its arms brethren at the greatest distance; and
> not only such as are known, but such as are unknown, even the
> whole family of God upon earth. Neither is it necessary to social
> prayer that all who are present should be believers. Were this the
> case, we must restrain prayer in our congregations, and in our
> families. The worship of the primitive churches had in it both
> prayer and singing, and that in a language that might be under-
> stood; yet it was open to unbelievers, or any person who chose
> to join in it, 1 Cor 14:15, 23–25. If either prayer or praise was a
> *positive institution*, we might be under the necessity of refusing
> admission to some characters, as is the case in other positive

63. Fuller, *Works*, 1:576–77.
64. Fuller, *Works*, 1:577. Emphasis original.

institutions; but if they are immediately binding on all men, whatever be their characters, any man has a right to be present. If he can join in either, let him; and if not, it is to himself only. Our only concern in such cases is, not to give unbelievers to understand that they are considered differently from what they are; and this may be avoided, without refusing to pray or praise in company with them.[65]

These appear to be the very principles that undergirded Fuller's freedom in encouraging the united efforts of prayer throughout the association even though they were separated geographically. Likewise, these principles undergirded his freedom to exhort those within his association to pray for the interest of Christ's kingdom and not their association only.

Fifth, and finally, on January 2, 1785, Fuller wrote in his diary,

> Very tender in reading more of Mr. Bunyan's *Holy War*, particularly that part where the four captains agree to petition the King for more force. Felt a great satisfaction in my principles concerning preaching to sinners and a desire to pray like them for help from on high to render the word effectual.[66]

The above is a particularly clear correlation between Fuller's developing principle regarding appeals to sinners to repent and believe in Christ and his growing desire to pray for the lost. Nearly five years prior in Soham, he wrote, "Found a heart to pray for the conversion of the congregation."[67] Perhaps this is evidence that the heart Fuller found in Soham to pray for the salvation of sinners in his congregation was now being stoked further to pray not only for the interest of his congregation, but for the interest of sinners around the globe.

Implications for Doctrine

Calling on the Name of Jesus

Calling on the name of Jesus, as Fuller understood it, was a defining mark of the New Testament saint.[68] Fuller understood the church universal to be

---

65. Fuller, *Works*, 1:579.

66. Fuller, *Complete Works: Diary*, 1:100.

67. Fuller, *Complete Works: Diary*, 1:13.

68. "Calling on the name of the *Lord*," though, it seems was a defining mark of God's people not only in the New Testament. Fuller understood the reference to calling on the name of the Lord in Gen 4:26 as not marking the beginning of prayer but a more "*visible* form" of "true religion"—that is, "the seed of the woman, afterwards called 'the

made of all those past, present, and future who call on the name of Jesus. Thus, if a congregation is made up of "faithful men," then faithful men are those men and women who have been saved by the atoning work of Christ and have called on his name. In a letter to Samuel Palmer, "Agreement in Sentiment the Bond of Christian Union," Fuller wrote that the "dissent from the Church of England, or any other church" gave "no proper ground of religious union."[69] The basis of unity relies entirely on areas of "agreement" and "forbearance."[70] Fuller held that both agreement and forbearance were required for unity. Fuller stated that since differing sentiments will always exist, then unity must be built on the positive affirmations of first principles of the gospel and "consent to exercise forbearance towards each other in every thing [sic] else."[71] One must consider then, what were Fuller's first principles of the gospel that were necessary for Christian unity?

For Fuller, calling on the name of Jesus was *the* shibboleth of belonging to the kingdom of Christ. In his letter to Palmer, he described calling on the name of Jesus as "*the* characteristic of a primitive believer."[72] Those who do not call on the name of Christ cannot be rightly understood as being gathered unto Christ through his atoning sacrifice on the cross. Fuller held that one may be properly called "a Christian brother," belonging to the kingdom of Christ, if he believed in the deity and work of Christ. Without these two principles positively confessed, Fuller stated, "I had reason to believe . . . that he did not call upon the name of the Lord Jesus, or rely upon his atoning sacrifice for acceptance with God."[73] Speaking of the deity and atonement of Christ, Fuller stated, "Without the former, we cannot with any consistency call on the name of Jesus Christ our lord, which is characteristic of a primitive believer; and without the latter, I need not say to you, sir, that the gospel is rendered of none effect."[74] Fuller knew such a stance would bring

---

sons of God,' assembling together to worship him." Fuller, *Works*, 3:24. Some, such as Gary Millar, argued for this passage to be "the first prayer in the Bible." He convincingly argued that this key phrase in Genesis 4 is a neglected "methodological point" of understanding the nature and purpose of prayer as developed throughout Scripture. Millar, *Calling on the Name of the Lord*, 19. From Fuller's exposition, one may be able to conclude that Fuller saw this as representing the first prayer meetings rather the first prayers.

69. Fuller, *Works*, 3:489.
70. Fuller, *Works*, 3:489–92.
71. Fuller, *Works*, 3:491.
72. Fuller, *Works*, 2:492.
73. Fuller, *Works*, 3:490.
74. Fuller, *Works*, 3:492.

on accusations of that he incorrectly inferred principle from practice. Fuller preemptively responded:

> Possibly you may think it unfair to reason as I have done from practices to principles, and that we ought to make a wide difference between the one and the other. But the difference, as it appears to me, is only as the difference between root and branch. Faith is not a mere speculation of the understanding, nor unbelief a mere mistake in judgment. They are both of a moral nature, or salvation would not be connected with the former, and final condemnation with the latter.[75]

Contrary to his normative method of reasoning from principle to practice, Fuller understood the practice of calling on the name of Jesus as tantamount to affirming his deity and work on the cross.[76] Likewise, calling on the name of Jesus, which is unmistakably a prayer, was tantamount to one's belonging to the gathered covenant community of faith. Indeed, calling on the name of Jesus was vital for Fuller's understanding of the nature of the church as a congregation of gathered faithful men; that is, faithful men who call on his name.

"The Commencement of the Angel's Flight"[77]

Nearly two months prior to his death, Fuller penned, with hints of optimism, the preface to his *Expository Discourses on the Apocalypse*. In the preface he stated that the work had been nearly complete for four or five years, but he continued to rework, edit, and add material along the way. And even though he had seen a number of dear friends pass away in the past four to five years, he concluded optimistically, "we have seen enough, amidst all the troubles of our times, to gladden our hearts; and trust that our children will see greater things than these."[78] Fuller's optimistic outlook persisted throughout the discourse.

---

75. Fuller, *Works*, 3:492.

76. By using the phrase "normative method," the researcher is recalling Fuller's order of reasoning described in his covenant of renewal, "This day I see, and have all along found, that holy practice has a necessary dependence on sacred *principle*." Fuller, *Works*, 1:20. Thus, typically, Fuller argued that practice is built upon principle and not the other way around.

77. The title of the subheading is taken from a line in Fuller's exposition of Rev 14:6–20. Fuller, *Works*, 3:270.

78. Fuller, *Works*, 3:202.

One reason in particular for Fuller's optimism was the united efforts in prayer. In commenting on the angel's flight in Revelation 14, Fuller stated, "I am aware that this commission of the flying angel has been generally understood as addressed to papal idolaters, and the passage of course applied to the evangelical labours of the reformers."[79] However, Fuller believed, "There are other things, . . . which have led me to consider 'the angel flying in the midst of heaven' as sent to pagan rather than to papal idolaters."[80] Despite the fact that "we are in danger of magnifying the events of our times," Fuller stated that such an application "appears to be its most natural meaning."[81] Fuller understood the recent unified efforts in prayer and use of means for the expansion of Christ's kingdom to be on a scale not seen "since the Reformation." Commenting still on the angel's flight, Fuller stated:

> The desire which has been kindled of late years to carry the gospel among the heathen does not appear to be an object unworthy of a place in prophecy. It has engaged the attention of a larger portion of the Christian church, and excited more earnest prayer and disinterested exertion, than perhaps any thing [sic] which has occurred since the Reformation. Nor ought we to consider what has hitherto been done as any thing [sic] more that [sic] the commencement of the angel's flight. It has indeed for its *object* the evangelizing of "*every* nation, and kindred, and tongue, and people"; but at present this is far from being accomplished. We have seen enough, however, to convince us with what ease the great God, by touching the hearts of a few individuals, can accomplish it.[82]

If the mission of the church was the great place of evangelical unity and forbearance for Fuller, then nowhere was this unity more tangibly manifest

79. Fuller, *Works*, 3:269.

80. Fuller, *Works*, 3:269. Fuller's interpretation seems to comport with elements of John Gill's exposition of the same passage. With respect to the meaning of the angel's flight in Rev 14:6, Gill stated, "I think a set of Gospel preachers are intended, who will appear at the beginning of the spiritual reign of Christ, and will be a means of ushering it in; and these are the watchmen of Zion, who will give the Lord no rest till he has made Jerusalem the praise of the whole earth." Gill, *An Exposition of the New Testament*, 3:799.

81. Fuller, *Works*, 3:269.

82. Fuller, *Works*, 3:270. Emphasis original. Fuller's own estimation of the impact of the recent prayer and gospel efforts seems to be equally as bold as Elwyn's. From a much later historical vantage point, Elwyn concludes that "this prayer call of 1784 to the Northamptonshire Association was one of the most decisive events in the life of Dissent in that period, and probably for all Christendom." Elwyn, *Northamptonshire Association*, 18.

than in the united efforts in prayer for the advancement of the gospel. The Prayer Call of 1784 was the catalyst for this united effort within the Northamptonshire Baptist Association, but this concerted gospel-interest in prayer quickly spread to other Baptist associations.[83] Charles Deweese, in his historical survey of *Prayer in Baptist Life*, observes that "the 1784 prayer call of the Northampton Baptist Association in England significantly altered the nature of Baptist prayer meetings by adding a strong missionary character to them."[84] Fuller was without a doubt a principle figure responsible for embedding a missional focus in Baptist prayer meetings.[85] Yet from their

83. Edwards, *Works*, 2:279.

84. Deweese, *Prayer in Baptist Life*, 45–46.

85. Since it has been well-catalogued that the united efforts stemming from the Prayer Call of 1784 extended beyond Baptist interests, there is room for further consideration on how the Prayer Call of 1784, and perhaps Fuller's unique influence in that movement, extended beyond the Baptist denomination with respect to increased focus on missions in prayer and spirituality. As noted in chapter 4, Fuller's influence outside the bounds of the Baptist denomination is clearly observable in Thomas Binney's inclusion of Fuller's sermon preached at Sutcliff's funeral on praying in the Spirit. See chapter 4, 157n88.

Additionally, further research may be undertaken tracing Fuller's influence on Baptist Spirituality at large. Without supplying evidence, E. Glenn Hinson claims that "Baptist spirituality shifted from a contemplative to a conversionist mode during the Great Awakening (c. 1720–1750), which accentuated the experience of conversion. Baptists now meditated on Scriptures and prayed, whether individually or corporately, not so much for their impact on their entire spiritual lives as on the front end of them—conversion, whether one's own experience or the conversion experiences of others. In effect they focused on the pilgrim's *beginning* rather than the pilgrim's *progress*." See Hinson, "Baptist Spirituality." While the Great Awakening refers explicitly to the revival in the British American colonies, one may ask if Fuller's influence in America in the eighteenth century furthered the alleged transformation in Baptist spirituality. How might Fuller's missional focus in prayer nuance Hinson's claim? On cursory analysis, Morden's work on Fuller's spirituality may challenge or nuance Hinson's claim that seems to imply that the missional focus in prayer and Scripture reading was detrimental to Baptist spirituality. Indeed, Morden may claim the opposite for Fuller's case. Note Morden's summative observation: "In the first year of the BMS's existence the two halves of our chapter come together. Through his work as the Society's secretary Fuller found a focus for his spirituality that was more conducive to his temperament than morbid introspection; and through missional activity his love for God increased and he found a greater and more settled degree of happiness than hitherto. He had found a cause, one to which he could be increasingly devoted. He would remain the very active secretary of the BMS for the rest of his life." Morden, *Life and Thought of Andrew Fuller*, 123. If Morden is correct, then Fuller's experience contradicts Hinson's description of the shift within Baptist Spirituality. To borrow Hinson's words, Fuller's conversionist shift is what furthered his progress on the pilgrim's journey.

Another possible area of further study is the correlation between Grant's thesis in *Andrew Fuller and the Evangelical Renewal of Pastoral Theology* and the infusion of a missional character within Baptist prayer meetings. Grant argues that Fuller's renewal

origin, both Fuller and Sutcliff envisioned united prayer in gospel efforts extending beyond the Baptist interest. For example, in the preface to the 1789 English edition of Jonathan Edwards's *An Humble Attempt*, Sutcliff stated, "O for thousands upon thousands, divided into small bands in their respective cities, towns, villages, and neighbourhood, all met at the same time, and in pursuit of one end, offering up their united prayers, like so many ascending clouds of incense before the Most High!—May he shower down blessings on all the scattered tribes of Zion!"[86] Prayer was a catalyst for mission-oriented unity between evangelical Baptists, but these efforts extended well beyond the Baptist interests. Through prayer, the scattered tribes of Zion, regardless of denominational sentiments, were united in mission. Although one cannot reasonably determine that the one caused the other, nonetheless, for the Northamptonshire Baptist Association, their unity in prayer preceded their unity in sending missionaries to the utter most parts of the earth.[87] The commencement of the angel's flight was on the heels of united efforts in prayer. Edwards shared this perspective with respect to the revival in New England nearly a century prior. Edwards stated, "So is God's will, through his wonderful grace, that the prayers of his saints should be one great and principal means of carrying on the designs of Christ's kingdom in world. When God has something very great to accomplish for his church, it is his will that there should precede it the extraordinary prayers of his people."[88]

Conclusion

Doctrine's Influence on Prayer

In considering the nature of the church, Fuller's distinction between positive institutions and moral obligations was essential for encouraging public

---

of "pastoral theology was particularly expressed in his preaching, and that the character of that renewal can be substantiated and defined with reference to his key convictions about preaching: *plain* in composition and delivery, *evangelical* in content and concern, and *affectionate* in feeling and application." Grant, *Andrew Fuller*, 8. One may be able to argue in connection with Grant's thesis that Fuller's renewal of pastoral theology was also expressed in his stimulating the growth and transformation of prayer meetings toward a more evangelical, or missional, focus.

86. Edwards, *Humble Attempt*, 2:278–79.

87. Morden made a similar observation regarding the order of events within the Northamptonshire Baptist Association. "The period in question also saw Fuller and his friends become increasingly committed to the spread of the gospel around the globe. This commitment was fed by wider reading and manifested itself firstly in prayer and then in action." Morden, *Life and Thought of Andrew Fuller*, 97.

88. Edwards, *Works*, 1:426.

prayers to be offered in the home and church regardless of whether unbelievers were present. Fuller held resolute convictions regarding baptism and the Lord's Supper, but these, he considered, are positive institutions for the church. Prayer is the moral obligation of all persons. So rather than restricting prayer to only those contexts where believers are present, Fuller felt that prayers freely offered in the home and church in the presence of unbelievers encouraged the person not yet a believer to consider their duty to God.

In considering the mission of the church, Morden correctly states, "Mission was the outworking of his [Fuller's] prayer and devotion but it was also the essential context which shaped that devotion, providing the content for his prayers and moulding [sic] the different ways he related to God."[89] Fuller, like many noble ministers within the Northamptonshire Baptist Association, held their commitment to the expansion of Christ's kingdom of greater worth that the expansion of the Baptist interest. Fuller alongside his fellow Northamptonshire Baptist ministers led the charge in calling for united prayer for the expansion of Christ's kingdom to the ends of the earth.

Prayer's Influence on Doctrine

Regarding the nature of the church, Fuller equated calling on the name of Jesus with belonging to the kingdom of Christ. He described the practice of calling on the name of Jesus as "*the* characteristic of a primitive believer."[90] As such, Fuller understood the church universal to be made up of those who have called on the name of Jesus. Arguing from practice to principle, Fuller held that if one had not, or could not on account of their conviction, call on the name of Jesus then he had reason to doubt their truly belonging to the kingdom of Christ.

Fuller's belief and practice of prayer influenced his understanding of the mission of the church. His experience in the growing prayer movement and success in efforts of the Baptist Missionary Society influenced the way that Fuller interpreted the meaning of the angel's flight in Rev 14:6. Following the Prayer Call of 1784, the widespread commitment of churches to concerted prayer for the expansion of Christ's kingdom likely provided the impetus for concerted effort in founding and sending missionaries through the BMS.[91] Fuller saw these advances as only the beginning of what God

89. Morden, *Life and Thought of Andrew Fuller*, 193–94.

90. Fuller, *Works*, 2:492.

91. Financing the mission was, as Nigel Wheeler states, a "herculean" task. Wheeler states that "the whole initiative of a foreign mission was founded on a solid base of at least nine years of prayer and in like manner prayer was at the foundation of their

had in store. Thus, Fuller concluded that the recent years of "earnest prayer and disinterested exertion" for the expansion of Christ's kingdom to the ends of the earth may very well be "the commencement of the angel's flight."[92]

fundraising activities." Wheeler, "Eminent Spirituality and Eminent Usefulness," 50–51. More work could be done to connect these two activities, prayer and fundraising.

92. Fuller, *Works*, 3:270.

7

Eschatology and Prayer

The desire which has been kindled of late years to carry the gospel among the heathen does not appear to be an object unworthy of a place in prophecy. It has engaged the attention of a larger portion of the Christian church, and excited more earnest prayer and disinterested exertion, than perhaps any thing [sic] which has occurred since the Reformation. Nor ought we to consider what has hitherto been done as any thing [sic] more that [sic] the commencement of the angel's flight. It has indeed for its *object* the evangelizing of "*every* nation, and kindred, and tongue, and people"; but at present this is far from being accomplished. We have seen enough, however, to convince us with what ease the great God, by touching the hearts of a few individuals, can accomplish it.

—Andrew Fuller, *Expository Discourses on the Apocalypse*[1]

Explanation of the Doctrine

Optimistic Eschatology: "The Time Is at Hand"

In "Eschatology and Missions," Don Fanning states, "The anticipation of a special intervention of God in time and history whether it was His First

1. Fuller, *Works*, 3:270.

Coming or will be His Second Coming has had a significant effect on the worldview, lifestyle and ministry strategy of believers throughout history."[2] Fuller was no exception. One of Fuller's final published works was a critical expansion of his expositions of Revelation titled *Expository Discourses on the Apocalypse*.[3] Fuller's *Expository Discourses on the Apocalypse* was permeated with eschatological implications for his church.[4] Fuller saw his study of Revelation as a subject of a necessity for his church. He stated, "The reason also assigned why we should study this part of the Holy Scriptures in particular—that 'the time is at hand,' seemed to have greater force after a lapse of above seventeen hundred years than it could have at the time of its being written." Thus Fuller believed that "events of the present times . . . called for a special attention to prophecy."[5]

His interpretation of Revelation and his views regarding the second coming had a significant effect on his life and ministry. As Fanning stated, "One of the reasons that early Protestant and Evangelical missionaries were so bold to advance the gospel into primitive and often hostile countries was their Calvinistic (God had predestined this to happen) and Postmillennial theology (God was building His kingdom), thus nothing could stop this from happening." While Fanning did not refer to Fuller specifically, he did cite Fuller's friend and the BMS's first missionary as being motivated by a "postmillennial vision of victory."[6] Carey's postmillennial optimism was ubiquitous among his fellow Particular Baptist ministers and most evangelicals in the eighteenth century.[7] According to Bebbington, "The equivalent

2. Fanning, "Eschatology and Missions," 1.

3. Fuller, *Works*, 3:201–307; Roberts, "Andrew Fuller," 45.

4. Ryland recorded Fuller's subtitle in his list of Fuller's publications: *Expository Discourses on the Apocalypse, Interspersed with Practical Reflections.* Ryland, *Work of Faith*, 144.

5. Fuller, *Works*, 3:201.

6. Fanning, "Eschatology and Missions," 37.

7. Bebbington, "Early Developments of the Baptist Movement," 7. Bebbington claimed that Carey's eschatological optimism represents the wider optimism permeating from "the optimism of the Enlightenment." Bebbington, "Early Developments of the Baptist Movement," 6. Bebbington's more comprehensive treatment of the correlation between the Enlightenment and evangelicalism is represented in Bebbington, *Evangelicalism in Modern Britain*. Bebbington's boldest thesis related to the Enlightenment and Evangelicalism was that evangelicalism was "created by the Enlightenment." Bebbington, *Evangelicalism in Modern Britain* 74. Other scholars have noted numerous correlations and affinities between the Enlightenment and evangelicalism. For example, Mark Noll explained how enigmatically evangelicalism's "general stance . . . clearly opposed some expressions of the Enlightenment," while at the same time being "an authentic expression of Enlightenment principles." Noll, *Rise of Evangelicalism*, 150–51. Similarly, Michael Haykin, in "Evangelicalism and the Enlightenment: A

among Evangelicals was postmillennial doctrine." Fuller, also no exception to this evangelical commonality in the eighteenth century, shared in Carey's optimism. Or, more chronologically appropriate, Carey shared in Fuller's optimism.[8] While the postmillennial optimism was commonly shared, Fuller's own unique postmillennial views were not embraced ubiquitously.[9]

Fuller's Unique Postmillennialism

Fuller's optimistic eschatology was rooted in what Phil Roberts calls "a historicist view of the Apocalypse"; that is, "believing along with Edwards that history was then in the period of the sixth vial . . . the period of the overthrow of the temporal power of Antichrist and the introduction to the final vial when God's truth and morality will exercise 'its spiritual dominion, or the hold which it has on the minds of men.'"[10] Like Roberts, Chris Chun also recognizes the significant influence of Edwards's interpretation of Revelation on Fuller's unique optimistic postmillennial views.[11] Chun specifically

Reassessment," challenged Bebbington's thesis that evangelicalism was "a product of the Enlightenment," while recognizing that the "shared characteristics clearly indicate that there are close ties between the eighteenth-century evangelicalism and the Enlightenment." He continued, "The older interpretation of these two movements as intrinsically hostile to each other needs to be scrapped, as does the view that the eighteenth-century evangelicalism was largely insulated from its cultural environment." Haykin, "Evangelicalism and the Enlightenment: A Reassessment," 48, 52.

8. Elwyn, *Northamptonshire Association*, 17. Roberts's evaluation of Fuller's eschatology is particularly telling. Roberts states, "His [Fuller's] eschatology, however unpopular it might be at present, was nonetheless his because he believed it was the accurate biblical position which in turn went the furthest to encourage the evangelization of the world." Roberts, "Andrew Fuller," 45.

9. For example, Chun proposed that in the endorsement of the English edition of Edwards's *An Humble Attempt* (1789), Sutcliff "distances himself from 'some of the prophecies.'" According to Chun, Sutcliff's distancing "may be yielding to the former preface (1748 edition) as written by five evangelical members of the Boston clergy. In other words, in aligning himself with the more established interpretation of Revelation 11, Sutcliff could be perceived as disassociating himself from the Edwardsean interpretation of prophecy." Chun, *Edwards in the Theology of Fuller*, 78.

10. Roberts, "Andrew Fuller," 45.

11. Chun's chapter, "Fuller's Missiological Optimism and *Humble Attempt*," is the most comprehensive analysis of Edwards and Fuller's eschatological views to date. Chun, *Edwards in the Theology of Fuller*, 71–83. Interestingly, his comparison chart of the seven seals indicated that nonconformist minister, Moses Lowman, was as influential, if not more so, as Edwards on some of Fuller's interpretations regarding the dating of the seals. See Table 3.2.2 *The Seven Seals* in Chun, *Edwards in the Theology of Fuller*, 73. The influence of Moses Lowman on other aspects of Fuller's interpretation of Revelation may be an area for further study. Chun clearly indicates that "Lowman's apocalyptic interpretations on Fuller's thinking . . . was greater than Lowman on Edwards."

centered Fuller's optimistic postmillennialism on what Chun describes as a "minority viewpoint" in Fuller's day respecting the slaying of the witnesses in Revelation 11.[12] "By far," according to Chun, "the prevailing interpretation during that era was that the horrendous persecution was yet to be seen."[13] Nonetheless, Fuller agreed with Edwards that the slaying of the witnesses represented the persecution of the church prior to the Reformation.[14]

Implications for Prayer

Optimistic Prayers

Chun's analysis of Fuller's appropriation of Edwards's optimistic eschatology concludes confidently that "there is no doubt that in the wellspring of Andrew Fuller, the missiological theologian, was the Edwardsean optimistic worldview that underpinned his exhortation in the Prayer Call of 1784."[15] Chun supports his claim by citing the frequent quotation of Edwards in Fuller's *Expository Discourses on the Apocalypse*, a shared minority view regarding the slaying of the witnesses in Revelation 11, and Fuller's quotation of Edwards's *An Humble Attempt* in the discourse on Revelation 11. Chun correctly states, "The acknowledgment of the *Humble Attempt* as an inspiration for the Prayer Call of 1784 is generally recognized in the secondary literatures [*sic*], but the apocalyptic portion that drove this eschatology, which in some sense was the engine for the optimism of this missionary effort, is often ignored."[16]

Another significant piece of evidence ought to be added to Chun's analysis regarding Fuller's appropriation of Edwards's eschatological optimism. In the initial publication of his *Persuasives*, Fuller stated:

> Might we not plead now with Christ, *Awake*, awake, put on strength, O arm of the Lord! awake, as in the ancient of days! art thou not it that didst cut the foe when hanging on the cross, that didst wound his interest in the day of Pentecost? And may we not plead that as God destroyed Babylon and delivered his

---

Chun, *Edwards in the Theology of Fuller*, 74. What remains to be seen is who, whether Lowman or Edwards, exercised a greater degree of influence on Fuller's interpretations. Chun's study is an excellent starting point.

12. Chun, *Edwards in the Theology of Fuller*, 79.

13. Chun, *Edwards in the Theology of Fuller*, 76–77.

14. Fuller, *Works*, 3:251; Chun, *Edwards in the Theology of Fuller*, 79.

15. Chun, *Edwards in the Theology of Fuller*, 80.

16. Chun, *Edwards in the Theology of Fuller*, 71.

church, so he would destroy the power and principles of mystical Babylon? He preserved a people, namely the *Waldenses,* who in the worst of times bowed not the knee to the image of this idol, and when they were nearly extirminated [*sic*] by persecution, raised up a set of men at the reformation [*sic*] who gave it a deadly wound, a wound which it has never recovered to this day.[17]

Note the similarity between Fuller's statement in his *Persuasives* and Edwards's *An Humble Attempt.*[18] Curiously, the entire quotation above is not included in the *Persuasives* published within Fuller's *Works.*[19] The paragraph may have been edited out in later editions due to its overt connection to Edwards and Fuller's minority view regarding the slaying of the witnesses in Revelation 11 as a past event.[20] Believing that the severe persecution of the church prophesied in Revelation 11 had already passed with victory over Rome in the Reformation, Fuller was optimistic that the prayers of the church would continue the work begun prior to the Reformation with the Waldenses.[21] As Fuller stated:

17. Fuller, *Persuasives*, 43. Emphasis original. Chun referred readers to Fuller's *Works* to note the similarities between Fuller's *Persuasives* and Edwards's *An Humble Attempt*. If Chun was aware of the abridgment in the *Works*, then he did not note as such. Chun, *Edwards in the Theology of Fuller*, 70.

18. Edwards stated in Part 3, Section 3, in *Humble Attempt*, that united efforts in prayer for revival were not premature but in line with the present times and prior fulfillment of prophecy in Rev 11:7–10; that is, "the time wherein the *witnesses lie dead in the streets of the great city*, doubtless signifies the time wherein the true church of Christ is lowest of all, most of all prevailed against by antichrist, and nearest to an utter extinction; the time wherein there is left the least visibility of the church of Christ yet subsisting in the world." Edwards, *Humble Attempt*, 299. Emphasis original. Fuller quoted this quotation from Edwards's *An Humble Attempt* in his expository discourse on Revelation 11. Fuller concluded then, "I cannot therefore but think with him that the persecution and slaughter of the witnesses *preceded the Reformation*." Fuller, *Works*, 3:251. Emphasis original.

19. Fuller, *Works*, 3:667. In addition to the quotation cited below, one other large quotation is not included in Fuller's *Works*. Compare Fuller, *Persuasives*, 44–45; Fuller, *Works*, 3:668. Chun states that Fuller preached two sermons at the association meeting in Nottingham, *The Nature and Importance of Walking by Faith* and *Persuasives to General Union in Extraordinary Prayer*. While the two works were published together, Chun probably misidentifies Fuller's *Persuasives* as a sermon. If Fuller's *Persuasives* was a second sermon preached at the association meeting, then the second sermon was curiously left out of the minutes, an exclusion particularly unlikely considering that this was the circular letter from which issued the fabled Prayer Call of 1784.

20. Chun, *Edwards in the Theology of Fuller*, 80.

21. Chun, *Edwards in the Theology of Fuller*, 79–80. Chun made a similar point in his analysis of Fuller's *Apocalypse*. Chun states, "Like Edwards, Fuller saw them as the faithful witnesses who were persecuted prior to the Reformation, and among many

> O let us pray to the Lord Jesus that the work may be carried
> on—*that antichrist may be consumed with the spirit of his mouth,
> and destroyed by the brightness of his coming!*—that the king-
> doms of this world may become the kingdoms of our Lord and
> of his Christ, and that he may reign forever and ever.[22]

The affinity of Fuller's *Persuasives* with elements of Edwards's *An Humble
Attempt* may further support Chun's confident claim.[23] With respect to his
optimistic postmillennialism, Fuller found a theological ally in Edwards.
Fuller's heart was stoked through reading Edwards's *An Humble Attempt*,
along with Sutcliff in particular, to reissue a call to prayer within his denomination and "to any others who love and long for the coming of Christ's
blessed kingdom, and whose hearts may be inclined to unite in seeking its
welfare."[24] It is important to note that Fuller's theology of prayer expressed
a strong eschatological dimension nearly thirty years prior to his *Expository
Discourses on the Apocalypse*.

The Lord's Prayer and Prayer's Eschatological End

A strong eschatological dimension to Fuller's theology of prayer can also
be seen in his exposition of the Lord's Prayer. Fuller's exposition of the Sermon on the Mount began on June 6, 1784, immediately after the prayer
call was issued and his return to Kettering from the association meeting at
Nottingham.[25] Fuller drafted his *Persuasives*, a publication already noted to
be full of eschatological optimism, after he expounded on the Lord's Prayer
in Matthew 6. On August 10, 1784, Fuller wrote in his diary, "Occupied in

---

others he also identified them as the Waldenses, Albigenses and Bohemians." Chun,
Edwards in the Theology of Fuller, 80.

22. The italicized text is not included in Fuller's *Works*. Compare Fuller, *Persuasives*,
43; Fuller, *Works*, 3:667.

23. Chun in particular notes the similarity of Fuller's *Persuasives* with themes
"throughout *Humble Attempt* . . . especially . . . in Part II." Chun, *Edwards in the Theology of Fuller*, 70n19. The above evidence highlights the similarity between the eschatology laden in the *Persuasives* that is especially seen in Part 3, Section 3 of Edwards,
Humble Attempt.

24. The quotation is from Fuller, *Persuasives*, 41. Sutcliff has been credited with the
actual issuing of the call after Fuller's sermon, *The Nature and Importance of Walking
by Faith*—the same sermon to which Fuller's *Persuasives* were appended for publication
shortly after the association meeting. Haykin, *One Heart and One Soul*, 164–65; Ryland,
Nature, Evidences, and Advantages, 11–12.

25. See Appendix 2 for a proposed date for Fuller's exposition of the Lord's Prayer
on July 25, 1784. If correct, then the exposition of the Lord's prayer took place just one
month after the prayer call was issued at Nottingham on June 2, 1784.

writing some *persuasives to united prayer for the revival of real religion*, for the press."[26] The two works not only share chronological proximity, they also share a thematic correlation with respect to the eschatological purpose of prayer.

In expounding on the "order" of the Lord's Prayer, Fuller noted that two things "must have . . . precedence in all of our prayers."[27] The first item is "the glory of God's character."[28] The second item is "the coming of his kingdom." These two were held in equal value. In Fuller's estimation, they together "stand first in all his works."[29] Respecting this order, Fuller expounded on the priority of praying for the coming of Christ's kingdom:

> We are taught to pray for even the coming of God's kingdom, and the universal prevalence of righteousness in the world, in subserviency to the honour of his name. It is to this end that God himself pursues these great objects; to this end therefore we must pray for them. But though they a placed [*sic*] *after* the hallowing of his name, yet they stand *before* any private petitions of ours, and in this order each requires to be sought. Why is it that so little has been done, from age to age, for the general interest of Christ? Is it not owing to a practical error on this subject? Placing our own private interests before his, dwelling in our ceiled houses, while the temple of God has been in ruins, or at most seeking the prosperity of a small part of the church which happens to be connected with us, to the utter neglect of the general kingdom of the Redeemer?[30]

The similarity of themes between Fuller's exposition and *Persuasives* can be clearly seen here. In the first persuasive, Fuller stated, "Yea he even *commands* us to pray for the coming of his kingdom before we ask for our *daily bread*."[31] Fuller bolstered his congregation's assurance that God would certainly answer the prayers of those who prioritize what God, himself, had prioritized. Fuller stated, "Christ would not have directed us to ask for a specific object, and without any proviso, when he knew it would never be granted."[32] Thus, whether praying for the coming of Christ's kingdom

26. Fuller, *Complete Works: Diary*, 1:66. Compare with the timeline in Appendix 2.
27. Fuller, *Works*, 1:579.
28. Fuller, *Works*, 1:579. The importance of the glory of God's character in Fuller's theology of prayer was explored in chapter 2.
29. Fuller, *Works*, 1:579.
30. Fuller, *Works*, 1:580. Emphasis original.
31. Fuller, *Works*, 3:666.
32. Fuller, *Works*, 1:580.

meant "the Messiah's kingdom, or . . . that state of things when the kingdom shall be delivered up to the Father, and God shall be all in all, it makes no difference."[33] Fuller understood that his listeners may hold differing opinions regarding the meaning of Jesus's command to pray for the coming kingdom of Christ. The difference, in Fuller's thinking, neither lessened the immediacy of the command nor the optimism under which such a prayer should be undertaken. He stated:

> The coming of the latter supposes the gradual completion of the former: to pray therefore what is ultimate in the system is to pray for whatever is intermediate. At present God's name, instead of being sanctified in the earth, is disregarded and blasphemed. He reigns in the heart of but few of the children of men. Instead of earth resembling heaven, as to obedience to the Divine will, it bears a much nearer resemblance to hell. But it shall not be thus always. He who taught us thus to pray was manifested to destroy the works of the devil, and destroyed they will be. And as the grand means by which this great end will be accomplished is the preaching of the cross, we have abundance of encouragement to persevere in that arduous employment.[34]

A great deal of Fuller's optimism in prayer and evangelism was linked to his faith that God will bring about the ultimate end of which he promised; namely, the exaltation of the glory of his character and the coming of the victorious kingdom of Christ.[35] Therefore, to pray for what God has promised to do ultimately is to pray with the greatest degree of assurance and optimism that God will bring about that which one has prayed.[36] As Fuller encouraged his congregants while expounding Matt 7:7–12, "It is of great account in prayer to lay hold of the *promises*. It is this [that] constitutes it the prayer of faith."[37] The postmillennial optimism of Fuller's prayer can be nuanced as an optimism that was rooted in the promises of Scripture; in particular, the glory of God's character and the coming of Christ's kingdom. As such, Fuller encouraged in his *Persuasives*:

---

33. Fuller, *Works*, 1:580

34. Fuller, *Works*, 1:580.

35. In his sermon "The Nature and Importance of Walking by Faith," Fuller stated, "Our hope of a *better state, when this is over*, is built on faith in God's testimony." Fuller, *Works*, 1:131.

36. The link between prayers and the promises of God was also seen clearly in Fuller's short paper on the harmony between God's commands and promises and the prayers of saints in Scripture. Fuller, "Harmony of Scripture."

37. Fuller, *Works*, 1:587.

For an absolute impossibility we can have no hope, and for what God hath declared shall never come to pass, we can have no warrant to pray; but when we pray for the spread of Christ's kingdom, our object is clogged with neither of these difficulties. On the contrary, it is accompanied with the strongest assurances of success. Let us not imagine that God has yet done all he intends to do for his church; or that Christ has yet seen of the travail of his soul so as to be *satisfied*.[38]

Fuller firmly believed that the prayers of the saints were to be an instrumental means for bringing about God's eschatological ends for the earth and the establishment of his kingdom. That which has preeminence in God's order for prayer, likewise, has preeminence in man's hope for fulfillment. Following the order of the Lord's Prayer, just as "God's name and cause in the world" have supremacy in all things, "the three petitions in respect of God's name and cause in the world" precede those "which regard our own immediate wants."[39]

Example of Fuller's Practice of Prayer

"Faith penetrates futurity," preached Andrew Fuller to the Devonshire Square congregation in London on June 26, 1796.[40] He also preached, 12 years prior for those gathered in Nottingham at the 1784 association meeting, "a life of faith will ever be a life of prayer."[41] This was the same association meeting from which the Prayer Call issued and the same sermon to which Fuller appended his *Persuasives*. He called his listeners to join him in praying that "all . . . in every place call upon the name of Jesus Christ our Lord, both theirs and ours!"[42] According to Fuller, followers of Jesus can persist prioritizing God's name and cause in the world with their prayer when their faith rests on the promises of God's word. When, in prayer, people prioritize God's name and cause in the world their faith "penetrates futurity." As Fuller more fully stated, "Faith penetrates futurity; it rends the veil and pierces into an unknown world; it fixes its eye on eternity."[43] Fuller made faith in God's

38. Fuller, *Persuasives*, 45.

39. Fuller, *Works*, 1:581.

40. Fuller, *Works*, 1:362–67. The sermon taken from Phil 4:7 and the surrounding verses was titled, "The Peace of God."

41. Fuller, *Works*, 1:131.

42. Fuller, *Works*, 1:131.

43. Fuller, *Works*, 1:365–66.

eschatological promises a centerpiece of the prayer movement he aided in
launching and sustaining through his ministry.

Fuller, likewise, made faith in God's eschatological promises a centerpiece of his personal prayer life and anchor through life's most painful
trials. Recall the agonizing circumstance of Fuller watching the health of
his daughter Sarah eroding. Fuller turned to the promise in Rev 7:16–17
to encourage his daughter, and, surely, to encourage his own heart.[44] Fuller
commented that the promise aided "to stimulate the servants of God in this
world to persevere."[45] "Written about the same time" in an undated letter to
Ryland, Fuller stated that he could not imagine the anguish of nursing a sick
child without "the hope of the gospel."[46] Fuller continued:

> Sure [*sic*] I know something more than I did, of the meaning of
> "Thanks be to God for his unspeakable gift!" and "Underneath
> are the everlasting arms!" with many other passages. And yet,
> after all, O what shall I say? I am not without hope—hope, as I
> said, with which I would not part for ten thousand worlds; but I
> have, as well, painful fears.[47]

With raw honesty, Fuller admitted that the certainty of hope he possessed
in the gospel was plagued frequently by fear.[48] Fuller expressed in his diary
how his fears, to the detriment of his confidence in prayer, undercut his
hope in the promise of the gospel. Fuller wrote:

> For this month past I have had great exercise of heart on account
> of my poor little girl . . . Sometimes pleading hard with God
> on account of her, at other times ready to despair, and to fear
> God would never hear me. Lord's day March 19 was a distress-
> ing day to me. My concern for the loss of her body is but trifling
> compared with that of her soul! Preached & prayed much from
> Matthew 15.25, Lord help me! On the Monday I carried her to-
> wards Northampton . . . was exceedingly distressed on the Mon-
> day night . . . Went to prayer with a heart almost broken. Some
> encouragement from a conversation with dear Brother Ryland.
> I observed "God had not bound himself to hear the prayers of
> anyone for the salvation of the soul of another." He replied, "But
> if he has not, he very frequently does so, and hence perhaps
> through grace does not run in the *blood*, yet we frequently see it

---

44. Ryland, *Work of Faith*, 273.

45. Fuller, *Works*, 3:229.

46. Ryland, *Work of Faith*, 278–79.

47. Ryland, *Work of Faith*, 279.

48. Fuller believed fear to be the opposite of faith.

does in the *line*. Many more of the children of God's children are gracious than others." I know neither I nor mine have any claim upon the Almighty for mercy, but as long as there is life it shall be my business surely to implore it![49]

Ryland's correction reminded Fuller that while the promises of God did not entitle him to come before God as a claimant with a demand, the promises of God provided a warrant for Fuller to come before God as a petitioner imploring for the salvation of his daughter. Ultimately, Fuller's prayers for his daughter modeled, albeit imperfectly, the "faith penetrating futurity" by imploring God for more than her temporal healing. In prayer, he sought to fix his eyes on eternity, the glory of God's name, and expansion of God's cause within his home.

Implications for Doctrine

Prayers of the Saints: Revelation 8:1–5

Fuller finished his *Expository Discourses on the Apocalypse* after nearly thirty years of seeing churches within and outside of his denomination unite in prayer for the expansion of Christ's kingdom. There is a reason to believe that Fuller's interpretation of Scripture's eschatological promises, in particular, those within Revelation, were colored by events stemming from the Prayer Call of 1784. The surging activity in prayer appears to bear implications for Fuller's postmillennial, optimistic eschatology. As he admitted in commenting on the commencement of the angel's flight, "We are in danger of magnifying the events of our own times."[50] Nonetheless, recent events led Fuller to a greater degree of confidence regarding the impending victorious reign of Christ.

Chun correctly states that "Edwards is willing to speak explicitly about the end time being near" more than Fuller.[51] Even so, Fuller was not bashful regarding his belief that the recent rise of prayer and disinterested gospel effort was a sign that the end was drawing near.[52] In expounding on the Seventh Seal in Revelation 8, Fuller stated:

49. Fuller, *Complete Works: Diary*, 1:169–70.

50. Fuller, *Works*, 3:269.

51. Chun, *Edwards in the Theology of Fuller*, 75.

52. One of the clearest examples of Fuller interpreting prophecy in light of current events was his understanding of the "earthquake" in Revelation 11 to refer most likely to the French Revolution. He stated, "All things considered, I know of no event that seems to correspond so well with the prophecy as *late revolution in France*." Fuller,

Our great High Priest, having offered himself without spot to God, passed into the heavens, where he ever liveth to make intercession for us. Through him our prayers ascend with acceptance before God.

The "prayers" here referred to appear to have a special relation to the events about to be predicted by the sounding of the trumpets. The events would occur in answer to those prayers; which might be so many intercessions for the success of Christ's cause, and against that of its adversaries. Heathen Rome was overthrown in answer to the prayers of the souls under the altar, and Christian Rome may fall in the same manner.[53]

Chun correctly observes that, like Edwards, "Fuller equally stressed prayer as the means to expedite the kingdom."[54] The quotation also clearly demonstrates that Fuller understood prayer to be part of expediting the judgment of adversaries to Christ's kingdom.[55] The theme of victory and judgment are also present in Fuller's exposition regarding the slaying of the witnesses in Revelation 11.

From the Edge of Darkness to Brightness

The inauguration of the kingdom clearly goes hand-in-hand with the inauguration of judgment. And here, too, prayer has a role. Fuller expounded regarding the authority of the witnesses to shut the sky or call down plagues:

Their having "power to shut heaven that it rain not in the days of their prophecy, to turn waters into blood, and to smite the earth with plagues as often as they will," denotes the influence of prayer when presented in faith and in conformity to the will of

---

Works, 3:252.

53. Fuller, *Works*, 3:230.

54. Chun, *Edwards in the Theology of Fuller*, 75. Neither explicitly addressed by Chun nor dealt with in the present work, Fuller treated prayer in his *Expository Discourses on the Apocalypse* as a means for ushering the coming victory and *judgment* of the Eschaton. Fuller did not divide the coming of Christ's kingdom and judgment into two chronological happenings, but, nonetheless, the theme of judgment is distinguishable from the theme of victory brought about through prayer.

55. Not explicitly addressed by Chun, nor dealt with in the present work, Fuller seems to have understood prayer to be a means for ushering the coming victory and *judgment* of the Eschaton. Fuller did not divide the coming of Christ's kingdom and judgment into two chronological happenings, but, nonetheless, the theme of judgment is distinguishable from the theme of victory brought about through prayer. From the researcher's perspective, little has been done regarding Fuller's correlation between prayer for the kingdom and the judgment of sinners.

God. There is a reference no doubt to the prayer of Elijah against apostate Israel, which prayer was answered with a dearth: but, without any thing [sic] properly miraculous, the prayers of God's suffering servants may draw down both temporal and spiritual judgments on persecuting nations. The terrible things which God is now in righteousness inflicting on the nations may be in answer to the prayers of his servants of former ages, who century after century have been crying, "How long, O Lord, holy and true, dost thou not judge and avenge our blood on them that dwell on the earth?" Such cries enter the ears of the Lord of hosts, and must be answered.[56]

Fuller believed that the "witnesses" in Revelation 11 signified the severe persecution "principally found in that of the *Waldenses* and *Albigenses*."[57] Thus, the current judgment—"the terrible things which God is now in righteousness inflicting on the nations"—was in answer to the prayers of the Waldenses, Albigenses, and other saints who concurrently or preceding them persevered through persecution. Fuller rejected the notion of "Bishop Newton" that witnesses symbolized only "councils, princes, and eminent men."[58] Fuller countered:

They will be found, I doubt not, in great numbers amongst those who were unknown, and consequently unnoticed by historians. God hath chosen the *things that are not* to bring to naught the things that are. Let a church history of our own times be written on the principles of that of Mosheim, and the great body of the most faithful witnesses would have no place in it.[59]

What a fitting perspective for a Baptist pastor spearheading a prayer and mission movement among Nonconformist congregations throughout the British Empire. The Baptists, like the majority of Nonconformity, were disqualified from most noble accolades and services that belonged to those within the Church of England. Nonetheless, their prayers just like the prayers of the witnesses before them availed much in the power of God.

While Fuller's confidence in the prominent role of prayer to inaugurate the kingdom was consistent for upwards of thirty years, his perspective regarding the nearness of Christ's coming kingdom may be observably more optimistic near the end of his life. Fuller could encourage the fledgling

56. Fuller, *Works*, 3:245.

57. Fuller, *Works*, 3:246.

58. Fuller, *Works*, 3:245.

59. Fuller, *Works*, 3:245–46. Johann Lorenz Mosheim was a German church historian of the early-to-mid-eighteenth century. Stroup, "Mosheim, Johann Lorenz."

prayer movement in its infancy, "consider *what God has promised to do for his church in times to come.*"[60] Consider that the promise was not given to councils, princes, nor eminent men only. The promise was given to the church. Fuller's interpretation of Revelation 11 that God was currently answering the prayers of the witnesses in aiding the coming kingdom but ushering in righteous judgment furthered his confidence to invite others to unite in prayer. Fuller knew, "*It will not be in vain, whatever be the immediate and apparent issue of it.*"[61] He was assured, like the witnesses represented in Revelation 11, their prayers were not in vain. Fuller stated, "But suppose we should never live to see those days, still our labour shall not be in vain in the Lord. To say the least of it, God would be glorified, and that would be no little thing. It would convey this piece of intelligence to the world, that God has yet some hearty friends in it, and who will continue to pray to him in the darkest times."[62]

Nearing the end of his life, Fuller's confidence and optimism appeared to reach its zenith. Expounding on Revelation 14 and considering the increase in "earnest prayer and disinterested exertion," Fuller stated, "We have seen enough . . . to convince us with what ease the great God, by touching the hearts of a few individuals, can accomplish it."[63] Albeit optimistic regarding the future and prayer's effect, in 1784 Fuller viewed the church as standing on the edge of the darkest of times. In 1814, Fuller viewed the church as standing on the edge of the brightest of times, the inauguration of the kingdom through "the evangelization of *every* nation, and kindred, and tongue, and people."[64] Fuller's shift in seeing the nearness of the kingdom seems to be in relationship to the success of the prayer movement, and activities that sprouted it, that started at Nottingham in 1784.[65]

60. Fuller, *Persuasives*, 45. Emphasis original.
61. Fuller, *Persuasives*, 46. Emphasis original.
62. Fuller, *Persuasives*, 46–47.
63. Fuller, *Works*, 3:270.
64. Fuller, *Works*, 3:270.
65. Perhaps Fuller would have agreed with E.A. Payne's general sentiment that June 1784, the issuing of the Prayer Call, should be remembered as equally significant in the minds of Baptists with October 1792, the founding of the Baptist Missionary Society. Payne, "Prayer Call of 1784," 19–30.

Conclusion

Doctrine's Influence on Prayer

The postmillennial optimism of Edwards's *An Humble Attempt* permeated Fuller's *Persuasives*.[66] An abridged version of Fuller's *Persuasives* appeared in Fuller's *Works*. The abridgements appear to reflect the removal of specific references to prophetic fulfillment associated with historical events. The early influence of Edwards's *An Humble Attempt* and his eschatological views may be further supported by the content preserved in the first edition of *Persuasives*. Fuller's eschatological convictions in *Persuasives* undergirded his case for *A General Union in Prayer for the Revival of Real Religion*.[67] Commenting on the postmillennial views espoused by both Edwards and Fuller, Chun states, "For good or ill, it is in this eschatological climate, that BMS and the Modern Missionary Movement was born."[68] One may add, it was also in this eschatological climate that the Prayer Call of 1784 originated.

Fuller's strong eschatological convictions also permeated his exposition of the Lord's Prayer, which was likely composed and delivered near the same time as his writing and publication of *Persuasives*.[69] God's eschatological end of glorifying his name and cause permeated Fuller's understanding of the "order" of the Lord's Prayer. Since his conviction was that Lord's Prayer was a model prayer for all prayers to follow, Fuller believed that the order of glorifying God's name and cause out to be preeminent in all prayers.

Prayer's Influence on Doctrine

Fuller's experiences stemming from the Prayer Call of 1784 clearly sustained, and perhaps even increased, his certainty regarding Christ's imminent postmillennial reign. The sustained efforts in prayer, connected with recent advances in missionary efforts throughout the Empire, appear to have increased Fuller's certainty that the time of Christ's reign was drawing

66. Wheeler claimed that the influence of Edwards's *An Humble Attempt* could be seen with the mention of the work in his diary. The ubiquity of *Humble Attempt* in Fuller's *Persuasives* further supports Wheeler's claim. Wheeler, "Eminent Spirituality and Eminent Usefulness," 33n64.

67. Further study could be done respecting the paragraphs excluded from Fuller's works. There may be other reasons beyond reference to specific historical events. Above, the researcher has analyzed the paragraph excluded from Fuller's second persuasive. The largest exclusion is the second, third, and fourth paragraphs of the third persuasive. Fuller, *Persuasives*, 43–45.

68. Chun, *Edwards in the Theology of Fuller*, 81.

69. See Appendix 2 for probable dating of Fuller's exposition of the Lord's Prayer.

near. Based on his interpretation of the witnesses' prayers in Revelation 8, Fuller believed that prayer did, and would continue to, play a role in exacting righteous judgment on opponents of Christ's kingdom.[70] Fuller understood prayer as a vital means for ushering both the victory of Christ's kingdom and the judgment of his opponents. The sustained efforts in prayer stretching from 1784 through Fuller's death likely increased his already optimistic outlook that the end was near.

70. The correlation in Fuller's thinking between coming judgment, eschatology, and prayer has not been otherwise recognized by prior studies.

Conclusion

Evaluation of the Multifaceted Approach

THE MULTIFACETED DOCTRINAL APPROACH to constructing Fuller's theology of prayer demonstrates that Fuller's theology of prayer—both his belief and practice of prayer—informed and was informed by aspects of six major doctrines. As one may expect, Fuller's doctrine of God bore the most significant influence in answering critical questions related to the nature and moods of Christian prayer. Even so, other doctrines bore a significant amount of influence on Fuller's theology of prayer as a whole. The following paragraphs survey the major findings with respect to the six select corollary doctrines.

The Father and Prayer

Considering "the Father and Prayer" as principally exploring the correlation between Fuller's doctrine of God and prayer, Fuller's doctrine of the knowledge of God demonstrated the most significant influence upon Fuller's theology of prayer. Fuller's doctrine of the knowledge of God answered questions regarding the why, who, and how of prayer:

> *Why should one pray?*—The glory of the divine character provides enduring motivation for all worship and prayer.

> *Who should pray?*—The harmony of God's moral government obligates all humans to pray.

> *How should one pray?*—Each person ought to pray out of a spirit of love for God according to the will of God.

The why, who, and how questions are the most critical questions to answer regarding a Christian theology of prayer. Without a proper motivation, object, or proper means for praying, further construction of a theology of prayer would be reduced merely to academic exercise. Each of these critical questions are informed chiefly by Fuller's doctrine of the knowledge of God.

Conversely, the influence of Fuller's theology of prayer on his doctrine of God may be observed in the priority of prayer as the appointed means for gaining a proper love and knowledge of God. Prayer is the God-ordained means for tasting, feeling, and handling the word of life. Without prayer, one's knowledge of, communion with, and love for God would be utterly stifled.

The Son and Prayer

Fuller's doctrine of the Trinity, in particular his doctrine of the Son, informed Fuller's understanding of the entire Godhead as the proper object of prayer. In particular, prayers offered to Christ were not only warranted but encouraged through Fuller's systematic reflection on the deity and work of Christ. Fuller's doctrine of the work of Christ also informed his theology of prayer regarding the ongoing work of Christ as intercessor and the proper attitude of one approaching God in prayer. Fuller held that a purely commercial view of the atonement violated the proper posture of the heart for one approaching God in prayer. With a commercial understanding, one may approach God as a claimant rather than a supplicant for mercy. In Fuller's understanding, the commercial view also truncated Christ's ongoing work as intercessor and mediator before the Father as superfluous. Entitled claimants, unlike supplicants, have no need for a mediator or intercessor to advocate on their behalf.

Fuller's interpretation of prayers in Scripture directed to Christ clearly informed or augmented his arguments for the deity of Christ. Stephen's prayer in Acts 7, the prayer of the Canaanite woman, and the general practice of primitive Christians to call out to Christ in prayer were primary biblical evidences in Fuller's arguments for the deity of Christ.

The Spirit and Prayer

Fuller's doctrine of the Spirit, perhaps more than any other doctrine, demonstrated the most reciprocity with Fuller's theology of prayer. The two are so closely related that the researcher struggled to see a clear line between the doctrine's influence on Fuller's theology of prayer, and *vice versa*. Fuller's doctrine of the Spirit undergirded his theology of prayer. Equally, he believed that the Spirit's influences were in direct correlation with one's praying for the outpouring of God's Spirit. Building upon the memorable adage credited to William Carey—expect great things from God; attempt great things for God—the researcher proposes that Fuller's great expectations and attempts for the kingdom of Christ were borne and sustained in the interplay between his doctrine of the Spirit and theology of prayer. Stated another way, prayer was the vital connection between Fuller's use of means and utter dependence on the Spirit for any effect to come from human efforts. You ought not to have the one without the other.

Humanity and Prayer

Fuller's doctrine of humanity informed his theology of prayer with respect to answering the proto-Modern Question—whether it be the duty of the unregenerate to pray. Fuller's positive affirmation—that prayer is the duty of all persons regardless of their spiritual state—safeguarded first principles of the gospel. According to Fuller, denying one's obligation to pray may lead to the denial of one's obligation to repent and believe in Christ.

Fuller's practice of prayer, poignantly captured in his diary entries in 1780, demonstrated the significant reciprocity between Fuller's doctrine of human depravity and his theology of prayer. Within four years of recording that he found a heart for praying for the lost in his congregation, Fuller, likewise, found a heart for, and called his association to join him in, praying for the interest of the lost around the world. Fuller's own experience with his depravity and private prayer life in 1780 may have laid the stalwart foundation needed to sustain a prayer movement starting in 1784 and missionary movement starting in 1792.

Two writings in particular articulated the influence of Fuller's theology of prayer on his doctrine of human depravity and human inability. In *The Backslider*, Fuller argued, among other things, that prayer was the God-ordained means for sustaining a proper view of one's inability and dependence on the power of God. Also in *The Backslider*, Fuller described prayer as central to not only combatting sin, but also maintaining a proper view of oneself before God. As such, prayer is the vital means for restoring full communion and peace with God. Similarly, in his paper, "The Harmony of Scripture Precepts, Prayers, and Promises," Fuller argued that the prayers of saints in Scripture testified to "the moral *insufficiency* of the creature" and "the *all-sufficiency* of the God of Grace."[1] Fuller's own practice of

---

1. Fuller, "Harmony of Scripture," 221. Emphasis original.

prayer comported with such an understanding of recognizing both his own insufficiency, while, at the same time, also recognizing the all-sufficiency of Christ. Prayer modeled after the examples of Scripture affirms both.

The Church and Prayer

Fuller's ecclesial distinction between positive institutions and moral obligations informed Fuller's theology of prayer.[2] Fuller's ecclesial distinction comported with his conviction that prayer was the duty of all persons. The distinction also provided a helpful explanation for why public prayers in the church and home were not offerings of false security for those who had not yet called on the name of Christ. Stated differently, praying with or inviting them to pray was not inviting them to partake in a closed institution of the church. As such, Fuller practiced and encouraged free prayer in the home and in public gatherings. Considering the mission of the church, Fuller's convictions influenced his activism with respect to the Prayer Call of 1784, even at its infancy, being a call to all who have an interest in the expansion of the kingdom of Christ. Fuller's commitment to the expansion of Christ's kingdom superseded his commitment to expand the Particular Baptist interests.

The example of primitive believers in Scripture calling on the name of Christ informed Fuller's understanding of the nature of the church. Fuller notably described the practice of calling on the name of Jesus as "*the* characteristic of a primitive believer."[3] The practice of New Testament saints informed Fuller's understanding of the nature of the church as a congregation of faithful men who called properly on his name.

The Last Things and Prayer

Fuller's postmillennial optimism certainly informed his theology of prayer. *Persuasives*, Fuller's first major publication, was perhaps the clearest reflection of such a postmillennial influence on his theology of prayer. The work also demonstrated the early influence of Edwards's *An Humble Attempt* on Fuller's eschatological views. While Fuller's postmillennial expectations may no longer be in vogue, Chun states correctly, "it is in this eschatological

---

2. In a circular letter, "The Practical Uses of Christian Baptism" (1802), Fuller used the imagery of a "garden enclosed" to describe the nature of the church as separated and set apart from the world. Fuller, *Works*, 3:343.

3. Fuller, *Works*, 3:492.

climate, that the BMS and the Modern Missionary Movement was born."[4] To Chun's observation, the researcher adds that it was in this eschatological climate that the Prayer Call of 1784 was, likewise, born. The influence of the former on the latter cannot be overstated.

Fuller's strong eschatological convictions, likewise, permeated his exposition of the Lord's Prayer. Not coincidentally, Fuller expounded on the Sermon on the Mount within the same time frame as writing *Persuasives*. Fuller's first major publication was saturated with the eschatological expectations and language of the Sermon on the Mount.[5]

Fuller's eschatological optimism was furthered by the success of the events stemming from the Prayer Call of 1784. Fuller made these observations near the end of his life in one of his last publications, *Expository Discourses on the Apocalypse*. Fuller's expository commentary on Revelation expressed how the sustained efforts in prayer and recent advances in mission efforts around the globe increased his certainty that the time of Christ's victorious reign was at hand. Indeed, Fuller saw these events as truly "the commencement of the angel's flight."[6]

Evaluation of Fuller's Theology of Prayer

Fuller's belief and practice regarding prayer were shaped chiefly by elements within his doctrine of God; namely, his doctrine of the knowledge of God, the glory of the divine character, and harmony of God's moral government. Considering who God is and the way he works in the world informed Fuller's theology of prayer respecting the proper object, motivation, and disposition of the heart for prayer.

Consider how Fuller's doctrine of the Spirit comported with his belief that prayer is the vital connection between the use of means and total dependence on the Spirit. Fuller's doctrine of humanity influenced his understanding that a person ought to come before God as a supplicant for mercy rather than as a claimant. His doctrine of humanity bore significant implications for the proper posture of the heart in one's approach to God in prayer.

Conversely, Fuller's theology of prayer bore a significant amount of influence reciprocally with these major Christian doctrines. Fuller's doctrine of the Son and the church were influenced by his interpretation of

4. Chun, *Edwards in the Theology of Fuller*, 81.

5. There is room here for further analysis detailing the exact phrases and expositions from which Fuller's *Persuasives* were drawing upon. Nonetheless, the researcher is confident in his observation.

6. Fuller, *Works*, 3:270.

the primitive Christians' calling on the name of Christ. Fuller interpreted the prayers of New Testament saints, calling on the name of Christ, as supporting evidence for the deity of Christ and as the defining characteristic of those who belong to the kingdom of Christ. Calling on the name of Christ, for Fuller, was a shibboleth of orthodox Christology and belonging to the kingdom of Christ.

Fuller's systematic reflection on prayer concerning multiple doctrinal points also corroborates the claims made by Fuller scholars that prayer was a vital aspect of his spirituality and theological reflection. The work failed to answer some questions related to Fuller's theology of prayer. Specifically, further consideration should be given to Fuller's theology of prayer as reflected in his diary and letters. The appendix of quotations from Fuller's diary is a good starting point. The researcher supposes that Fuller's diary would illuminate some aspects of Fuller's practice of prayer. The findings far exceeded the researcher's expectations. More work could be done to extract and expound on the entries related to prayer from Fuller's diary. For at least two reasons, Fuller's diary represents, in the researcher's estimation, a rare preservation of an often undocumented aspect of Baptist spirituality.[7] First, prayers were rarely written or preserved within the seventeenth- and eighteenth-century Baptist tradition of free, or extemporaneous, prayers. Such was Fuller's practice. Second, in Fuller's day, many spiritual diaries where thoughts on prayer or specific prayers may have been recorded were destroyed at the author's request. Such was Fuller's request. Thankfully, Fuller's friends did not completely honor his dying wish.[8]

Correlating perhaps to the purpose of Fuller's spiritual diary, the study did not explore Fuller's understanding or concern for "watchfulness." Watchfulness was a theme that developed alongside a number of Fuller's works concerning prayer.[9] Watchfulness was a frequently referenced spiritual discipline of the seventeenth-century Puritans.[10] A future work could consider the differences between Fuller's understandings of watchfulness in relation to prayer. Likewise, one could consider the similarities and

7. For more on the difficulties surrounding the study of prayer within Baptist spirituality, see Ellis, "From the Heart," 104. Ellis's study could be enhanced by contrasting what is stated about prayer, principally from Bunyan's practice and writings, with the practice of prayer recorded in Fuller's diary.

8. For more details on the preservation of Fuller's diary, see McMullen and Whelan, "Introduction," xiii.

9. See, for instance, his essay "On Spiritual Declension and the Means of Revival" and *The Backslider* in Fuller, *Works*, 3:620–21, 637, 646, and 652.

10. For more on watchfulness in seventeenth-century Puritanism, see Hedges, *Watchfulness*.

differences between the seventeenth-century Puritan practice and understanding of watchfulness with that of the eighteenth-century Particular
Baptists.

Finally, further attention can be given to prayer within Fuller's pastoral
theology.

Nigel Wheeler argues that "effective prayer was a [sic] considered to be
as much as a gift as the ability to preach well."[11] The present study did little
to corroborate his claim. The multifaceted approach did not consider the
broader opinions of Particular Baptist ministers or congregants regarding
their emphasis on prayer in pastoral leadership. The study did demonstrate
Fuller's critical role in providing leadership to a budding prayer movement
that emphasized the role of prayer for all members of the church rather than
the priority of prayer for officers, especially elders, of the church. One may
consider if the pastor's public prayer still feature as prominently in Fuller's
day among his circle of friends or more broadly among Particular Baptists
in the eighteenth century. Grant proposed, in *Andrew Fuller and the Evangelical Renewal of Pastoral Theology*, that "Fuller's renewed pastoral theology
was particularly expressed in his preaching."[12] If correct, does it stand to
reason that the evangelical renewal of preaching muffled his prayer? Or,
more likely, did Fuller's theology of prayer, likewise, go through an evangelical renewal concurrent with his preaching? If the latter, then the renewal
may be manifest principally in the more missional focus of prayer meetings
within Fuller's congregation, the Northamptonshire Baptist Association,
and Baptist congregations at large on either side of the Atlantic.[13]

11. Wheeler, "Eminent Spirituality and Eminent Usefulness, " 149.

12. Grant, *Andrew Fuller*, 8.

13. One could compare Hinson's proposal that Baptist spirituality shifted from a
contemplative to a conversionist agenda in the mid-eighteenth century with Deweese's
observation that the Prayer Call of 1784 "significantly altered the nature of Baptist
prayer meetings by adding a strong missionary character to them." Compare Hinson,
"Baptist Spirituality," 292; Deweese, *Prayer in Baptist Life*, 45–46. In recent decades,
Christian spirituality, spiritual formation, and spiritual theology have become important concepts in the global evangelical community. Consequently, an accessible and
reliable academic resource is needed on these topics—one that will offer a discerning
orientation to the wealth of ecumenical resources available while still highlighting the
distinct heritage and affirming the core grace-centered values of classic evangelical
spirituality. The Dictionary of Christian Spirituality reflects an overarching interpretive
framework for evangelical spiritual formation: a holistic and grace-filled spirituality
that encompasses relational connecting. "Baptists," Hinson states, "now meditated on
Scripture and prayed, whether individually or corporately, not so much for their impact
on their entire spiritual lives as on the front end of them—conversion." Hinson, "Baptist
Spirituality," 292. Deweese further observes, "Emphasizing regular monthly meetings
and having wide influence among Baptists in several parts of the world, this prayer call
appeared at a teachable moment in the story of Baptists." Deweese, *Prayer in Baptist*

Critical Analysis for Contemporary Use

In 1986, Deweese lamented the waning emphasis of prayer meetings within Baptist life. "In recent years," he said, "the multiplication of other midweek meetings in churches has weakened the status of prayer meetings in many churches." Despite some exceptions, the trend, three decades later, continues in the same direction.[14] While Deweese looked to the multiplication of midweek services as a possible reason for such decline, Fuller's multifaceted theology of prayer may provide a more nuanced explanation and corrective to the waning interest in corporate prayer.

The Prayer Call of 1784 was not the first call to prayer. Several prayer calls for revival were issued before 1784 within the Northamptonshire Baptist Association.[15] What made the difference in the Prayer Call of 1784? Why did this prayer movement mushroom into the seed of the Modern Missionary Movement and not the prior prayer calls? What is stifling such a movement in our own day? Perhaps the multifaceted study demonstrates the need for systematic reflection on one's belief and practice of prayer with respect to a wide range of doctrinal points. The glory of God's character motivated Fuller to pray. His pneumatology and eschatology infused a prayer movement with hope that God would pour out his Spirit in direct response to the prayers of his people.

"Eschatology," according to Benjamin Gladd and Matthew Harmon, "not only enriches how pastors lead their churches; it also energizes and informs how the church interacts with God and the world around us."[16] The same could be said of Fuller's eschatology and a number of other doctrinal points. Doctrines operate in a cyclical relationship informing and being informed by one another, motivating, and, at times, correcting where needed. Harmon, in his chapter on eschatology and prayer, asked a question that corresponds in theme with a number of Fuller's *Persuasives*: "What difference might it make in our prayer lives if we embraced the reality of what God has *already* done for us in Christ as the foundation for trusting him for what is *yet to come*?"[17] In principle, the same question could be asked regarding one's doctrine of the Father, Son, Spirit, humanity, or the church. For example, the reciprocity of Fuller's doctrine of the Spirit and theology

---

Life, 46. Perhaps the emphasis on monthly prayer meetings unintentionally led to a minimization of the pastoral priority of prayer in all areas of his ministry.

14. For an example of one such exception, see Dever, "On the Use and Importance of Corporate Prayer," 5–9.

15. For more on these prayer calls, see Elwyn, *Northamptonshire Association*, 16.

16. Harmon, "Prayer," 115.

17. Harmon, "Prayer," 133.

of prayer begs the question for today, "What difference might it make in our praying if we embraced the reality that we can do nothing apart from the Spirit?" Fuller would say this ought to provide great encouragement for us to pray all the more earnestly. Consider also the doctrine of humanity: "What difference might it make in our praying if we embraced the reality of our own inability and depravity before God?" Fuller would say this ought to encourage us to maintain the proper posture in prayer as a supplicant for mercy rather than an entitled claimant. The doctrinal implications for prayer are clear.

A decline in prayer, whether personal or corporate is troubling. Churches will need more than a fervent call or "ought" from the pastor if the prominence of corporate prayer is to return. Sound theological reflection and teaching are needed to sustain a church's vision for prayer. Yes, a proper understanding of providence is vital for one's prayer life. Yet, confidence in the person and work of Christ, dependence on the Spirit, humble acknowledgment of human inability and depravity, proper understanding of the nature of the church, and hopeful anticipation of God's ultimate victory in Christ's coming kingdom are equally vital elements of one's prayer life.

Appendix 1

Chronology of Prayer Quotations or Entries Associated with Prayer in Fuller's Diary, January 1780–July 1800

THIS LIST OF CHRONOLOGICAL quotations from Fuller's diary highlights the prominence of prayer in public and private sectors of his life. As noted in the first chapter, Fuller's diary contains at least 188 entries concerning prayer. The count may vary depending on what one qualifies as an entry concerning prayer. For example, even though Monday evening meetings were not all dedicated to prayer, the researcher included these entries because a number of them did comment on prayer that took place during the meeting. For example, on October 18, 1784, Fuller wrote, "Much depressed in spirit tonight on account of my little spirituality. Prayed at the evening meeting with tenderness of spirit—sensibly felt my entire dependence on the Spirit of God for carrying on the work of grace as well as for the beginning of it."[1] The Monday meeting, unlike the first Mondays of the monthfollowing the Prayer Call of 1784, was not devoted entirely to prayer. The meeting was a regularly planned service. Much like services that were held on Sunday in the "morning, afternoon, and evening," the Kettering congregation held services also on "Monday and Friday each week."[2] While these midweek meetings did not have prayer as their chief reason for gathering, there is little reason to doubt that prayer was nonetheless a central part of the worship service just as on Sundays. In many of the entries, Fuller simply expressed

1. Fuller, *Complete Works: Diary*, 1:83.
2. For more on the monthly prayer meetings and regularly schedule church meetings, see McMullen and Whelan, "Introduction," xxii–xxiv.

his general feeling after the meeting. These entries have been included for
the sake of representing how Fuller felt leaving a worship service where
leading in public prayer was a principal aspect of his duties as the pastor.

The chronology of quotations has three columns. The first column provides the date and quotation. Most quotations have been abridged. While
not grammatically conventional, the researcher placed ellipses at the beginning of quotations to signal that entry has content preceding the relevant
quotation. The second column provides an explanatory note. Where possible, the researcher provided context, explanation, or succinct description
of the quotation. Some quotations required no explanation or the researcher
was unable to provide a satisfactory contextual point of reference. The third
column provides the volume and page number of the quotation from *The
Complete Works of Andrew Fuller*, abbreviated as *TCWAF*.[3]

Date and Quotation	Explanatory Note	Reference

January 10, 1780, "O my God . . .
 	
    O Lord God! . . .
 	
    One thing in particular I would pray for; namely, that I may not only be kept from erroneous principles, but may so *love* the truth as never to keep it back. O Lord, never let me under the specious pretence of preaching *holiness*, neglect to promulgate the truths of thy word; for this day I see, and have all along found, that holy practice has a necessary dependence on sacred *principle*. O Lord, if thou wilt open mine eyes to behold the wonders of thy word, and give me to feel their transforming tendency, then shall the Lord be my God; then let my tongue cleave to the roof of my mouth, if I shun to declare, to the best of my knowledge, the whole counsel of God."
	Fuller's vow of renewal. The renewal covenant is predominantly in the form of a prayer	*TCWAF* 1:1

---

3. Fuller, *Complete Works: Diary*. The quotations retained all spacing, punctuation,
spelling, and emphases from the source publication.

Date and Quotation	Explanatory Note	Reference
June 22, 1780, "O that I might feel more the power of religion, and know more of the love of Christ, which passeth knowledge! I think I see divine excellence in such a life. O that thou wouldest bless me indeed, enlarge my coast! I am going, God willing, to visit a friend today. O that a spirit of watchfulness, savour, and fellowship with Christ, may attend me!"	Prayer for more love and presence of Christ. Scripture quotation from the prayer of Jabez, 1 Chron. 4	*TCWAF* 1:4
June 26, 1780, "Dull and unaffected. How soon do I sink from the spirit of the gospel! I have need of thine intercession, O Lord Jesus, that my faith fail not."	Prayer for Christ's intercession	*TCWAF* 1:4
June 27, 1780, "O how difficult is my situation! Providence seems to go against me, yet I am in a strait what to do. Lord, and what shall I do? O that thine hand might be with me, and that thou wouldst keep me from evil, that it may not grieve me!"	Fuller is working for meager wages each year as the pastor of the Baptist church in Soham	*TCWAF* 1:4
June 28, 1780, "Have found my heart tenderly affected several times, especially tonight, in prayer respecting my critical situation. Oh! Providence, how intricate! If rough roads are marked out for me, may my shoes be iron and brass! I found, today, a peculiar sympathy toward poor people under trying providences; thinking I may have to go that road. 'Teach me to do thy will, for though art my God: thy Spirit is good, lead me into the land of uprightness!'"	Prayer acknowledging God's meticulous providence and for help in doing God's will. Scripture quotation from Ps 143:10	*TCWAF* 1:5
June 29, 1780, "My heart has been much affected today, in thinking on my situation. I prayed to the Lord earnestly, that, if there were any thing in this world which might direct me, he would lead my mind to it. Here I must wait. The Lord may have designed to lead me in a way that I have not known."		*TCWAF* 1:5

Date and Quotation	Explanatory Note	Reference
July 1, 1780, "My soul has been dejected today, in thinking on the plague of the human heart; but I have been sweetly refreshed tonight, by a hymn of Dr. Watts, (85th, Second Book,) . . . This was my dear Brother Driver's funeral hymn. I had a sweet time in prayer, tonight. Through the glass of my depravity, I see, O I see the preciousness of that blood which flowed on Calvary! O that the ideas I have had tonight were written indelibly on my heart! But, alas! One hour of sin will, I fear, efface them all."	Reflection on human depravity and his own depravity stirred his heart to prayer and deeper gratefulness of Christ's atonement	*TCWAF* 1:6
July 4, 1780, " . . . I fear some trial is at hand. O may the Lord keep me!"	Prayer for the Lord's sustainment	*TCWAF* 1:6
July 6, 1780, "Dull and unaffected. I sometimes feel a spirit of idle, skeptical despair; as if the difficulties that attend the finding out what is truth and duty were insurmountable. O Lord, keep up in me a spirit of activity, and teach me to know and do thy will. May I know what is that good, perfect, and acceptable will of God."	Prayer to know and do God's will. Prayer for a spirit of activity may be of particular significance regarding Fuller's future work with the BMS. Scripture quotation from Rom 12:2	*TCWAF*1:7

July 7, 1780, "Heaviness of heart makes me stoop.
    O time, how clogg'd with cares!
    How pregnant life with ills!
    Sin, like some poisonous spring, my cup
    With dregs of sorrow fills.
    But why do I cry by reason of my *affliction*? On account of mine *iniquities* do these things come upon me. O Lord, how justly mightiest thou open ten thousand springs of woe, ten thousand floodgates of sorrow, and let them all in upon me. Yet thy mercies are new every morning: it is of the Lord's mercies that I am not consumed."
	McMullen and Whelan proposed that the poem was "Fuller's own composition." Scripture quotations appear to be from Lam 3	*TCWAF* 1:7

Date and Quotation	Explanatory Note	Reference
July 11, 1780, "O my dear Brother Diver! Very pleasant has thou been to me. I am distressed for the loss of thee! Earth seems a lonely place without thee! But, Lord, *thy* presence will more than make amends for *his* absence. Give me that, or I sink! The cares of the world have engrossed my attention this afternoon; but the cares of the church return this evening. O now I feel the loss of my dear Brother Diver!"	Diver was a deacon at Soham and close confidant of Fuller's during his early years as a minister	*TCWAF* 1:8
July 12, 1780, "O wretched man that I am! . . . Oh may the remembrance of *this* make thee shrink back from sinning! Surely the renewal of a fresh conflict with old corruptions is not the trial I feared? Lead me not into temptation, but deliver me from evil, O Lord!"	Scripture quotation is from the Lord's Prayer, Matt 6	*TCWAF* 1:8
July 15, 1780, "Alas! with what can I go forth tomorrow? My powers are shackled, my thoughts contracted. Yesterday and this morning, . . . Bless the Lord! Tonight, I have felt a melting sense of the heinous nature of backsliding from the Lord, while thinking on Jeremiah 2:5, 31–33. Bless the Lord, O my soul, and all that is within me, bless his holy name. He maketh me to renew my strength like the eagle, dissolve my hardness, disappoints my fears, and touches my lips as with a live coal from his altar. Bless the Lord, O my soul!"	Further evidence demonstrating the way Fuller contentiously infused Scripture into his prayers	*TCWAF* 1:9
July 20, 1780, "O peace! Thou inestimable jewel! The Lord grant I may never enter the polemical lists!"	Prayer regarding his upcoming publication. Likely a reference to the work undertaken in composing *The Gospel Worthy of All Acceptation*	*TCWAF* 1:10

Date and Quotation	Explanatory Note	Reference
July 21, 1780, "Dejected, through worldly and church concerns; but had some relief, tonight, in casting all my care upon the Lord, hoping that he careth for me. The Lord undertake for me! O thou that manages worlds unknown, without one disappointment, take my case into thy hand, and fit me for thy pleasure. If poverty must be my portion, add thereto contentment."	Poor conditions in Soham. A prayer for contentment. Scripture quotation from 1 Pet 5:7	*TCWAF* 1:10
July 22, 1780, "Ah! how heavily do I drag on without the Lord! I can neither think, nor do any thing to purpose. Lord, help me! Sin, how deceitful! While we may obtain an apparent victory over one sin, we may be insensibly enslaved to another . . . "	Prayer of confession	*TCWAF* 1:10
September 3,1780, "Had a good day, in preaching from the above, and from Lamentations 3:40, 41. O that God might write the things delivered today, in indelible characters, on all our hearts! Found a heart to pray for the conversion of the congregation."	Prayer of intercession. A pastoral prayer for his people. The second time that Lam 3 appears to influence Fuller's prayer (see entry from July 7, 1780)	*TCWAF* 1:13
September 5, 1780, "I longed, in prayer tonight, to be more useful. Oh that God would do somewhat by me! Nor is this, I trust, from ambition; but from a pure desire of working for God, and the benefit of my fellow sinners."	Prayer for usefulness	*TCWAF* 1:14
September 10, 1780, "Earnest in prayer with God, this afternoon. Humbled for our little love: yet found such desire, that, could I obtain my wish, the brightest seraph should not outvie me in love to my Lord. I saw, plainly, that my salvation must be, from first to last, of free grace."	Prayer for richer love for and communion with God	*TCWAF* 1:14
September 11, 1780, "Much affected, this morning, in reading Edwards's thoughts on evangelical humility, in his *Treatise on the Affections*. Surely there are many that will be found wanting in the great day. 'Lord, is it I?'"	Influence of Jonathan Edwards in personal reflection. Prayer of searching his own heart and desires	*TCWAF* 1:14

Date and Quotation	Explanatory Note	Reference
September 12, 1780, " . . . I think, of late, I cannot, in prayer, consider myself as a Christian, but as a sinner, casting myself at Christ's feet for mercy."	Prayer of searching and petition for mercy	*TCWAF* 1:14
September 23, 1780, "O blessed by God, he has appeared once again. Tonight, while I prayed to him, how sweet was Colossians 1:19 to me . . . O for some heavenly clue, to guide me to the fullness of Christ! O for an overcoming faith!"	Prayer of thankfulness for God's communion through Christ. Another clear indicator of Fuller's prayer life being stimulated and infused with Scripture	*TCWAF* 1:15
October 11, 1780, " . . . But feel myself full of darkness, deadness, and pollution. The Lord have mercy upon me!"	Petition for mercy	*TCWAF* 1:16
October 13, 1780, "Much concerned with the state of things among us, and with my own state. Went to the Lord in prayer: found a solemnity of spirit. The Lord direct me to the land of uprightness!"	Prayer for his own sanctification, maturity, and growth	*TCWAF* 1:16
October 22, 1780, " . . . Was in some doubt, whether I should preach any lectures at all: went to the Lord, laid the case before him, and had some freedom in pleading that he would bless me. Preached, this evening, from Romans 7:12, and had a very affecting time. I love to vindicate his equity, and 'justify the ways of God to man.'"	It appears from the entry that this was either the first time Soham undertook to include evening lectures on Sunday or it was the first during Fuller's tenure as pastor	*TCWAF* 1:17
October 24, 1780, " . . . Somewhat concerned, today, about the state of the church, and my own state. Surely I do not pray to the Lord enough! Surely I am too careless about matters of so great concern!"	Lamenting his own lack of prayer	*TCWAF* 1:17
November 9, 1780, "Found a heart to pray today—Into thine hands I commit my spirit. Enlighten my judgement, guide my choice, direct my conscience, and keep it tender. Found my heart disposed to ask counsel of God, and leave him to guide me in his own way."	Fuller felt his desire for prayer was God-given	*TCWAF* 1:19

Date and Quotation	Explanatory Note	Reference
November 10, 1780, "O that I might be guided in some way! My heart is much perplexed, but found liberty in prayer. Towards night, was affected in 23rd and 24th chapters of Jeremiah, and earnest in prayer."	Prayer for guidance	*TCWAF* 1:19
December 22, 1780, "I am far from happy. I cannot feel settled where I am; yet I cannot remove. Lord, let not duty hang thus in doubt!"	Expression of frustration and sadness in prayer	*TCWAF* 1:21
January 24, 1781, "Today, visited my father again, but he seems to have no thought of death. I found my heart much drawn out, tonight, to pray for him."	Concern for the depleted health of his father	*TCWAF* 1:22
January 26, 1781, "Much affected, today for my dear father. Oh his immortal soul! How can I bear to bury him unconverted! Father, if it be possible let this cup pass from me! I have had many outgoings of soul for him, and some little conversation with him . . . "	Prayer for physical healing and salvation of his father	*TCWAF* 1:23
January 27, 1781, "Father if it be possible, let this cup pass from me! Give me some good hopes of the welfare of his soul! then I could almost be willing to part with him. This would be letting the cup pass from me. 'But, O the soul, that never dies,' &c. The woman of Canaan made her daughter's case her own, and cried, 'Lord, help me!' Surely I may do likewise by my father."	Further prayer for his father	*TCWAF* 1:23
February 3, 1781, " . . . O that the Holy Spirit would open my eyes, and let me into the things that I have never yet seen!"	Prayer for illumination of the Spirit	*TCWAF* 1:24
February 8, 1781, "O would the Lord the Spirit lead me into the nature and importance of the work of the ministry! Reading a wise spiritual author might be of use: yet, could I, by divine assistance, but penetrate the work myself, it would seek deeper, and be more durable."	Prayer for the Spirit's guidance in the work of the ministry	*TCWAF* 1:24

Date and Quotation	Explanatory Note	Reference
March 11, 1781, "I had an affecting day especially in singing and prayer. The revival nature, at this season of the year, seemed to kindle an earnest desire for the revival of religion."	The Lord's Day and prayer for revival	*TCWAF* 1:25
March 26, 1781, ". . . I had an affecting time in prayer on these subjects. I thought, what an immense fullness of light and happiness dwelt in God; how easily could he inform my mind, and comfort my heart: what fullness in the Holy Scriptures, enough to furnish the man of God thoroughly, for every good work. All I want is to find something that suits my case."	Wrestling with his station at Soham and the invitation to Kettering	*TCWAF* 1:25–6
April 2, 1781, "Affected in prayer. Oh for an unerring guide! Oh that I knew the Lord's will! Verily, if I know mine own heart, I would do it. I had rather, I think, much rather, walk all my days in the most miserable condition, than offend the Lord, by trying to get out of it."	Prayer for God's guidance.	*TCWAF* 1:27
April 10, 1781, "The thoughts of my situation now return and over power me. Tonight, I was exceedingly affected in prayer, earnestly longing that I might know the will of God."	Wrestling with his station at Soham and the invitation to Kettering. Praying for knowledge of God's will	*TCWAF* 1:27
April 18, 1781, "Earnest outgoings to God, in prayer. Tomorrow seems a day of great importance. Then I must give my reasons to the church, for what I have intimated concerning my removal. The Lord guide and bless them and me!"	Decision is made to remove to Kettering	*TCWAF* 1:27
April 19, 1781, ". . . My heart is overwhelmed! Lead me to the Rock that is higher than I! I have been pouring out my heart to the Lord, since I came from the meeting. Thinking I could rather choose death than departure! My heart is as if it would dissolve. It is like wax—it is melted in the midst of my bowels."	Soham mourns over his news of departing	*TCWAF* 1:28

Date and Quotation	Explanatory Note	Reference
May 1, 1781, "Have been praying to the Lord, that I may keep to that direction which has been so much to me ten or eleven years ago—'In all thy ways acknowledge him, and he shall direct thy paths.' This passage has been, several times, like a present help in time of need. O that it may be so now!"	Prayer for direction and peace. Scripture quotation from Prov 3:6. The verse had a vital influence on Fuller's prayers for upwards of eleven years	*TCWAF* 1:28
May 2, 1781, " . . . My heart and flesh faileth! O that God may be the strength of my heart, and my portion for ever!"	Prayer for comfort and strength Scripture quotation from Ps 73:26	*TCWAF* 1:28
May 3, 1781, "A painful melancholy lies heavily upon me all this day. Have been trying to pray, but can get no manner of ease. 'Withhold not thou tender love,' has been my plea."	Prayer for comfort. Scripture quotation possibly from Ps 40:11 if one substitutes "love" for "mercies" as the King James renders it	*TCWAF* 1:28
May 7, 1781, "Tender thoughts towards the church. Several verses of the 122nd Psalm, towards the latter part, exceedingly move me. The welfare of this part of Zion lies exceedingly near me. Earnest, very earnest longings for it, and for direction to myself, in prayer."	Fuller had been sick the day priorand unable to preach on the Lord's Day. Scripture infused devotion and prayer from Ps 122	*TCWAF* 1:29
May 10, 1781, "O that I might arrive at a greater degree of satisfaction! Earnest longings for this, tonight, in prayer."	Wrestling with a desire to leave Soham	*TCWAF* 1:30
May 14, 1781, "My load seems heavier than I can bear! O Lord, for thine own sake, suffer me not to act contrary to thy will! O for an unerring guide!"	Prayer for guidance	*TCWAF* 1:30
May 22, 1781, "One thing I desire of the Lord: whatever be my portion here—if it be to wear out my years in pining sadness—let me so walk, as to enjoy his approbation. Into thy hands I commit my spirit."	Reflection on his station at Soham	*TCWAF* 1:30
June 29, 1781, "Well—it is by the grace of God I am what I am: nor is any sin so black or so detestable, but I am liable to fall into it. Lord, keep me!"	Reflecting on the Yoke of Christ versus the Yoke of Satan	*TCWAF* 1:31
July 1, 1781, "A fervent day in prayer, in preaching from Isaiah 53:6, and Ecclesiastes 8:11, . . . "	The Lord's Day	*TCWAF* 1:32

Date and Quotation	Explanatory Note	Reference
July 3, 1781, "Was very ill, tonight; but felt tenderhearted and earnest in prayer."		TCWAF 1:32
July 12, 1781, ". . . God knows my heart. I have been trying to pray; and sure it is my sincere desire, if I am wrong, to be set right."	Plans to announce his departure within a quarter of a year at the Thursday evening meeting	
July 14, 1781, "Waked, this morning with great heaviness of heart. Have been trying to pray, 'O send out thy light and truth . . .' My soul seems at a distance from God . . ."	Praying for nearness with God. Scripture quotation from Ps 43:3	TCWAF 1:33
September 21, 1781, "Earnestly affected in prayer, that, if it would be most pleasing to God for me to stay, I might do so after all . . . 'Unto thee I lift up mine eyes, O thou that dwellest in the heavens!'"	Scripture quotation from Ps 123:1	TCWAF 1:34
September 22, 1781, "My heart much moved this morning. Psalm 123:1, 2, was somewhat to me. Overcome in prayer, that God would shine upon my path. O God, thou knowest that I am willing to be any thing. It is my unfeigned desire, that not my will, but thine be done . . ."	Prayer for direction. Continued to reflect the next day on Ps 123:1	TCWAF 1:35
December 20, 1781, "Religion appeared to me to be full of *greatness*. A *great* God, possessed of *great* excellencies, whence arise *great* obligations . . . O that I had a *great* sense of the importance of divine things! Lord, increase my faith!"	Prayer for increased faith	TCWAF 1:36
December 28, 1781, "Thought, today, . . . what a matter of importance is the birth of a child. . . . But, O that God would accept of my new-born child, and let its end be 'to glorify God, and enjoy him for ever!'"	Prayer for a soon-to-be-born child. His prayer reflects a probable influence from the Westminster Shorter Catechism's Question 1	TCWAF 1:36
January 3, 1782, ". . . O wretch that I am! Is this to have my speech seasoned with grace? O Lord forgive me! Some humbling thoughts, tonight, for the above, in prayer."	Prayer of confession and petition forgiveness	TCWAF 1:37
January 4, 1782, "Very tender, this morning, in remembering the above circumstance. Lord, make me more spiritual in time to come!"	Prayer of confession and petition forgiveness	TCWAF 1:37

Date and Quotation	Explanatory Note	Reference
There is a gap in diary entries from January 1782 till April 1784 for the first few years of his ministry at Kettering.		*TCWAF* 1:38
April 11, 1784, "A tender forenoon in public prayer. My heart aches for the congregation young and old, especially for some who seem to be under concern. O, if Christ might but be formed in them!"	Pastoral prayer for his congregation at Kettering	*TCWAF* 1:38
April 19, 1784, "Visited Mr. E. and rode to Carlton today—preached there tonight with great tenderness. Felt my heart very tender in prayer—and disposed to deal plainly with them as a people."	Public prayer for a congregation in Carlton. McMullen and Whelan suggest this could be John Evans of Northampton	*TCWAF* 1:41
April 25, 1784, "A very good forenoon in prayer & preaching on *walking by faith*—not much savor at the Lord's Supper. Expounded the 4th chapter of Matthew this evening on *Christ's temptation.* Took notice of its *importance, time, circumstances, nature,* and *issue,* & concluded with 2 uses—Christ did not *run into* temptation but was *led up*—let not us, Christ bids us to pray that *we* enter not into it."	Fuller's mention of preaching from Matthew provides rough estimations as to when he preached through the Sermon on the Mount in Matthew's Gospel	*TCWAF* 1:42
April 28, 1784, "Rode to Winick today—preached there tonight—felt sacred pleasure in prayer . . . "		*TCWAF* 1:43
April 30, 1784, "Very little exercise today—what reason have I to pray for a revival in my soul! . . . My soul cleaveth to the dust, quicken thou me."		*TCWAF* 1:43
May 8, 1784, "Conversation with R. H. on various subjects. Some tenderness and earnestness in prayer after his departure. O could I but keep more near to God! How *good* it is to draw near to him! 'Where should my foolish passions rove? where can such sweetness be?'"	McMullen and Whelan identify "R. H." as Robert Hall Sr.	*TCWAF* 1:46

Date and Quotation	Explanatory Note	Reference
May 11, 1784, "This day I have devoted to fasting & prayer, in conjunction with several other ministers, who have agreed each at home by himself to fast & pray the second Tuesday in every month for the revival of real religion and the extending of Christ's Kingdom in the world.—Feel very unhappy to think that my heart should be no more in it. But very little real prayer throughout the day."	2nd Tuesday of the Month, Fasting and Praying with other Ministers. McMullen and Whelan noted that Ryland's account stated, "little of the true spirit of prayer" as opposed to "very little real prayer"	TCWAF 1:47
May 16, 1784, "A good forenoon—tender in prayer for the revival of religion and the carrying on of a good work in our young people . . . "	The Lord's Day	TCWAF 1:48
May 30, 1784, "Rode home tonight—much dispirited on account of my Stupidity and Carnality. Some outgoings of heart to God in prayer."	The Lord's Day	TCWAF 1:52
June 1, 1784, " . . . Heard the Letters from the Churches. Found many of them are in a low condition, destitute of Pastors. The Lord see, and provide!"	Regarding the association meeting in Nottingham	TCWAF 1:52
June 3, 1784, "Some sweet solemnity of spirit this morning hearing Mr. Hopper speak his exercise & conclude in prayer. O for a revival of real religion in the churches of Christ! . . . "	Regarding the close of the association meeting in Nottingham	TCWAF 1:53
June 13, 1784, "A poor, cold day, except in the evening—I am weary of being out from home so much—I want to be more at home that I may be more with God."	Fuller seems to connect being on the road with not being able to be near to God	TCWAF 1:55
June, 18, 1784, "Conversation with Mr. Ryland chief part of the day—preached this afternoon a lecture with him at Bugbrook with some pleasure—returned—felt sweetly tonight in prayer for ardor in Christ's cause."		TCWAF 1:56
June 19, 1784, "Tender in prayer again this morning—but O what a poor, carnal, stupid wretch nearly throughout the day. Some little fervor tonight in meditation on Christ's mercy."		TCWAF 1:56

Date and Quotation	Explanatory Note	Reference
June 20, 1784, "A good forenoon—some tenderness in prayer, but feel myself wretchedly cold this afternoon. Tender again tonight on *watchfulness* from I Thessalonians 5.6."	The Lord's Day	*TCWAF* 1:56
June 27, 1784, "A tenderish forenoon on *waiting* upon God—but a poor cold heart this afternoon even though commemorating the Lord's death!"	The Lord's Day	*TCWAF* 1:58
July 1, 1784, " . . . Returning home tonight, some exercise on David's prayer renew a *constant* spirit within me! O what need have I of that!"	Scripture quotation possibly from Ps 51:10	*TCWAF* 1:58
July 9, 1784, " . . . Read a part of Mr. Edwards's *Attempt to promote explicit agreement in God's people in prayer for the revival of religion* to our friends this evening to excite them to the like practice. Felt my heart profited by what I read, and much solemnized."	Definite influence of Jonathan Edwards and his work *An Humble Attempt*	*TCWAF* 1:60
July 12, 1784, " . . . Found earnest desire this morning in prayer that God would heart the *right* in regard to them and hear our prayers which the churches agree to unite in for the spread of Christ's Kingdom."	Monday, a new day established for prayer meetings originating with the Association meeting on June 3, 1784 (see, *TCWAF* 1:61n174)	*TCWAF* 1:61
July 13, 1784, "Spent this day in fasting and prayer in conjunction with several of my brethren in the ministry, for the revival of Christ's kingdom in the world and in the churches. Some tenderness and earnestness in prayer several times in the day. Wrote some few thoughts on the desirableness of the coming of Christ's Kingdom."	2nd Tuesday of the Month	*TCWAF* 1:62
July 18, 1784, "A good forenoon in preaching on *All my springs are in thee*, but a better time in prayer—found my heart go out for the children and youth of the congregation—owing perhaps to my having spoke at the grave last night of a little boy mentioned June 21. Poor Child! . . . "	The Lord's Day	*TCWAF* 1:63

Date and Quotation	Explanatory Note	Reference
July 19, 1784, " . . . Read some more of Edwards on prayer, as also last Monday night with sweet satisfaction."	Another example of Edwards's influence	*TCWAF* 1:63
July 20, 1784, "Read the 9th chapter of John this morning with pleasure—went to prayer after it with solemn pleasure . . . "	Fuller's prayer life infused with Scripture	*TCWAF* 1:64
July 26, 1784, "Very little exercise today—and but a cold heart tonight at evening meeting."	Monday evening meeting.[4]	*TCWAF* 1:65
July 27, 1784, "I find myself so unaffected with things, nothing seems to lay hold of me. Some fear tonight in prayer. An accident that has befallen my youngest child now lays sufficient hold of me—fear lest he should be taken from me. Very much moved in prayer for him. O Lord! I must have something trying to move me! How I shall endure this I know not! O prepare him, & prepare me!"	Prayer for his youngest son, petition for physical healing	*TCWAF* 1:65
August 1, 1784, "A very tender forenoon especially in prayer, occasioned by the death of Mrs. B's child . . . "	Lord's Day	*TCWAF* 1:66
August 2, 1784, "Some tenderness of heart today—especially tonight at evening meeting, when we met together to *pray for the revival of religion*."	Monday evening prayer meeting	*TCWAF* 1:66
August 10, 1784, "Occupied in writing some *persuasives to united prayer for the revival of real religion*, for the press."	Fuller's first publication is on prayer	*TCWAF* 1:66

4. At this point, Fuller began to comment more about Monday evening meetings. While the main purpose of these meetings, as distinct from the first Monday of each month, was not concerted prayer for revival, there is reason to believe that prayer was a central piece of each of their meetings as a congregation. Cf. Nigel David Wheeler, "Eminent Spirituality and Eminent Usefulness: Andrew Fuller's (1754–1815) Pastoral Theology in His Ordination Sermons" (PhD diss., University of Pretoria, 2009), 114–15; with Michael D. McMullen and Timothy D. Whelan, "Introduction," in *The Complete Works of Andrew Fuller: The Diary of Andrew Fuller, 1780–1801*, vol. 1 (Berlin: De Gruyter, 2016), xxii–xxiv.

Date and Quotation	Explanatory Note	Reference
August 21, 1784, " . . . Surely I am more brutish than any man, and have not the understanding of a man! O that I might be led into divine truth! . . . The Lord direct my way in respect to publishing! . . . "	Prayer for God's guidance with respect to publishing his writings. Likely in reference to publishing his first edition of *The Gospel Worthy of All Acceptation*	TCWAF 1:69
August 23, 1784, " . . . The Lord keep me! Wish to suspect my own spirit, and go forth leaning upon him for strength! . . . "	Wrestling with the decision to publish or not	TCWAF 1:70
August 24, 1784, "Some tenderness in prayer of late . . . The Lord keep me, and lead me into all truth!"	Scripture quotation from John 16:13	TCWAF 1:70
August 25, 1784, "Some sweetness for some days in reading over the *Acts* of the *Apostles*, before family prayer. Sweet times in that duty. O that we might see some such blessed times come over again! . . . "	Scripture's influence on the family prayers in the Fuller household	TCWAF 1:70
August 29, 1784, "A very tender and affectionate time in prayer for the congregation, especially for the young people! . . . The Lord lead me into the Spirit of the gospel, and keep me from extremes!"	The Lord's Day, pastoral prayer and concern for the youth at Kettering	TCWAF 1:71
September 2, 1784, "Low in my feelings today. O that God would bless me indeed! Wearied out today with writing."	Prayer for strength in writing	TCWAF 1:72
September 6, 1784, " . . . But a poor evening meeting."	Monday evening prayer meeting	TCWAF 1:73
September 14, 1784, " . . . But very little spirituality through the day, though it was a day on which I fasted & prayed."	2nd Tuesday	TCWAF 1:75
September 15, 1784, "Nothing of any remarkable exercise for these two or three days except some little tenderness in prayer. Last Tuesday I found some heart to pray for God's *Holy Spirit* that it might not be taken from us, and on some seasons since then have felt that desire renewed . . . "	Connection between prayer and the Spirit	TCWAF 1:75–76
September 20, 1784, "Pretty much depressed in spirit on account of the state of S—m Church—But a poor evening meeting tonight."	Monday evening meeting	TCWAF 1:76

Date and Quotation	Explanatory Note	Reference
October 4, 1784, " . . . The ministers met tonight in the vestry being the monthly exercise of prayer for the revival of religion, and joined us in it. Heard *Mr. Ryland jun.* pray with much pleasure and satisfaction, and several others united."	Monday evening prayer meeting	*TCWAF* 1:79
October 5, 1784, " . . . Some pleasure tonight on hearing Mr. Hall sen. Speak on *a right use of the law in preaching the gospel*, and in concluding the opportunity in prayer."	Fuller made note of Hall's prayer	*TCWAF* 1:80
October 7, " . . . Much depressed in spirit and grieved . . . in a certain person . . . Felt my heart go out in prayer for that person."	Intercession	*TCWAF* 1:80
October 8, 1784, "Waked exceedingly depressed in spirit partly from what grieved me last night, and partly from a *dream* . . . O the danger that mankind are in! What thousands of them are every hour precipitated into an eternal world! Rose and went to prayer alone with some tenderness . . . "	Connection between prayer and the condition of humanity	*TCWAF* 1:80–81
October 11, 1784, " . . . But a poor cold time at the evening meeting."	Monday evening meeting	*TCWAF* 1:81
October 18, 1784, "Much depressed in spirit tonight on account of my little spirituality. Prayed at the evening meeting with tenderness of spirit—sensibly felt my entire dependence on the Spirit of God for carrying on the work of grace as well as for the beginning of it."	Monday evening meeting. Connection between prayer, human inability, and dependence on the Spirit	*TCWAF* 1:83
October 21, 1784, "Had I not the satisfaction that 'tis *the Cause of God and truth*, I would drop all thoughts of printing. The Lord keep me meek and lowly in heart!"	The prospect of printing *The Gospel Worthy of All Acceptation*	*TCWAF* 1:83
October 22, 1784, "This day the Lord has been merciful to me in delivering my wife who has miscarried. A saying of Mr. Hall's has been pretty much to me of late which I heard him use in prayer, 'Lord, said he, we are bound this night to love thee more than ever we were before!' Our sins and mercies how they accumulate! Spake tonight from 'My *words are Spirit & life*,' occasioned by reading the *Review*. O the *Bible*, the *Bible*!"	Wife's miscarriage	*TCWAF* 1:84

Date and Quotation	Explanatory Note	Reference
October 31, 1784, "Heard this morning that Mr. Gotchsen. Is dying! . . . he said to me to this effect, 'Remember and pray for a poor old man for I cannot be long in this world!' Much affected with the news—sung the 90th Psalm—tender in prayer, . . . O, to know more of, and live upon Christ! He must be our *daily bread*! . . . "	The Lord's Day. Scripture quotation from Matt 6:11 or Luke 11:3	*TCWAF* 1:86
November 1, 1784, "But little spirituality today. I seem almost to have lost my views of yesterday. Tonight we met for prayer for the revival of religion. Felt but a poor time compared with what I have heretofore."	Monday evening prayer meeting	*TCWAF* 1:86
November 9, 1784, "Employed chiefly in writing. Some tenderness in private prayer."	Record of private prayer	*TCWAF* 1:88
November 10, 1784, "Rode to Braybrook and preached and prayed with a good deal of warmth of heart on Jesus *crying to every one that thirsteth, let him come unto me and drink*! . . . "	Scripture quotation from John 7:37	*TCWAF* 1:88
November 12, 1784, "Feel my mind earnestly engaged in longing for the salvation of souls—earnest in prayer for this . . . "	Connection between prayer and the conversion of the lost	*TCWAF* 1:88
November 15, 1784, "Chiefly employed in finishing a MS for the press. But a poor opportunity at evening meeting."	Monday evening prayer meeting	*TCWAF* 1:89
November 22, 1784, "Walked to Northampton today. Some prayer that God would bless that about which I am goin.— viz. the printing of a MS on *Faith in Christ being the duty of unregenerate sinners*. But feel myself a poor, barren creature."	Preparing to publish *The Gospel Worthy of All Acceptation*	*TCWAF* 1:91
November 26, 1784, "Some reflections of late in prayer for my strange propensity to depart from God—and many discouraging thoughts concerning praying and preaching for the promotion of Christ's kingdom. It seems almost, as if the Lord, if he hath not forsaken the earth, has nearly forsaken me, and would not regard my petitions."	Connection between praying, preaching, and the expansion of Christ's kingdom. Fuller experienced doubt regarding his own prayers	*TCWAF* 1:92

Date and Quotation	Explanatory Note	Reference
December 3, 1784, "A tender evening meeting tonight in speaking from—*Continue in prayer, and watch* &c. but little of anything else all day."	Scripture quotation from Col 4:2	*TCWAF* 1:93
December 6, 1784, " . . . A very tender evening meeting of prayer for the revival of real religion. Much pleasure in singing, and freedom with God in prayer—prayed against my late skeptical feelings."	Monday evening prayer meeting	*TCWAF* 1:94
January 2, 1785, " . . . Very tender in reading more of Mr. Bunyan's *Holy War*, particularly that part where the four captains agree to petition the King for more force. Felt a great satisfaction in my principles concerning preaching to sinners and a desire to pray like them for help from on high to render the word effectual."	The Lord's Day. Evidence of the probable influence of John Bunyan on Fuller's conviction to pray for the conversion of sinners	*TCWAF* 1:100
January 3, 1785, "Felt very sensibly tonight at our monthly meeting for prayer, how far off a Christian life I live—how little real fellowship with Christ! How little of holy boldness can I use in prayer! Surely, if I were more to frequent the throne of grace in private it would be better with me!"	Monday evening prayer meeting. The centrality of prayer in the Christian life	*TCWAF* 1:101
January 8, 1785, "Much affected today in hearing my little girl say, 'How soon Sabbath day comes again!' . . . Was led to importune God at the throne of grace on her behalf."	Prayer for his family, particularly his daughter	*TCWAF* 1:101
January 9, 1785, "A goodish day upon the whole. Preached in the forenoon on being *quickened when we were dead in Trespasses and sins* and in the afternoon on the petition of the *blind man* in the tenth [chapter] of Mark. Expounded the 6th chapter of Acts this evening. One verse in particular caries in it conviction to me, *That we may give ourselves wholly to prayer and the ministry of the Word!*"	The Lord's Day. On this Sunday, Fuller preached two sermons on or related to prayers from Scripture	*TCWAF* 1:102

Date and Quotation	Explanatory Note	Reference
January 11, 1785, "Some outgoings of the heart in prayer today for the revival of real religion first in my own soul, and then in the churches in general. . . . Went several times to the Lord with some satisfaction but not much tender nearness."	2nd Tuesday of the Month	*TCWAF* 1:102
January 17, 1785, "Employed today in reading *Cotton Mather's Student and Preacher*, with some profit—but a poor evening meeting."	Monday evening prayer meeting	*TCWAF* 1:103
January 27, 1785, "Some outgoings in prayer for Brother Ryland for the cause of Christ which suffers much by his father's conduct . . . "	Intercession for a friend and fellow minister	*TCWAF* 1:105
February 7, 1785, "But little exercise today. Some tenderness this evening at the meeting of prayer for the revival of Christ's cause."	Monday evening prayer meeting	*TCWAF* 1:107
February 9, 1785, " . . . The Lord keep me!"	Possible scriptural petition from Num 6:24	*TCWAF* 1:107
February 14, 1785, "Not much exercise of a religious kind today. Some tenderness tonight at evening meeting wishing I could walk nearer to God—but it seems to be little more than wishing!"	Monday evening meeting	*TCWAF* 1:109
February 21, 1785, " . . . A poor evening meeting."	Monday evening meeting	*TCWAF* 1:110
February 22, 1785, "Some tenderness in private prayer—attended with shame. Had an agreeable visit with Mr. B. Wallis at Mr. Timms. Found the conversation very serious & profitable chiefly on closet-prayer, and experimental subjects."	Example of Fuller practicing and conversing on private prayer	*TCWAF* 1:111
February 25, 1785, " . . . Visited M. Daniels of Burton this afternoon . . . conversed & prayed with her as well as I knew how, but with but little savor."	Pastoral visitation included prayer	*TCWAF* 1:111
February 27, 1785, "Preached today and prayed with some fervor, on Christ as the *Wisdom* and the *Word* of God . . . "	The Lord's Day	*TCWAF* 1:112

Date and Quotation	Explanatory Note	Reference
March 7, 1785, "... Some tenderness tonight in the monthly prayer meeting, in speaking a little on *Continuing in prayer*; and in going to prayer—though I felt wretchedly cold before I began."	Monthly Prayer Meeting	*TCWAF* 1:113
March 24, 1785, "... Preached tonight on the ways of sin like the adulteress, being *movable* &c. some earnestness and solemnity of spirit in prayer and preaching."	Traveled to Woodford	*TCWAF* 1:117
March 25, 1785, "... Some tenderness in prayer with Mrs. Askew who is very ill. Damped in a little conversation with T. A. whom I thought to be a good man but find it is very doubtful whether he ever prays either in his family or in private ... "	Return from Woodford	*TCWAF* 1:117
March 30, 1785, "... My wife now lies ill of a miscarry, how does goodness and mercy follow us in delivering her in times of trouble!"	Wife's Miscarriage	*TCWAF* 1:118
March 31, 1785, "Felt myself vile tonight— Being at Mr. H.'s and hearing of a meeting of prayer there. Surely my evidences of real Christianity are very small! What should I think if I knew that of another which I know of myself! Should I think they had any real religion? Surely I could not!"	Prayer meeting at a Mr. Heighton's	*TCWAF* 1:119
April 6, 1785, "Taken up in Mr. H.'s company. Feel much dejected in viewing the state of the churches. O that God would revive us! O that we could pray for it with more fervor! ... "	Mr. Hall of Arnsby visiting Kettering	*TCWAF* 1:120
April 7, 1785, "This afternoon met at Mr. G.'s—went to prayer and from thense Mr. Hall & I went to break the unhappy affair of Mr. B to Mrs. B.—Found her in an amiable spirit indeed. A most affecting evening to us all!"	Pastoral Confrontation	*TCWAF* 1:121
April 11, 1785, "... But a poor time at evening meeting."	Monday evening prayer meeting	*TCWAF* 1:121
April 24, 1785, "... Some outgoings of heart of late in prayer. Feel myself tender tonight in that duty."	Lord's Day	*TCWAF* 1:123

Date and Quotation	Explanatory Note	Reference
April 30, 1785, "Thought today I could wish to die if I had but done my generation work. Last Monday I heard a young man at Northampton speak of the advantage of mixing prayer with reading the word. This morning I have been trying to read in that way. Read over the second chapter of Hosea in this way. O that I could call him *Ishi*, my husband, in a way of sweet & holy freedom! Oh that I could dwell nearer to him! I fear something unhappy should take place 'ere long in the church. O that I may but be kept near to God—then shall I be able to bear anything!"	Interesting that Fuller mentions his trying this practice when numerous entries reflect his prayer life as permeated with Scripture. Perhaps Fuller had separated previously the two disciplines into a time of reading and a time of prayer	*TCWAF* 1:125
May 1, 1785, " . . . Felt my heart go out in prayer this morning that God would make some use of me for good. Praying that I might not labour in vain and spend my strength for nought . . . On this I found much outgoing of heart in pleading *Christ's merits*, and the *welfare of souls* as the ground . . . "	The Lord's Day. Prayer for strength and success in his efforts	*TCWAF* 1:125
May 2, 1785, " . . . Tonight we met for prayer for the revival of religion. Felt tender all the time; but in hearing Mr. B. Wallis pray for me I was overcome. His having a better opinion of me than I deserve cuts me to the heart! Went to prayer myself, and felt more than ordinarily drawn out in prayer for revival of religion. I had felt many skeptical thoughts as 'What profit shall I have if I pray to God?' for which I felt grieved. Found a great satisfaction in these monthly meetings even supposing our requests should never be granted. Prayer to God is its own reward! Felt many bitter reflections for my stupid, carnal way of living."	Monthly Prayer Meeting. Note Fuller's statement, "Prayer to God is its own reward!"	*TCWAF* 1:126
June 12, 1785, " . . . Some earnestness & tenderness in prayer. But a poorish time in the afternoon from Psalm 65:2, *Thou that hearestprayer* &c . . . "	The Lord's Day	*TCWAF* 1:134

Date and Quotation	Explanatory Note	Reference
June 14, 1785, "Taken up in Mr. H's company—feel much pain for him. The Lord, in mercy to him and his churches in this country, keep him in the path of truth and righteousness."	Visiting with Mr. Robert Hall, Jr.	*TCWAF* 1:134
June 26, 1785, "This day has been one of the best that I have experienced I think for years. Most tenderly and earnestly affected in prayer and in preaching both. Could scarcely go on for weeping in the morning, preaching from Acts 4:33, *Great grace was upon them all!* Not quite so tender in the afternoon, though on the *excellency of the knowledge of Christ*—nor at the ordinance. Yet I felt a sweet serenity at the Lord's Supper, and spake of it under the idea of a feast."	The Lord's Day	*TCWAF* 1:137–8
July 3, 1785, "Another exceeding melting Sabbath—very tender and earnest in prayer & in preaching on casting our *care* on the Lord . . . "	The Lord's Day	*TCWAF* 1:139
July 4, 1785, "Very little exercise today and a poor time tonight at meeting though it was the night for the prayer meeting."	Monday evening prayer meeting	*TCWAF* 1:140
July 8, 1785, " . . . Some free conversation with a friend tonight (J/C) affords me some relief."	McMullen and Whelan noted that the "phrase may refer to Fuller's private prayer time, with 'J/C' an abbreviation for 'Jesus Christ'" (see *TCWAF* 1:41n295)	*TCWAF* 1:141
July 11, 1785, " . . . Rode home, but had a poor evening meeting."	Monday evening meeting	*TCWAF* 1:141
July 16, "Some pleasure in thinking on God's power to do abundantly more than we can ask or think. Surely he had need have more power in giving that I have in asking."	Scriptural allusion and motivation to pray from Eph 3:20	*TCWAF* 1:142
July 19–21, 1785, " . . . The Lord in mercy lead me into all truth! . . . "	In reference to his recent publication	*TCWAF* 1:143

Date and Quotation	Explanatory Note	Reference
July 24, 1785, "A pretty god forenoon on the above subject. Much solemn feeling in prayer on the ruined state of man by nature—was helped to deplore it before God on behalf of myself and the congregation . . . "	The Lord's Day. Connection between prayer and total depravity	*TCWAF* 1:143
July 25, 1785, "Very tender this morning in reading some remains of Mr. Mason's, author of *Songs of praise to Almighty God*. This appeared to me to be a life of prayer! but mine, O what is it? Went tonight to see M. Daniels of Barton—poor woman she is not likely to be here long, and much in the dark. Very solemn and affected in conversing and praying with her."	Influence of another work on Fuller's prayer life (room for further exploration). Prayer included in a pastoral visit	*TCWAF* 1:144
July 31, 1785, "A pretty good forenoon in preaching . . . Some tenderness in prayer. A poor time at the Lord's Supper."	The Lord's Day	*TCWAF* 1:145
August 1, 1785, "Some very tender feelings and outgoings of heart in prayer tonight at the monthly prayer meeting. Surely *Unbelief* damps our near addresses to God—and something of that spawn "What profit shall we have if we pray unto him?" lies at the bottom of our indifference to this duty."	Monthly Prayer Meeting	*TCWAF* 1:145
August 2, 1785, "Was very much affected today in calling on J. Daniel's wife and praying with her. She is a most wretched, miserable object indeed! . . . "	Visiting a difficult person and praying with her	*TCWAF* 1:146
September 5, 1785, "Feel myself guilty today on account of barrenness in spiritual conversation. A tender opportunity tonight in prayer at the monthly prayer meeting."	Monthly Prayer Meeting	*TCWAF* 1:150
September 7, 1785, "Set off for home—preached at Irchester tonight on God being *able to do more than we can ask or think*."	Preached on Eph 3:20. The verse was previously cited as motivation for prayer	*TCWAF* 1:151
September 20, 1785, "Today I thought to have devoted to fasting & prayer! but some complaints attending my body I not do the former—attended in some degree to the latter."	Example of Fuller's practice of fasting and praying	*TCWAF* 1:153
September 28, 1785, " . . . Heard Mr. Heighton pray with most pleasure."	Ministers' meeting at Kettering	*TCWAF* 1:154

Date and Quotation	Explanatory Note	Reference
September 30, 1785, " . . . The best part of the day was I think in conversation. A question was put and discussed, to the following purport . . . 'To what causes in ministers may much of the want of their success be imputed?' The answer much turned upon the want of *personal* religion—particularly the want of close dealing with God in *closet prayer*. Jeremiah 10:21 . . . Another reason assigned was, the want of reading and studying the Scriptures more as *Christians*, for the edification of our own souls. We are apt to study them merely to find out something *to say to others*, without living upon the truth ourselves . . . Another reason was, our want of being emptied of *self-sufficiency*. In proportion as we lean upon our own gifts, or parts, or preparations, we slight the Holy Spirit and no wonder that being grieved he should leave us to do our work alone! . . . Oh that I may remember these hints for my good!"	Minister's meeting at Northampton	*TCWAF* 1:154–5
October 2, 1785, " . . . Preached in the morning from Acts 2:41, and in the afternoon from verse 42."	The Lord's Day. Fuller baptized four persons this day	*TCWAF* 1:155
October 3, 1785, "This was the evening for our monthly prayer meeting . . . I felt very tender, and was much affected in prayer. When I come to these opportunities it has been frequent for me to be much affected, and yet I have so little heart to wrestle with God alone. I cannot tell how to account for this!"	Monthly prayer meeting	*TCWAF* 1:156
November 21, 1785, " . . . On the Lord's day the 20th I preached on . . . Also, on *soul prosperity* from 3 John 2. Had a tender & earnest mind."	Lord's Day, Returned from intenerate preaching circuit	*TCWAF* 1:159
November 30–December 6, 1785, "Had a very affecting time in prayer at our monthly prayer meeting. O for *Christ's sake* was enabled to plead."	Monthly prayer meeting	*TCWAF* 1:160
December 25, 1785, " . . . Felt tenderly in prayer with Mr. Lillyman who appears to be in dying circumstances . . . "	The Lord's Day. Pastoral prayer with sick member of his congregation	*TCWAF* 1:163

Date and Quotation	Explanatory Note	Reference
January 1–8, 1786, "Some painful reflec-tions in thinking on my vast deficiencies. Another year is gone, and what have I done for God?—O that my life was more devoted to God! . . . Exceedingly distressed on Wednesday night. I fear God will take away my little girl. I have reason to fear some awful chastisement is at hand—either *spiritual* or *natural*. Methought I was like the Israelites who had little or no heart to call upon God except in times of trouble. I tried however to pray to him now. I think I could be will-ing to submit to God in all things, and bear whatever he should lay upon me, though it were the loss of one of the dearest parts of myself, provided I could but see Christ formed in her! I know also I have no demand on the Lord for this, but surely I ought to bless his name that he does not require me to be willing to be lost, or that that should be the end of any that he has put under my care! The chief exercise of my mind this week has been about my poor child. Methought I felt somewhat of resignation to divine providence, 'The Lord liveth . . . *and blessed by my rock'* &c."	Prayer for healing and strength during the sickness of his daughter	*TCWAF* 1:164
January 8–January 15, 1786, "Very tender and earnest this morning at public prayer. O that God may work upon the tender minds of our youth and children . . . "	Lord's Day	*TCWAF* 1:164
January 29–February 5, 1786, " . . . Our dear little girl has this week much alarmed our fears. On Thursday morning she broke out with the measles, and we hop the ill-ness may be hereby carried off. As I sat by her that morning alone she requested me to go to prayer with her, saying though she was greatly afflicted with pain, 'she would try to lie still.' I did so, and found some tenderness of heart on her behalf . . . "	Praying for and with his daughter	*TCWAF* 1:166

Date and Quotation	Explanatory Note	Reference
March 12–April 16, 1786, "For this month past I have had great exercise of heart on account of my poor little girl . . . Sometimes pleading hard with God on account of her, at other times ready to despair, and to fear God would never hear me. Lord's day March 19 was a distressing day to me. My concern for the loss of her body is but trifling compared with that of her soul! Preached & prayed much from Matthew 15.25, Lord help me! On the Monday I carried her towards Northampton . . . was exceedingly distressed on the Monday night . . . Went to prayer with a heart almost broken. Some encouragement from a conversation with dear Brother Ryland. I observed 'God had not bound himself to hear the prayers of anyone for the salvation of the soul of another.' He replied, 'but if he has not, he very frequently does so, and hence perhaps through grace does not run in the *blood*, yet we frequently see it does in the *line*. Many more of the children of God's children are gracious than others.' I know neither I nor mine have any claim upon the Almighty for mercy, but as long as there is life it shall be my business surely to implore it! Methought I saw on Tuesday (21st) the vanity of all created good. I saw if God were to cut off my poor child, and not to afford me some extraordinary support under it, I should be next to dead to the whole creation, and all creation dead to me! O that I were but thus dead as Paul was *by the cross of Christ!* On Thursday preached at Woodford from Psalm 50.15, Call upon me in the day of trouble &c . . . On Monday [March] 27th, riding towards Northampton I think I felt greater earnestness and freedom with God than I ever had before in this matter. I seemed likewise more willing to leave her in the hands of God. Some tender opportunities in prayer with her & for her.	Fuller's daughter, her healing, and his strength to endure the suffering were major themes during the extended season of sickness that his daughter	*TCWAF* 1:169–70

Date and Quotation	Explanatory Note	Reference
April 28, 1786, "Riding to Towcester was exceedingly affected and importunate with God in prayer for her soul. I felt indeed the force of those words 'To whom Lord shall we go? Thou has the words of eternal life!' . . . My heart seemed to be dissolved in earnest cries for mercy, particularly so on the other side of Blisworth . . . "	Prayer for the salvation and healing of his daughter	*TCWAF* 1:171
May 14–May 21, 1786, "Death! Death is all around me! . . . At times I feel reconciled to whatever may befall me . . . But at other times, I am distressed beyond due bounds. On Thursday the 25th in particular . . . I lay before the Lord weeping like David, and refusing to be comforted. This brought on I have reason to think a bilious cholic, a painful affliction it was, and the more so as it was it has prevented me ever seeing my child alive again! Yes, she is gone!"	His daughter's death and his own sickness	*TCWAF* 1:172
May 30, 1786, "I heard as I lay very ill in bed in another room I heard a whispering. I enquired . . . and all were silent!—but all is well! I feel reconciled to God! I called my family round my bed—I sat up & prayed as well as I could. I bowed my head &worshipped, and blessed a taking as well as a giving God."	Fuller still ill after his daughter's death	*TCWAF* 1:172
June 1, 1786, " . . . Often she requested me to pray with her and for her that God, as she expressed it, would 'bless her and keep her and save her soul!' She took great delight in some verses composed for her by Mr. Ryland. These she would repeat over to herself prayer-wise, and would ask me to *sing* them to her when we were alone."	Reflecting on his late daughter's life and piety	*TCWAF* 1:173

Date and Quotation	Explanatory Note	Reference
October 3, 1789, "For upwards of a year & a half I have wrote nothing . . . Two or three years ago my heart began wretchedly to degenerate from God. Soon after my child Sally died I sunk into a sad state of carnality; . . . I feel at times some longing after the lost joys of God's salvation, but cannot recover them. I have backslidden from God; and yet I may rather be said to be habitually dejected on account of it than earnestly to repent for it . . . My spiritual enemies have been too much for me. Some time ago I set apart a day for fasting & prayer; and seemed to get some strength in pleading with God. The very next day, as I remember, I found my heart so wretchedly strayed away, such a load of guilt contracted, that I was frightened at my own prayer the preceding day—and I have not set apart a day to fast and pray since. But surely this was one of Satan's devices by which I have been be-fooled. Perhaps also I trusted too much to my fasting &praying, and did not on that account follow it with watchfulness. During this summer I have sometimes thought what *Joy* Christians might possess in this world were they but to improve their opportunities & advantages . . . I have preached two or three times upon this subject. . . . Once from John 15:11, . . . Another time from Nehemiah 8:10 . . . And again from Mark 11:24, Whatsoever things ye desire when ye pray, believe ye shall receive them, & ye shall receive them. In which the chief sentiment on which I insisted was how *confidence in God's goodness was necessary to our success in prayer . . .* "	The Lord's Day. Fuller had an extended season of silence in his diary after the death of his daughter and other happenings	*TCWAF* 1:176–77

Date and Quotation	Explanatory Note	Reference
January 20, 1790, "During the last quarter of a year I seem to have gained some ground on spiritual things. I have read some of President Edwards's sermons, which have left a deep impression upon my heart. Have attended more constantly than heretofore to private prayer, and feel a little renewed strength. Sometimes also I have been much affected in public prayer, particularly on Monday evening January 4, at the monthly prayer meeting . . . "	The beginning of Fuller's spiritual renewal after an extended season of neglecting private prayer	*TCWAF* 1:178
March 27, 1790, "Some weeks ago, I thought I felt to gain ground by closet prayer; but have lately relapsed again too much into indifference . . . "	Still struggling in private prayer	*TCWAF* 1:179

Date and Quotation	Explanatory Note	Reference

[No specific date], 1791, "In the spring of this year there appeared a religious concern amongst five or six of our young people. I proposed to meet them once a week at the Vestry to talk and pray with them. I hope that has been of use to both me and them.
 	
    Towards the latter end of this summer I heard of some revival of religion taking place in certain individuals about Walgrave and Guilsborough and that the means of it were their setting apart days for fasting and prayer. From hence I thought, we had been long praying for revival of God's cause, the spread of the gospel amongst the heathens &c. and perhaps God would begin with us at home first. I was particularly affected with this thought by finding it in the 67th Psalm which I was expounding about the same time—'that God being merciful to *us*& blessing *us* might be the means of his way being known upon earth, and his saving health among all nations'; at least amongst a part of them.
 	
    O to be spiritually alive amongst ourselves! One Monday evening meeting, I think in October, I told our friends of some things and prayed with them with more than usual affection—I was particularly encouraged by the promise of giving the Holy Spirit to them that ask. Surely if ever I wrestled with God in my life I did so then for *more grace*, for *forgiveness*, for the restoration of the joys of salvation; and that not only for myself, but for the generality of Christians amongst us, who I plainly perceived to be in a poor lukewarm state when compared with the primitive Christians.
 	
    December 27th I set apart for fasting and prayer. I felt tender in the course of the day . . . "
	A year in review entry. Key entry for Fuller's theology of prayer related to God's answer of long seasons of prayer and the giving of the Spirit for those who ask, presumably for those who ask in prayer. Also of interest is the role of expounding the Psalms during this season of renewed passion for prayer for revival of religion	*TCWAF* 1:181–82

Date and Quotation	Explanatory Note	Reference
[No specific date], 1792, "This year was begun, or nearly so, with a day of solemn fasting & prayer as a church. It was a most affecting time with me, and many more. Surely we never had such a spirit of prayer amongst us! On April 2 we lost our dear and worthy Mr. Beeby Wallis; the next church meeting was kept as a day of solemn fasting and prayer, and a very tender opportunity it was. . . . Had a good deal of religious concern among the young people of the congregation. I set up a private meeting in which I might read and pray & converse with them—& have found it good both to them and me . . . "	Reflection on first quarter to half of the year	*TCWAF* 1:183
July 25, 1792, "O my God, my soul is cast down within me! The afflictions in my family seem too heavy for me. O Lord I am oppressed, undertake for me! My thoughts are broken off and all my prospects seem to be perished! I feel however some support from such Scriptures as these—All things shall work together for good &c. God, even our own God, shall bless us. It is of the Lord's mercy that I am not consumed. One of my friends observed yesterday, that it was a difficulty in many cases to know wherefore God contended with us? But I thought that was no difficulty with me! I have sinned against the Lord; and it is not a little affliction that will lay hold of me, but it seems God is determined to prove me. Those words have impressed me of late, *It was in mine heart to chastise them!*"	Struggling with wife's diminished state during her final pregnancy	*TCWAF* 1:184
September 2, 1792, " . . . New scenes seem to be opening before me—new trials—O that I may glorify God in every stage! . . . "	Following the death of his wife	*TCWAF* 1:185

Date and Quotation	Explanatory Note	Reference
July 18, 1794, " . . . Of late my thoughts have turned upon another marriage. That passage, which has been with me in all my principal concerns though life—*In all thy ways acknowledge him, &he shall direct thy paths*—has recurred again. I found much of the hand of God in this concern, bot as to turning me from quarters on which my thoughts were employed, and guiding me to others where I hope to find a helper to my soul . . . It seemed a lovely thing which is said of Christ, *He went about doing good!* O that whatever I may possess at any time of this world's good, it might be consecrated to God! The Lord ever preserve me from the mean vice of Covetousness! . . . "	Reflection on the last two years	*TCWAF* 1:186–88
October 27, 1794, " . . . I devoted this day to fasting & prayer on account of my expected marriage, to entreat the blessing of God upon me, and upon her that may be connected with me, & upon all that pertains to us. This morning previous to family prayer I read the 8th chapter of the 1st Book of Kings, from verse 22 to the end. The 38th and 39th verses were much to me, as were also the 28th. I found a tenderness of heart in prayer after reading. My house keeper, on perceiving that I fasted, requested to join with me, & that her future life might be remembered before God in the supplications of the day."	Anticipation of a new marriage	*TCWAF* 1:188–89

Date and Quotation	Explanatory Note	Reference
May 12, 1796, " . . . I have found my marriage contribute greatly to my peace & comfort, & the comforts of my family for which I record humble and hearty thanks to the God of my Life. This day my eldest son Robert is gone to London, upon trial at a Warehouse belonging to Mr. Burles. My heart has been much exercised about him. The child is sober, & tender in his spirit; I find too he prays in private: but whether he be really godly I know not. Sometimes he has expressed a desire after the ministry . . . About a year & a half ago I felt a very affecting time in pleading with God on his behalf. Nothing appeared to me so desirable for him as that he might be a Servant of God. I felt my heart drawn out much to devote him to the Lord in whatever way he might employ him . . . I felt very tenderly last night & this morning in prayer. I cannot say, *God, before whom my Fathers Abraham & Isaac did walk;* but I can say, *God who hath fed me all my life long unto this day—The Angel which redeemed me from all evil, bless the Lad!* On January 10 this year God gave me another child which I pray may also be the Lord's."	Reflection on the past year	*TCWAF* 1:190–91
July 1796, " . . . I was lately earnestly engaged in prayer for him, that he might be renewed in spirit, and be the Lord's. Those words to my mind, and I prayed them over him many times, *Hear my prayer O Lord, that goeth not forth of my feigned lips!*	No specific day in July listed. Concern for his son Robert	*TCWAF* 1:191
October 2, 1799, " . . . I am the subject to many faults in company, and often incur guilt. The Lord keep me in the way I go, and enable me to keep my heart with all diligence. O that I may be spiritual, humble, and watchful, in all companies. May the God and Father of our Lord Jesus Christ prosper my way! May the God of Israel preserve my family, friends, and connections, during my absence . . . "	In prospect of leaving for fundraising in Scotland for the BMS	*TCWAF* 1:192

Date and Quotation	Explanatory Note	Reference
October 21, 1799, " . . . Returning to Glasgow that evening, we heard of the death of our beloved Pearce! O Jonathan, very pleasant has thou been to me. I am distressed for thee, my brother Jonathan! O Jonathan, thou wast slain on thy high places! . . . "	Fund raising in Scotland	*TCWAF* 1:201
July 21, 1800, " . . . The sorrows of my heart have been increased to an almost unsup-portable degree at different times. Yet I have hoped in God, and do still hope that I shall see mercy in the end. The Lord knows I have not sought *great things* for him; and that I have been more concerned when he has been among the soldiers, for the *wicked* course he was following on account of the *meanness* of his taste. O may the Lord bring me out of this horrible pit, & put a new song in my mouth!"	Concern for his son Robert	*TCWAF* 1:212

Appendix 2

Timeline of Fuller's Expositions,
June 6–August 29, 1784

The Sermon on the Mount (Matthew 5–7)

A PROBABLE TIMELINE OF Fuller's expositions of the Sermon on the Mount was constructed through a comparison of the expository divisions in *The Complete Works of the Rev. Andrew Fuller*, edited by Joseph Belcher, and the relevant diary entries in *The Complete Works of Andrew Fuller: The Diary of Andrew Fuller, 1780–1801*, edited by Michael D. McMullen and Timothy D. Whelan. All of the entries from Fuller's *Diary* are italicized and justified to the right in the date column. All other entries are extrapolated from Fuller's *Works*.[1]

Date	Sermon Text/Title or Diary Entry
Sunday, June 6—	Matt 5:1–12, "The Beatitudes"
Sunday, June 13 –	Matt 5:13–16, "Character of Christians and Christian Ministers"
Tuesday, June 15–	Next to this entry Fuller wrote in the margin "*Matt. 5.8.*"
Sunday, June 20 –	Matt 5:17–32, "Perpetuity and Spirituality of the Moral Law"
Sunday, June 27 –	Matt 5:33–37, "Oaths"
Sunday, July 4—	Matt 5:38–42, "Resisting Evil"

1. Fuller, *Works*, 1:561–92; and Fuller, *Complete Works: Diary*, 1:55–71.

Sunday, July 11 –	*"Expounded the last part of the 5th chapter of Matthew this evening."* Matt 5:43–48, "Love to Enemies"
Sunday, July 18 –	Matt 6:1–8, "Alms-giving, and Prayer"
Sunday, July 25—	Matt 6:9–15, "The Lord 's Prayer"
Sunday, August 1—	Matt 6:16–34, "Fasting, and Other Duties"
Sunday, August 8 –	Matt 7:1–6, "Judging Others, and Casting Pearls before Swine"
Sunday, August 15 –	*"Preaching today on divine goodness as laid up for us and laid out upon us . . . Preached this evening at Loddington, a sermon on Harvest."* Fuller's reference to *"laid up"* may be recalling material expounded already in Matthew 6. Matt 7:7–12, "Prayer and Equity"
Sunday, August 22—	Matt 7:13–20, "The Broad and Narrow Way; and How to Judge of Teachers"
Sunday, August 29 –	*"Expounded and finished Christ's Sermon on the Mount."* Matt 7:21–29, "The Last Judgment

Vita

Matthew C. Bryant

EDUCATIONAL

PhD, New Orleans Baptist Theological Seminary, 2019

ThM, New Orleans Baptist Theological Seminary, 2017

Graduate Certificate in Biblical Languages, New Orleans Baptist Theological Seminary, 2015

MDiv, Liberty Baptist Theological Seminary, 2013

BS, Liberty University, 2010

MINISTERIAL

Deputy Wing Chaplain, Maj, United States Air Force Reserve, 914th Air Refueling Wing, Niagara Falls Air Reserve Station, New York, 2020–present

Campus Pastor and Pastor of Discipleship, Village Baptist Church, Fayetteville, North Carolina, 2019–2020

Chaplain, Captain, United States Air Force Reserve, 403d Reserve Wing, Keesler Air Force Base, Mississippi, 2013–2020

Pulpit Supply, Alabama and Louisiana, 2015–2018

College Minister, King Street Church, Chambersburg, Pennsylvania, 2011–2015

Associate Minister of Pastoral Care, King Street Church, Chambersburg, Pennsylvania, 2013–2015

Interim Youth Pastor, King Street Church, Chambersburg, Pennsylvania, 2012–2013

PROFESSIONAL

Administrative Assistant to Dr. Craig Price, Dean of Online Learning, Professor of New Testament and Greek, New Orleans Baptist Theological Seminary, New Orleans, Louisiana, 2017–2019

Fellow to Dr. Michael H. Edens, Dean of Graduate Studies, Professor of Theology and Islamic Studies, 2016–2018

Professional Doctoral Recruiter and Administrative Assistant, Office of Student Enlistment, New Orleans Baptist Theological Seminary, New Orleans, Louisiana, 2015–2016

Graduate Assistant to Dr. Ben Gutierrez, Dean of Liberty University Online, Chair of Pastoral Leadership, Professor of Religion, Liberty University, Lynchburg, Virginia, 2010–2011

ORGANIZATIONAL

Member, Evangelical Theological Society, 2015–present

Member, Evangelical Homiletics Society, 2016–present

Bibliography

Allen, David L. *The Extent of the Atonement: A Historical and Critical Review*. Nashville: Broadman & Holman, 2016.

Ascol, Thomas Kennedy. "The Doctrine of Grace: A Critical Analysis of Federalism in the Theologies of John Gill and Andrew Fuller." PhD diss., Southwestern Baptist Theological Seminary, 1989.

Baelz, Peter. *Prayer and Providence: A Background Study*. London: SCM, 1968.

Bakke, Robert O. *The Power of Extraordinary Prayer*. Wheaton, IL: Crossway, 2000.

Ballitch, Andrew. "An Analysis of Andrew Fuller's *The Gospel Its Own Witness*." *Founders Journal* 101 (Summer 2015) 9–10.

Bayne, Peter. *Documents Relating to the Settlement of the Church of England by the Act of Uniformity of 1662: With an Historical Introduction*. London: W. Kent and Co., 1862.

Bebbington, David W. *Evangelicalism in Modern Britain: A History from the 1730s to the 1980s*. London: Routledge, 1989.

———. "The Early Developments of the Baptist Movement." In *150 Anni Di Presenza Battista in Italia (1863–2013)*, edited by S. Gaglian, 9–27. Guicciardiniana 4. Milan: Biblion Edizion, 2015.

Beck, Peter. "Trans-Atlantic Friendships: Andrew Fuller and the New Divinity Men." *The Journal of Baptist Studies* 8 (February 2016) 16–50.

———. "The Voice of Faith: Jonathan Edwards's Theology of Prayer." PhD diss., Southern Baptist Theological Seminary, 2007.

Benge, Dustin W., and Michael A.G. Haykin. "'A Most Blessed Exercise': Prayer in the Life of Andrew Fuller." Unpublished Paper, n.d.

Binney, Thomas. *The Closet and the Church: A Book for Ministers*. London: Jackson and Walford, 1849.

Box, Bart D. "The Atonement in the Thought of Andrew Fuller." PhD diss., New Orleans Baptist Theological Seminary, 2009.

Bradley, James E., and Richard A. Muller. *Church History: An Introduction to Research Methods and Resources*. 2nd ed. Grand Rapids: Eerdmans, 2016.

Brewster, Paul. "Andrew Fuller (1754–1815): Model Baptist Pastor-Theologian." PhD diss., Southeastern Baptist Theological Seminary, 2007.

———. *Andrew Fuller: Model Pastor-Theologian*. Nashville: Broadman & Holman, 2010.

———. "Andrew Fuller's Doctrine of God." *Founders Journal* 101 (Summer 2015) 22–47.

Briggs, John H.Y. *Pulpit and People: Studies in Eighteenth-Century Baptist Life and Thought.* Eugene, OR: Wipf & Stock, 2009.

Brine, John. *A Refutation of Arminian Principles, Delivered in a Pamphlet, Entitled, the Modern Question Concerning Repentance and Faith, Examined with Candour, etc. in a Letter to a Friend.* London: A. Ward, 1743.

Bruce, Dustin Blaine. "An Analysis of Andrew Fuller's Strictures on Sandemanianism." *Founders Journal* 101 (Summer 2015) 16–19.

———. "'The Grand Encouragement': Andrew Fuller's Pneumatology as a Reception of and Advancement on Orthodox, Puritan, and Evangelical Perspectives on the Holy Spirit." PhD diss., Southern Baptist Theological Seminary, 2018.

Bunyan, John. *Works of John Bunyan.* Edited by George Offor. Vols. 1–3. Bellingham, WA: Logos Bible Software, 2006.

Burnet, Gilbert. *An Exposition of the Thirty-Nine Articles of the Church of England.* Edited by James R. Page. New York: Appleton & Company, 1852.

Calvin, John. *Institutes of the Christian Religion.* Translated by Henry Beveridge. Peabody, MA: Hendrickson, 2008.

Calvin, John, and William Pringle. *Commentaries on the Epistles to Timothy, Titus, and Philemon.* Bellingham, WA: Logos Bible Software, 2010.

Carey, William. *An Enquiry into the Obligations of Christians to Use Means for the Conversion of the Heathens.* Edited by Ernest Alexander Payne. Facsimile. London: Carey Kingsgate, 1961.

Cathcart, William, ed. "Robinson, Robert." In *The Baptist Encyclopaedia.* Philadelphia, PA: Louis H. Everts, 1881.

Chan, Simon. *Spiritual Theology: A Systematic Study of the Christian Life.* Downers Grove, IL: InterVarsity Academic, 1998.

Chun, Chris. "Andrew Fuller on the Atonement: Was Fuller's Approach Nearer to That of Jonathan Edwards or the Younger?" *The Journal of Baptist Studies* 8 (February 2016) 51–71.

———. "The Greatest Instruction Received from Human Writings: The Legacy of Jonathan Edwards in the Theology of Andrew Fuller." PhD diss., University of St. Andrews, 2008.

———. *The Legacy of Jonathan Edwards in the Theology of Andrew Fuller.* Boston, MA: Brill, 2012.

———. "'Sense of the Heart': Jonathan Edward's Legacy in the Writing of Andrew Fuller." *Eusebeia* 9 (Spring 2008) 117–134.

Chute, Anthony L., Nathan A. Finn, and Michael A.G. Haykin. *The Baptist Story: From English Sect to Global Movement.* Nashville: Broadman & Holman, 2015.

Claude, Jean. *An Essay on the Composition of a Sermon.* Translated by Robert Robinson. 2nd ed. Vol. 2. London: J. Buckland, 1782.

Clipsham, E.F. "Andrew Fuller and Fullerism: A Study in Evangelical Calvinism." *Baptist Quarterly* 20, no. 3 (January 1, 1963) 99–114.

Cox, Francis A. *History of the English Baptist Missionary Society: From A.D. 1792 to A.D. 1842.* Philadelphia, PA: American Baptist Publication Society, 1844.

Crosby, Thomas. *The History of English Baptists.* Vols. 1–4. Bellingham, WA: Logos Bible Software, 2011.

Daniels, Brian. "The Doctrine of the Bible's Truthfulness in Andrew Fuller's Theology." *Journal of Baptist Studies* 8 (February 2016) 72–98.

Davies, Horton. *The English Free Churches*. 2nd ed. New York: Oxford University Press, 1963.

———. *Worship and Theology in England: From Watts and Wesley to Martineau, 1690–1900*. 2nd ed. Vols. 2–3. Grand Rapids: Eerdmans, 1996.

———. *Worship and Theology in England: From Watts and Wesley to Maurice, 1690–1850*. Vol. 3. Princeton: Princeton University Press, 2015.

———. *The Worship of the English Puritans*. 2nd ed. Morgan, PA: Soli Deo Gloria, 1997.

Dees, Jason Edwin. "The Way to True to Excellence: The Spirituality of Samuel Pearce." PhD diss., Southern Baptist Theological Seminary, 2015.

Dever, Mark. "On the Use and Importance of Corporate Prayer." *9Marks eJournal* 5.1 (February 2008) 5–9.

Deweese, Charles W. *Prayer in Baptist Life: A Historical Survey*. Nashville: Broadman & Holman, 1986.

Dockery, David S. "Looking Back, Looking Ahead." In *Theologians of the Baptist Tradition*, edited by Timothy George and David S. Dockery, 338–409. Nashville: Broadman & Holman, 2001.

Doggett, J.C. "Joseph Ivimey (1773–1834)." In Vol. 3, *The British Particular Baptists*, 113–131. Springfield, MO: Particular Baptist, 2003.

Edwards, Jonathan. *An Humble Attempt to Promote Explicit Agreement and Visible Union of God's People in Extraordinary Prayer, for the Revival and the Advancement of Christ's Kingdom on Earth*. In *The Works of Jonathan Edwards*, 2:278–312. Carlisle, PA: Banner of Truth, 1974.

———. *The Works of Jonathan Edwards*. Vols. 1–2. Carlisle, PA: Banner of Truth, 1974.

Ella, George. *Law and Gospel in the Theology of Andrew Fuller*. Durham, UK: GoPublications, 1996.

Ellis, Christopher J. "From the Heart: The Spirituality of Free Prayer." In *Gathering: A Theology and Spirituality of Worship in Free Church Tradition*, 103–24. London: SCM, 2004.

———. *Gathering: A Theology and Spirituality of Worship in Free Church Tradition*. London: SCM, 2004.

Ellis, Rufus. "Liturgical Worship and Free Prayer." *Monthly Religious Magazine*, 39.5 (May 1868) 354–61.

Elwyn, Thornton. "Particular Baptists of Northamptonshire Baptist Association as Reflected in the Circular Letters 1765–1820." *Baptist Quarterly* 36, no. 8 (1996) 368–81.

———. "Particular Baptists of Northamptonshire Baptist Association as Reflected in the Circular Letters 1765–1820." *Baptist Quarterly* 37, no. 1 (1997) 3–19.

———. *The Northamptonshire Baptist Association: A Short History 1764–1964*. London: Carey Kingsgate, 1964.

Evans, John. "The Circular Letter from the Baptist Ministers and Messengers Assembled at Carleton, Bedfordshire," June 1774. https://lib.ugent.be/nl/catalog/rug01:001144105.

———. "The Circular Letter from the Ministers and Messengers Assembled at Kettering, May 1765." In *The Northamptonshire Baptist Association: A Short History 1764–1964*, 12–4. London: Carey Kingsgate, 1964.

Fanning, Don. "Eschatology and Missions." *Themes of Theology that Impacts Missions* 8 (January 1, 2009). https://digitalcommons.liberty.edu/cgm_theo/8.

Fiddes, Paul S. "Mission and Liberty: A Baptist Connection." In *Tracks and Traces: Baptist Identity in Church and Theology*, 249–73. Studies in Baptist History and Thought. Eugene, OR: Wipf & Stock, 2007.

Finn, Nathan. "The Renaissance in Andrew Fuller Studies: A Bibliographic Essay." *Southern Baptist Journal of Theology* 17, no. 2 (February 8, 2014) 44–61.

———. "Review of The Legacy of Jonathan Edwards in the Theology of Andrew Fuller by Chris Chun." *Themelios* 37, no. 3 (2012) 536–38.

Floyd, Ronnie. *Pleading with Southern Baptists: To Humbly Come Together before God in Clear Agreement, Visible Union, & in Extraordinary Prayer for the Next Great Awakening and for the World to Be Reached for Christ*. https://www.ronniefloyd.com/am-site/media/pleading-with-southern-baptists---e-book.pdf.

Forsyth, Peter Taylor. *The Soul of Prayer*. Oak Harbor, WA: Logos Research Systems, Inc., 1999.

Francis, Keith A., and William Gibson, eds. *The Oxford Handbook of the British Sermon, 1689–1901*. Oxford: Oxford University Press, 2012.

Fuller, Andrew. *Antinomianism Contrasted with the Religion Taught and Exemplified in the Holy Scriptures*. 2nd ed. Bristol, UK: Button & Son, 1817.

———. *The Complete Works of Andrew Fuller: Apologetic Works 1, The Gospel Worthy of All Acceptation*. Edited by Robert William Oliver. Vol. 5. Berlin: De Gruyter, 2019.

———. *The Complete Works of Andrew Fuller: Apologetic Works 3, The Calvinistic and Socinian Systems Examined and Compared, as to Their Moral Tendency*. Edited by Thomas J. Nettles. Vol. 7. Berlin: De Gruyter, 2018.

———. *The Complete Works of Andrew Fuller: Apologetic Works 5, Strictures on Sandemanianism*. Edited by Nathan Finn. Berlin: De Gruyter, 2016.

———. *The Complete Works of Andrew Fuller: Memoirs of the Rev. Samuel Pearce*. Edited by Michael A.G. Haykin. Vol. 4. Berlin: De Gruyter, 2017.

———. *The Complete Works of Andrew Fuller: The Diary of Andrew Fuller, 1780–1801*. Edited by Michael D. McMullen and Timothy D. Whelan. Vol. 1. Berlin: De Gruyter, 2016.

———. *The Complete Works of the Rev. Andrew Fuller*. Edited by Joseph Belcher. Vol. 1–3. Harrisonburg, VA: Sprinkle, 1988.

———. "Confession of Faith." In *The Armies of the Lamb: The Spirituality of Andrew Fuller*, edited by Michael A.G. Haykin, 273–82. Dundas, ON: Joshua, 2001.

———. *The Dangerous Impact of Delay in Gospel Issues*. Edited by Michael A.G. Haykin and G. Stephen Weaver. Louisville, KY: Andrew Fuller Center for Baptist Studies, 2015.

———. "The Harmony of Scripture Precepts, Prayers, and Promises." In *The Work of Faith, the Labour of Love, and the Patience of Hope, Illustrated: In the Life and Death of the Rev. Andrew Fuller*, edited by John Ryland Jr., 218–21. 2nd ed. London: Button & Son, 1818.

———. "The Lord's Prayer." In *The Complete Works of the Rev. Andrew Fuller*, edited by Joseph Belcher, 1:577–83. Harrisonburg, VA: Sprinkle, 1988.

———. *Miscellaneous Pieces on Various Religious Subjects, Being the Last Remains of the Rev. Andrew Fuller*. Edited by John W. Morris. London: Wightman and Cramp, 1826.

———. "The Nature and Importance of Walking by Faith." In *The Works of the Rev. Andrew Fuller*, 7:9–38. New Haven: Sherman Converse, 1824.

————. "The Nature and Importance of Walking by Faith." In *The Complete Works of the Rev. Andrew Fuller*, 2:171–83. Boston: Lincoln, Edmands & Co, 1833.

————. "The Nature and Importance of Walking by Faith." In *The Complete Works of the Rev. Andrew Fuller*, edited by Joseph Belcher, 1:117–34. Philadelphia: American Baptist Publication Society, 1845.

————. *The Nature and Importance of Walking by Faith. A Sermon Delivered at the Annual Association of Baptist Ministers and Churches Met at Nottingham, June 2, 1784: To Which Are Added, A Few Persuasives to a General Union in Prayer for the Revival of Real Religion*. Northampton: T. Dicey & Co., 1784.

Garrett, James Leo, Jr., E. Glenn Hinson, and James E. Tull. *Are Southern Baptists "Evangelicals"?* Macon, GA: Mercer University Press, 1983.

Garrett, James Leo, Jr. *Baptist Theology: A Four-Century Study*. Macon, GA: Mercer University Press, 2009.

————. "Theology of Prayer." *Southwestern Journal of Theology* 14, no. 2 (1972) 3–17.

George, Timothy, and David S. Dockery, eds. *Theologians of the Baptist Tradition*. Nashville: Broadman & Holman, 2001.

George, Timothy, and Denise George, eds. *Baptist Confessions, Covenants, and Catechisms*. Nashville: Broadman & Holman, 1996.

Gill, John. *A Complete Body of Doctrinal and Practical Divinity: Or a System of Evangelical Truths, Deduced from the Sacred Scriptures*. 2 vols. London: Tegg & Company, 1839.

————. *An Exposition of the New Testament*. 3 vols. The Baptist Commentary Series. London: Mathews and Leigh, 1809.

Ginn, Richard J. *The Politics of Prayer in Early Modern Britain: Church and State in Seventeenth-Century England*. New York: Tauris, 2007.

Gombos, Chris S. "Divine Sovereignty, Divine Providence, and Prayer in the Thought of Evagrius Ponticus." PhD diss., Loyola University Chicago, 2013.

Gough, Thomas Talman. *On Prayer Meetings: The Circular Letter from the Ministers and Messengers of the Several Baptist Churches in the Northamptonshire Association, Assembled at Hackleton, on the 17th and 18th Days of May, 1842, etc.* Kettering, OH: Joseph Toller, 1842.

Grant, Keith S. *Andrew Fuller and the Evangelical Renewal of Pastoral Theology*. Studies in Baptist History and Thought 36. Milton Keynes, GB: Paternoster, 2013.

Grenz, Stanley J. *Prayer: The Cry for the Kingdom*. Rev. ed. Grand Rapids: Eerdmans, 2005.

————. *Theology for the Community of God*. Grand Rapids: Eerdmans, 2000.

Grudem, Wayne. *Systematic Theology: An Introduction to Biblical Doctrine*. Grand Rapids: Zondervan, 1994.

Hall, Robert. *Help to Zion's Travellers: Being an Attempt to Remove Various Stumbling Blocks out of the Way, Relating to Doctrinal, Experimental, and Practical Religion*. Philadelphia: American Baptist Publication Society, 1851.

Harkness, Georgia Elma. "Theology of Prayer." *Review & Expositor* 71, no. 3 (1974) 303–313.

Harmon, Matthew S. "Prayer: Pleading for the Consummation of the New-Creation Kingdom." In *Making All Things New: Inaugurated Eschatology for the Life of the Church*. Grand Rapids: Baker Academic, 2016.

Hastings, James. *The Christian Doctrine of Prayer*. Edinburgh: T&T Clark, 1915.

Haykin, Michael A.G. "Acknowledgements." In *The Complete Works of Andrew Fuller: Memoirs of the Rev. Samuel Pearce.* Vol. 4. Berlin: De Gruyter, 2017.

———. *The Armies of the Lamb: The Spirituality of Andrew Fuller.* Dundas, ON: Joshua, 2001.

———. "The Concert of Prayer in the 18th Century: A Model for Praying Together." In *Let Us Pray: A Symposium on Prayer by Leading Preachers and Theologians,* edited by Don Kistler, 123–45. Orlando, FL: Northampton, 2011.

———. "Editor's Introduction." In Vol. 4, *The Complete Works of Andrew Fuller: Memoirs of the Rev. Samuel Pearce,* 1–40. Berlin: De Gruyter, 2017.

———. "Eighteenth-Century Calvinistic Baptists and the Political Realm." In *Recycling the Past or Researching History? Studies in Baptist Historiography and Myths,* edited by Philip E. Thompson and Anthony R. Cross, 264–78. Eugene, OR: Wipf & Stock, 2006.

———. "Evangelicalism and the Enlightenment: A Reassessment." In *The Advent of Evangelicalism: Exploring Historical Continuities,* edited by Michael A.G. Haykin and Kenneth J. Stewart, 37–60. Nashville: Broadman & Holman, 2008.

———. "'A Great Thirst for Reading': Andrew Fuller the Theological Reader." *Eusebeia* 8 (Spring 2008) 5–25.

———. "An Historical and Biblical Root of the Globalization of Christianity: The Fullerism of Andrew Fuller's *The Gospel Worthy of All Acceptation.*" *The Journal of Baptist Studies* 8 (February 2016) 3–15.

———. "'The Honour of the Spirit's Work' Andrew Fuller, Dan Taylor, and an Eighteenth-Century Baptist Debate over Regeneration." *Baptist Quarterly* 47, no. 4 (October 2016) 152–61.

———. "Introduction." In *The Dangerous Impact of Gospel Issues,* edited by Michael A.G. Haykin and G. Stephen Weaver, 7–14. Louisville, KY: Andrew Fuller Center for Baptist Studies, 2015.

———. *One Heart and One Soul: John Sutcliff of Olney, His Friends and His Times.* Darlington, GB: Evangelical, 1994.

———. "'The Oracles of God': Andrew Fuller and the Scriptures." *Churchman* 103, no. 1 (1989) 60–76.

———. "Reading Andrew Fuller." *Founders Journal,* no. 101 (Summer 2015) 7–8.

———. "Review of *The Legacy of Jonathan Edwards in the Theology of Andrew Fuller.*" *Church History and Religious Culture* 94, no. 3 (2014) 389–91.

———. "A Socinian and Calvinist Compared: Joseph Priestley and Andrew Fuller on the Propriety of Prayer to Christ." *Dutch Review of Church History* 73, no. 2 (1993) 178–98.

———. "'To Devote Ourselves to the Blessed Trinity': Eighteenth-Century Particular Baptists, Andrew Fuller, and the Defense of 'Trinitarian Communities.'" In *One God in Three Persons: Unity of Essence, Distinction of Persons, Implications for Life,* edited by Bruce A. Ware and John Starke, 173–193. Wheaton, IL: Crossway, 2015.

———. "'Very Affecting and Evangelical': Review of Keith Grant, Andrew Fuller and the Evangelical Renewal of Pastoral Theology." *Southern Baptist Journal of Theology,* 17 no. 1 (2013) 42–45.

———, ed. *"At the Pure Fountain of Thy Word": Andrew Fuller as an Apologist.* Studies in Baptist History and Thought 6. Eugene, OR: Wipf & Stock, 2006.

———, ed. *The British Particular Baptists, 1638–1910.* 3 vols. Springfield, MO: Particular Baptist, 1998.

———, ed. "Confession of Faith." In *The Armies of the Lamb: The Spirituality of Andrew Fuller*, 273–82. Dundas, ON: Joshua, 2001.

———, ed. *Joy Unspeakable and Full of Glory: The Piety of Samuel and Sarah Pearce*. Kitchener, ON: Joshua, 2012.

Haykin, Michael A.G., David W. Bebbington, David L. Allen, Ian Hugh Clary, and Chris Chun. "The Southern Baptist Journal of Theology Forum: The Life and Ministry of Andrew Fuller." *Southern Baptist Journal of Theology*, 17, no. 1 (2013) 46–52.

Haykin, Michael A.G., and Kenneth J. Stewart, eds. *The Advent of Evangelicalism: Exploring Historical Continuities*. Nashville: Broadman & Holman, 2008.

Heath, Gordon L., and Michael A.G. Haykin, eds. *Baptists and War: Essays on Baptists and Military Conflict, 1640s–1990s*. Eugene, OR: Pickwick, 2015.

Hedges, Brian G. *Watchfulness: Recovering a Lost Spiritual Discipline*. Grand Rapids: Reformation Heritage, 2018.

Hefling, Charles, and Cynthia Shattuck, eds. *The Oxford Guide to The Book of Common Prayer: A Worldwide Survey*. New York: Oxford University Press, 2006.

Hinson, E. Glenn. "Baptist Spirituality." In *Dictionary of Christian Spirituality*, edited by Glen G. Scorgie, Simon Chan, Gordon T. Smith, and James D. Smith III. Grand Rapids: Zondervan, 2011.

Hooper, Thomas. *The Story of English Congregationalism*. London: Congregational Union of England and Wales, 1907.

Ivimey, Joseph. *A History of the English Baptists: Comprising Including an Investigation of the History of Baptism in England from the Earliest Period to Which It Can Be Traced, to the Close of the Seventeenth Century*. Vol. 1. London: Burditt, Button, Hamilton, 1811.

———. *A History of the English Baptists: Containing Biographical Sketches and Notices of above Three Hundred Ministers, and Historical Accounts, Alphabetically Arranged, of One Hundred and Thirty Churches, in the Different Counties in England: From about the Year 1610 till 1700*. Vol. 2. London: Button & Son, 1814.

———. *A History of the English Baptists: Comprising the Principal Events of the History of Protestant Dissenters from the Revolution in 1668 till 1760; and of the London Baptist Churches, During That Period*. Vol. 3. London: B.J. Holdsworth, 1823.

———. *A History of the English Baptists: Comprising the Principal Events of the History of the Protestant Dissenters, During the Reign of Geo. III and of the Baptist Churches in London, with Notices of Many of the Principal Churches in the Country During the Same Period*. Vol. 4. London: B.J. Holdsworth, 1830.

Jacobs, Alan. *The Book of Common Prayer: A Biography*. Princeton, NJ: Princeton University Press, 2013.

Jarvis, Clive R. "Growth in English Baptist Churches: With Special Reference to the Northamptonshire Particular Baptist Association (1770–1830)." PhD diss., University of Glasgow, 2001.

Keach, Benjamin. *An Exposition of the Parables and Express Similitudes of Our Lord and Saviour Jesus Christ*. London: Aylott and Co., 1858.

Kennedy, Rodney Wallace, and Derek C. Hatch, eds. *Gathering Together: Baptists at Work in Worship*. Eugene, OR: Wipf & Stock, 2013.

Kim, Sangwoo. "Embodied Prayer: The Practice of Prayer as Christian Theology." ThD diss., Duke University, 2016.

Kirkby, Arthur H. *Andrew Fuller*. London: Independent, 1961.

Kreider, Glenn R. "Jonathan Edwards's Theology of Prayer." *Bibliotheca Sacra* 160, no. 640 (October 2003) 434–56.

Lapsley, James N. "On Defining Pastoral Theology." *Journal of Pastoral Theology* 1, no. 1 (July 1, 1991) 116–24.

Laws, Gilbert. *Andrew Fuller, Pastor, Theologian, Ropeholder.* London: Carey Kingsgate, 1942.

Leclercq, Jean. "Theology and Prayer: The Education of Seminarians." *Encounter* 24, no. 3 (1963) 349–64.

Leithart, Peter J. "Freedom & Propriety." *Touchstone: A Journal of Mere Christianity* 22, no. 6 (August 7, 2009) 34–38.

Lumpkin, William. *Baptist Confessions of Faith.* Rev. ed. Valley Forge, PA: Judson, 1969.

Maeder, Tobias. "Towards a Theology of Prayer." *Worship* 40, no. 4 (April 1966) 218–30.

Maltby, Judith. "The Prayer Book and the Parish Church: From the Elizabethan Settlement to the Restoration." In *The Oxford Guide to The Book of Common Prayer: A Worldwide Survey*, edited by Charles Hefling and Cynthia Shattuck, 79–92. New York: Oxford University Press, 2006.

Manly Jr., B., ed. "Andrew Fuller's Confession of Faith (Delivered by Mr. Fuller, on the Occasion of His Installation as Pastor of the First Baptist Church at Kettering, October 7, 1783)." *American Baptist Memorial* 15 (1856) 346–48.

Martin, John. "The Circular Letter from the Ministers and Messengers Assembled at Kettering." *The Baptist History Homepage.* Accessed January 6, 2019. http://baptisthistoryhomepage.com/1770clbritish.html.

McBeth, H. Leon. *The Baptist Heritage: Four Centuries of Baptist Witness.* Nashville: Broadman & Holman, 1987.

McDonnell, Kilian. "Free and Formal Prayer in Protestant England." *Worship* 40, no. 8 (October 1966) 472–82.

McGlothlin, W.J. *Baptist Confessions of Faith.* Philadelphia: American Baptist Publication Society, 1911.

McKibbens, Thomas R. "Our Baptist Heritage in Worship." *Review & Expositor* 80, no. 1 (1983) 53–69.

McMullen, Michael D., and Timothy D. Whelan. "Introduction." In Vol. 1, *The Complete Works of Andrew Fuller: The Diary of Andrew Fuller, 1780–1801*, xi–xl. Berlin: De Gruyter, 2016.

Metzger, Bruce M., and Bart Ehrman. *The Text of New Testament: Its Transmission, Corruption, and Restoration.* 4th ed. New York: Oxford University Press, 2005.

Millar, Gary. *Calling on the Name of the Lord: A Biblical Theology of Prayer.* London: InterVarsity Academic, 2016.

Miller, Patrick D. *They Cried to the Lord: The Form and Theology of Biblical Prayer.* Minneapolis: Fortress, 1994.

Morden, Peter J. *The Life and Thought of Andrew Fuller (1754–1815).* Milton Keynes, GB: Paternoster, 2015.

——. *Offering Christ to the World: Andrew Fuller (1754–1815) and the Revival of Eighteenth Century Particular Baptist Life.* Milton Keynes, GB: Paternoster, 2003.

Morey, Robert A. *A Theology of Prayer.* Millerstown, PA: Faith Defenders, 2004.

Morris, John W. *Memoirs of the Life and Writings of the Rev. Andrew Fuller.* 1st ed. London: T. Hamilton, 1816.

——. *Memoirs of the Life and Writings of the Rev. Andrew Fuller.* 2nd ed. Boston: Lincoln & Edmands, 1830.

Mullins, Edgar Young. *The Christian Religion in Its Doctrinal Expression*. Providence, RI:: Roger Williams, 1917.

Nettles, Tom J. *The Baptists: Beginnings in America*. Vol. 2. Fearn, UK: Christian Focus, 2009.

———. *The Baptists: Beginnings in Britain*. Vol. 1. Fearn, UK: Christian Focus, 2005.

———. *The Baptists: The Modern Era*. Vol. 3. Fearn, UK: Christian Focus, 2007.

———. "The Influence of Jonathan Edwards on Andrew Fuller." *Eusebeia* 9 (Spring 2008) 97–116.

———. "Introduction: Two Hundred Years Ago, The World Lost a Good Friend." *Founders Journal*, no. 101 (Summer 2015) 4–6.

———. "On the Road Again: The Contributions of Andrew Fuller." In *By His Grace And for His Glory: A Historical, Theological and Practical Study of the Doctrines of Grace in Baptist Life*, 55–77. 2nd ed. Cape Coral, FL: Founders, 2006.

———. "Preface to the New Edition: Why Andrew Fuller?" In *The Complete Works of the Rev. Andrew Fuller*, edited by Joseph Belcher, 1:v–xviii. Harrisonburg, VA: Sprinkle, 1988.

Noll, Mark A. *The Rise of Evangelicalism: The Age of Edwards, Whitefield and the Wesleys*. Vol. 1. A History of Evangelicalism: People, Movements and Ideas in the English-Speaking World. Downers Grove, IL: InterVarsity Academic, 2003.

Nuttall, Geoffrey F. "Northamptonshire and 'The Modern Question': A Turning-Point in Eighteenth-Century Dissent." *The Journal of Theological Studies* 16, no. 1 (1965) 101–123.

Okholm, Dennis L. "Petitionary Prayer and Providence in Two Contemporary Theological Perspectives: Karl Barth and Norman Pittenger." PhD diss., Princeton Theological Seminary, 1986.

Owens, Jesse. "An Analysis of Andrew Fuller's Reply to Philanthropos." *Founders Journal* 101 (Summer 2015) 20–21.

Parker, Clinton, III. "Pastoral Role Modeling as an Antecedent to Corporate Spirituality." *Journal of Religious Leadership* 13, no. 1 (2014) 161–85.

Payne, Ernest A. *The Baptists of the World and Their Overseas Missions*. London: Carey Kingsgate, 1955.

———. *The Fellowship of Believers: Baptist Thought Yesterday and Today*. Enlarged. London: Carey Kingsgate, 1952.

———. "The Prayer Call of 1784." In *Ter-Jubilee Celebrations, 1942-4*, 19–30. London: Baptist Missionary Society, 1945.

Peaston, A.E. *The Prayer Book Tradition in the Free Churches*. London: James Clarke and Co., 1964.

Pelikan, Jaroslav. *The Christian Tradition: A History of the Development of Doctrine*. Vol. 1 of *The Emergence of the Catholic Tradition*. Chicago: University of Chicago Press, 1975.

Pittsley, Jeremy. "Christ's Absolute Determination to Save: Andrew Fuller and Particular Redemption." *Eusebeia* 9 (Spring 2008) 135–66.

Priest, Gerald L. "Andrew Fuller's Response to the 'Modern Question'—A Reappraisal of the Gospel Worthy of All Acceptation." *Detroit Baptist Seminary Journal* 6 (Fall 2001) 45–73.

Priestley, Joseph. *Notes on All the Books of Scripture: For the Use of the Pulpit and Private Families*. Vol. 3. Northumberland: Andrew Kennedy, 1804.

————. *Notes on All the Books of Scripture: For the Use of the Pulpit and Private Families.* Vol. 4. Northumberland: Andrew Kennedy, 1804.

Regal, Kevin Wayne. "Charles H. Spurgeon's Theology of Prayer." ThM, Southern Baptist Theological Seminary, 2000.

Roberts, Phil. "Andrew Fuller." In *Theologians of the Baptist Tradition*, edited by Timothy George and David S. Dockery, 34–51. Nashville: Broadman & Holman, 2001.

Robison, Olin. "The Particular Baptists in England, 1760–1820." DPhil diss., University of Oxford, 1963.

Ross, Melanie C. "Ecumenism after Charles Finney: A Free Church Liturgical Theology." PhD diss., University of Notre Dame, 2010.

Ryland, John, Jr. *The Circular Letter from the Baptist Ministers and Messengers Assembled at Nottingham, June 1784.* Boston, MA: Gale ECCO, 2010.

————. *The Nature, Evidences, and Advantages, of Humility, Represented in a Circular Letter from the Ministers and Messengers of the Baptist Association, Assembled at Nottingham, June 2, 3, 1784.* Northampton: T. Dicey and Company, 1784.

————. *The Work of Faith, the Labour of Love, and the Patience of Hope, Illustrated, in the Life and Death of Life and Death of the Reverend Andrew Fuller.* London: Button & Son, 1816.

————. *The Work of Faith, the Labour of Love, and the Patience of Hope, Illustrated: In the Life and Death of the Rev. Andrew Fuller.* 2nd ed. London: Button & Son, 1818.

Saliers, Don E. "Prayer and the Doctrine of God in Contemporary Theology." *Interpretation* 34, no. 3 (July 1980) 265–78.

————. "Theology and Prayer: Some Conceptual Reminders." *Worship* 48, no. 4 (April 1974) 230–35.

Schaff, Philip. *The Creeds of Christendom, with a History and Critical Notes: The Evangelical Protestant Creeds, with Translations.* Vol. 3. New York: Harper & Brothers, 1882.

Scorgie, Glen G. "Overview of Christian Spirituality." In *Dictionary of Christian Spirituality*, 27–33. Grand Rapids: Zondervan, 2011.

Selman, Francis. *Providence and Prayer.* Deeper Christianity. London: Catholic Truth Society, 2017.

Sheehan, Clint. "Great and Sovereign Grace: Fuller's Defence of the Gospel against Arminianism." In *"At the Pure Fountain of Thy Word": Andrew Fuller as an Apologist*, edited by Michael A.G. Haykin, 83–121. Studies in Baptist History and Thought 6. Eugene, OR: Wipf & Stock, 2006.

Smith, Erik. "An Analysis of Andrew Fuller's Letters to Mr. Vidler." *Founders Journal* 101 (Summer 2015) 14–15.

Sproul, R.C. *Does Prayer Change Things?* Vol. 3. Lake Mary, FL: Reformation Trust, 2009.

Spurgeon, Charles H. *Spurgeon on Prayer.* Alachua, FL: Bridge-Logos, 2009.

Taylor, Jeremy. *A Discourse Concerning Prayer Ex Tempore, or, by Pretence of the Spirit : In Justification of Authorized and Set-Forms of Lyturgie.* London, 1646.

Taylor, John. *The Scripture Account of Prayer: In an Address to the Dissenters in Lancashire : Occasioned by a New Liturgy Some Ministers of That County Are Composing for the Use of a Congregation at Liverpool.* London: J. Waugh and W. Fenner, 1761.

Thompson, Philip E., and Anthony R. Cross. *Recycling the Past or Researching History? Studies in Baptist Historiography and Myths.* Eugene, OR: Wipf & Stock, 2007.

Thomson, James G.S.S. *The Praying Christ: A Study of Jesus' Doctrine and Practice of Prayer*. Vancouver, BC: Regent College Publishing, 1995.

Tiessen, Terrance L. *Providence & Prayer: How Does God Work in the World?* Downers Grove, IL: InterVarsity Academic, 2000.

Timmons, Aaron Jason. "'The Cause of Christ and Truth: Arguments for the Deity of Christ in the Anti-Socinian Writings of John Gill, Dan Taylor, and Andrew Fuller." ThM, Southern Baptist Theological Seminary, 2008.

Toulmin, Joshua. *A Review of the Preaching of the Apostles: Or, the Practical Efficacy of the Unitarian Doctrine; Proved and Illustrated from the Acts of the Apostles, and the Epistle of Paul to Timothy and Titus*. London: Longman, 1819.

Ward, Matthew W. "Pure Worship: The Early English Baptist Distinctive." PhD diss., Southwestern Baptist Theological Seminary, 2013.

Watts, Isaac. *A Guide to Prayer: Or, A Free and Rational Account of the Gift, Grace and Spirit of Prayer*. 2nd ed. London: Emmanuel Matthews, 1716.

Weaver, G. Stephen, Jr. "C.H. Spurgeon: A Fullerite?" *Journal of Baptist Studies* 8 (February 2016) 99–117.

———. "An Unsung, but Influential Sermon." *Founders Journal* 101 (Summer 2015) 11–13.

Wheeler, Nigel David. "Eminent Spirituality and Eminent Usefulness: Andrew Fuller's (1754–1815) Pastoral Theology in His Ordination Sermons." PhD diss., University of Pretoria, 2009.

White, James F. *Protestant Worship: Traditions in Transition*. Louisville, KY: Westminster John Knox, 1989.

Willis, E. David. "Contemporary Theology and Prayer." *Interpretation* 34, no. 3 (July 1980) 250–64.

Wix, Samuel. *An Affectionate Address to Those Dissenters from the Communion of the Church of England, Who Agree with Her in the Leading Doctrines of Christianity: With a Postscript to the Rev. S. Newton, Occasioned by His Letter to the Author, Entitled "The Dissenters' Apology."* 2nd ed. London: F.C. & J. Rivington, 1820.

Yong, Jeremy Yuen Ming. "Tending to Love—'The Plant of Paradise': Andrew Fuller on Love and Its Role in Local Church Revival." DMin, Southern Baptist Theological Seminary, 2015.